IDENTITY, COMMUNITY, AND LEARNING LIVES IN THE DIGITAL AGE

Recent work on education, identity and community has expanded the intellectual boundaries of learning research. From home-based studies examining youth experiences with technology, to forms of entrepreneurial learning in informal settings, to communities of participation in the workplace, family, community, trade union and school, research has attempted to describe and theorize the meaning and nature of learning. *Identity, Community, and Learning Lives in the Digital Age* offers a systematic reflection on these studies, exploring how learning can be characterised across a range of 'whole-life' experiences. The volume brings together hitherto discrete and competing scholarly traditions: sociocultural analyses of learning, ethnographic literacy research, geospatial location studies, discourse analysis, comparative anthropological studies of education research and actor network theory. The contributions are united through a focus on the ways in which learning shapes lives in a digital age.

Ola Erstad is a professor in the Department of Educational Research, University of Oslo. Professor Erstad works across the fields of media and educational research and has published widely on issues of technology and education.

Julian Sefton-Green is an independent consultant and researcher. He is a principal research Fellow at the London School of Economics and an honorary professor at the Hong Kong Institute of Education. He has published widely on media education, informal learning and creativity.

Identity, Community, and Learning Lives in the Digital Age

Edited by

OLA ERSTAD

University of Oslo, Norway

JULIAN SEFTON-GREEN

London School of Economics and Political Science, UK

CAMBRIDGE UNIVERSITY PRESS
Cambridge, New York, Melbourne, Madrid, Cape Town,
Singapore, São Paulo, Delhi, Mexico City

Cambridge University Press
32 Avenue of the Americas, New York, NY 10013-2473, USA

www.cambridge.org
Information on this title: www.cambridge.org/9781107005914

First published 2013

Printed in the United States of America

A catalog record for this publication is available from the British Library.

Library of Congress Cataloging in Publication Data
Identity, community, and learning lives in the digital age / [edited by] Ola
Erstad, Julian Sefton-Green.
    p.   cm.
ISBN 978-1-107-00591-4 (Hardback)
1. Learning – Social aspects.   2. Educational sociology.   3. Digital communications.
4. Identity (Psychology)   I. Erstad, Ola.   II. Sefton-Green, Julian.
LC191.I34   2012
306.43–dc23   2012016497

ISBN 978-1-107-00591-4 Hardback

Contents

v

Illustrations

Contributors

Hans Christian Arnseth is an associate professor in the Department of Educational Research, University of Oslo. He is a member of the research group TransAction at the Faculty of Education. In his research, he explores computer-supported collaborative learning, the use of games and simulations in learning, interaction analysis of learning and identity construction in various contexts and transitions and boundaries between practices that young people participate in.

Karin Aronsson is a professor in the Department of Child and Youth Studies, Stockholm University. Her work focuses on how talk is used to build social organisation, with a particular focus on children's peer groups, family and institutional encounters. Other research interests include children's play, informal learning and second-language learning. She publishes internationally and is on the editorial board of several journals. She co-edited a recent book, *Children, Childhood and Everyday Life: Children's Perspectives* (Charlotte, NC: Information Age Publishing) with M. Hedegaard, C. Højholt and O. Skjær Ulvik.

Maria Lucia Castanheira is associate professor in the School of Education, Federal University of Minas Gerais, Brazil. Her research interests focus on the examination of literacy practices in and out of school, aiming to understand the meanings and consequences of being literate in specific contexts. She is particularly interested in examining the social construction of opportunities for learning, drawing upon discourse analysis and ethnographic approaches.

Lynne Chisholm holds the chair for education and generation at the University of Innsbruck (Austria) and is visiting professor at the University of Oslo (Norway). She specialises in comparative and interdisciplinary youth studies, together with the social and cultural analysis of education and learning across the life course (see http://homepage.uibk.ac.at/~c603207/).

Kirsten Drotner is a doctor of philosophy and professor of media studies at the University of Southern Denmark, where she also directs a national research centre, DREAM (Danish Research Centre on Education and Advanced Media Materials). Her research interests include audience studies, media uses, digital literacy formation and digital heritage studies. Among her publications are *The International Handbook on Children, Media and Culture* (2008; Sage, with co-editor Sonia Livingstone); *Informal Learning and Digital Media* (2008; Cambridge Scholars' Publishing, with co-editors Hans S. Jensen and Kim S. Schrøder) and *Digital Content Creation: Creativity, Competence, Critique* (2010; Peter Lang, with co-editor Kim S. Schrøder).

Ola Erstad is professor in the Department for Educational Research, University of Oslo, Norway. He has been working within both the fields of media and educational research, especially on media literacy/digital competence. He is leader of the research group TransAction: Learning, Knowing and Identity in the Information Society. He is involved in several research networks on digital media and education nationally, across the Nordic countries in Europe and internationally. Recent publications are 'The Learning Lives of Digital Youth – Beyond the Formal and Informal' (*Oxford Review of Education*, 2012) and 'Content in Motion: Remixing and Learning with Digital Media' (with Drotner & Schrøder, 2010).

Øystein Gilje is a postdoctoral researcher on the project 'Learning Lives' at the University of Oslo, Norway. His doctoral thesis 'Mode, Mediation and Moving Images: An Inquiry of Digital Editing Practices in Media Education' (2010) investigated young people's remixing practices by using a sociocultural and multimodal perspective. Gilje also led the research project 'Making a Filmmaker' (2007–9) on young filmmakers' learning trajectories in Scandinavia. Gilje has published his work recently in international journals, such as *Written Communication, Visual Communication* and *Nordicom Review*.

Judith Green is a professor at the University of California, Santa Barbara. Her research and teaching interests focus on teaching-learning relationships, disciplinary knowledge as socially constructed and ethnographic research and discourse studies of the patterns of everyday life in classrooms.

Shirley Brice Heath, Margery Bailey Professor of English and Dramatic Literature and professor of linguistics, emerita, Stanford University, studies youth in their own chosen learning environments all over the world. Her research theorises the processes of voluntary learning that advance young people's development of conceptual understanding and skills called for by art, mathematics, science and language development.

Jaakko Hilppö is a Ph.D. student working in the Department of Teacher Education at the University of Helsinki. His interest currently focuses on children's agency and well-being and participatory research methods.

Glynda A. Hull is a professor of education in language, literacy and culture at the University of California, Berkeley, and a visiting research professor at New York University. Her research focuses on sociocultural perspectives on literacy, the intersection of new media and literacy and school-university partnerships.

Kristiina Kumpulainen is professor of education in the Department of Teacher Education, University of Helsinki. Her scientific work focuses on socioculturally informed research on learning and education, classroom interaction, collaborative learning, formal and informal learning, learner agency and identity, learning environments and new technologies, innovative schools and their pedagogies, teacher professional development and video research methodologies, as well as on interdisciplinary research for the promotion of learning in the twenty-first century.

Jay L. Lemke is senior research scientist in the Laboratory of Comparative Human Cognition (LCHC) and adjunct professor of communication at the University of California, San Diego. Before coming to San Diego, he was professor in the School of Education at the University of Michigan, and previously professor and executive officer of the Ph.D. programme in urban education at the Graduate Center of the City University of New York. He is the author of *Talking Science: Language, Learning, and Values* and *Textual Politics: Discourse and Social Dynamics,* as well as of more than one hundred publications in the fields of discourse linguistics, multimedia semiotics and science and literacy education. His current research focus is on the integration of feeling and meaning in multimedia activity systems.

Lasse Lipponen is a professor of education, with special reference to preschool education, in the Department of Teacher Education, University of Helsinki. His research work is directed to teacher education, children's learning at the intersection of formal and informal learning environments and the development of children's agency.

Mark Evan Nelson is lecturer in English language and literacy education at Deakin University, in Victoria, Australia. He is an experienced teacher of art and design, as well as of literacy studies and language pedagogy, and he has also lived and worked in the United States, Japan and Singapore. He received his Ph.D. in language and literacy education from the University of California, Berkeley, and his current research interests are in applied linguistics, new literacies, multimodal communication and textual analysis and new media composing of children and youth in in-school and out-of-school contexts.

Helen Nixon is associate professor of education in the Children and Youth Research Centre at Queensland University of Technology in Brisbane, Australia. She has published in the fields of English and literacy education and cultural studies and education. Current projects focus on the effects of mandated literacy assessment on teachers' work and the changing literacy demands of schooling in the middle years.

Antti Rajala is a Ph.D. student working in the Department of Teacher Education at the University of Helsinki. He is funded by the Doctoral Programme for Multidisciplinary Research on Learning Environments and takes part in the doctoral training of the Centre for Research on Activity, Development and Learning. His interest currently focuses on classroom interaction and participatory pedagogy.

Julian Sefton-Green is an independent researcher working in education and the cultural and creative industries. He is currently principal research Fellow in the Department of Media and Communication, London School of Economics and Political Science, and a research associate at the University of Oslo. He is an honorary professor of education at the University of Nottingham, United Kingdom, and at the Hong Kong Institute of Education. His work explores aspects of media education, new technologies, creative practices and informal learning. Recent volumes include joint editing of *The International Handbook of Creative Learning* (2011) and *Researching Creative Learning: Methods and Approaches* (2010), both published by Routledge (www.julianseftongreen.net).

Kenneth Silseth is a research Fellow in the Department of Educational Research, University of Oslo. He is a member of the research group TransAction at the Faculty of Education and has, in previous work, been investigating a wide range of themes linked to young people's use of new media. In his thesis, Silseth explores constructions of learning, identity and intersubjectivity in young people's use of digital technology in and out of school.

Björn Sjöblom is a postdoctoral researcher in the Department of Child and Youth Studies, Stockholm University. His research revolves around children and youth's computer gaming, especially in co-located settings such as Internet cafés and LAN parties. Drawing primarily on video data, he studies situated and multimodal methods of communicating within such contexts. His dissertation 'Gaming Interaction: Conversations and Competencies in Internet Cafés' (Linköping University, 2011) deals with young players' interactional management of collaboration, disputes and gaming competence, and with how such interaction lies at the heart of participation in this gaming culture.

Audra Skukauskaite is an associate professor at the University of the Incarnate Word. Her research and teaching interests focus on discourse and ethnographic research in education, open-ended interviewing methodology, impact of reforms on teachers and student learning in diverse classrooms.

Randy Young (nom de plume RelixStylz) is a musician, composer and multimedia artist from Oakland, California. He translates perspectives on urban life into the verbal, visual and musical languages of hip-hop culture, producing critical understandings of social, political and aesthetic experience for social media audiences.

Acknowledgements

The editors would like to acknowledge the Norwegian Research Council's support of the project *Local Literacies and Community Spaces – Investigating Transitions and Transfers in the 'Learning Lives' of Groruddalen*, and, additionally the TransAction research group at the Faculty of Educational Sciences, University of Oslo, for their support and funding, which made the seminar at Soria Moria in 2009 possible.

We would also like to thank the editorial and production team at Cambridge and Naranee Ruthra-Rajan for her work on the index for this volume.

Chapter 1

Identity, Community, and Learning Lives in the Digital Age

Julian Sefton-Green and Ola Erstad

WHY LEARNING LIVES?

In some ways, learning is as commonplace (and complex) and banal as living. It is difficult to imagine a state of 'not learning', and it is a truism to state that, in all our lives, we constantly draw on and develop knowledge through experience. The authors of this book take this for granted. Similarly, a long tradition of scholarship in the sociocultural tradition distinguishes learning from the processes of schooling; whilst schools and schooling are *the* dominant educational institutions in contemporary societies and determine much of what constitutes, defines and frames learning, how learning works in schools is not the end all and be all of the issue.

We use the phrase *learning lives* to describe two discrete but interrelated concepts. First, in developing further the sociocultural position is the idea that learning needs to be situated intricately and intimately in a matrix of 'transactions': experiences, life trajectories, voluntary and involuntary learning contexts, affective frames and social groupings that make up experience across our life-worlds. Our subjectivities, interpersonal interactions, our developing sense of ourselves, how we construct learner identities and narratives about what we know and can do are all part of how the authors of this volume see learning within a 'whole-life' perspective. This poses complex challenges for research to identify, describe and understand learning within such a web of influences and determinants.

Our second use of the phrase *learning lives* describes more the idea of learning *for* life. Although all definitions of learning imply this prospective use, we are concerned with exploring how learning occupies the forefront of the new forms of 'liquid lives' (Bauman, 2005) in 'second' or 'late' modernity (see Chisholm, Chapter 5) lived by the young and now centrally mediated by a range of technologies, and how broader contemporary perspectives on learning alter our understanding of the role of learning in preparing and coping with changing life pathways and transitions.

The phrase *learning lives* grows out of a broad set of influential studies appearing from different disciplinary fields during the last decades. These studies do not represent a single unified field of research, but they address certain key challenges to the ways in which learning is embedded in our lives over time and which become more apparent as we move through the twenty-first century. These are studies of an ethnographic nature, documenting literacy practices in different cultures (Scribner & Cole, 1981; Heath, 1983; Barton & Hamilton, 1998), studies of media use among young people (Buckingham & Sefton-Green, 2004; Livingstone, 2002, Ito et al., 2010), studies of youth cultures (Fornäs, Lindberg & Sernhede, 1995; Pampols & Porzio, 2005), studies of place and space in children's and young people's geographies (Cresswell, 1996; Leander, Phillips & Headrick Taylor, 2010) or studies focusing on gender and schooling (McLeod & Yates, 2006; Rudberg & Bjerrum Nielsen, 2005). Few longitudinal studies have studied the timescales and pathways of learners (Lemke, 2000; Thomson 2009).

The rest of this introduction explores how our idea of *learning lives* might then be situated in a range of analytic and disciplinary perspectives and what its core elements might be in offering a series of *key concepts* to underpin the chapters that follow. This introduction also includes a discussion of why such ideas might be a useful corrective to contemporary approaches to education.

We first consider the relationship between theories of identity and theories of learning, and we follow this with a discussion about the meaning and nature of context. Next, we consider the meaning of learning for learners (and for researchers), thus leading to a consideration of debates about the purpose and nature of learning research in the current climate. We then describe the individual contributions to this volume, concluding with a section that poses a series of questions about the value of 'learning lives'.

LEARNER IDENTITIES

In many ways, it is very difficult to disentangle an attention to identity from an understanding of learning. Much of the focus of subsequent chapters explores the particular role of learning identity (see especially Arnseth & Silseth, Chapter 2). This role can describe the identity produced through or by learning, and/or the identity acting as a precondition or context for learning and/or the kind of identity required by the learner to be able to learn as part of the learning process (Sinha, 1999).

Contemporary research, especially that from within the lifelong learning and adult education tradition, is especially interested in the centrality of learning identity to identity per se: 'People must become individuals through constructing or reconstructing their own biographies and life courses' (Glastra, Hake & Schedler, 2004). An attention to biography and the processes of narrativising life in this tradition reveals an interest in modes of identity creation. Ecclestone et al., for example, contrast du Bois-Reymond's 'choice-biographies' with Denzin's 'epiphanies' or 'turning points' in an attempt to theorise the connections between biography and social structure in the emergence of lifecourse theory. The introduction to a recent collection (Ecclestone, Biesta & Hughes, 2009) focusing on the idea of transition as a way into the nitty-gritty of identity work is especially concerned with how 'changing notions of the self' under the conditions of reflexive modernity (Giddens, 1991) reveal new kinds of stress within individuals and between them and social structures. Forms of 'biographicity' (Alheit & Dausien, 1999) emerge from such tensions to dominate as the primary process of identity-making.

These approaches open up ways of putting people in the messy materiality of their lives at the centre of educational research and seeing learning as part of a very wide range of social processes. Research within this broad spectrum of approaches examines life histories – how people construct narratives of their learning lives – thus positioning learning experiences as episodes within varying timescales and relating the meaning and purposes of learning to other lifecourse trajectories: family, work and so on (see contributions by Nixon [Chapter 10], Gilje [Chapter 12] and Nelson, Hull and Young [Chapter 13]). Questions of gender and class, as well as other important social determinants such as religious affiliation or ethnicity, are also key lenses through which the nature and learning of individuals can be positioned.

Yet, it is perhaps true to say that such approaches have been used primarily with respect to older people, certainly with youth as opposed to children and younger cohorts. This is partly common sense: older people have 'more' biography, or at least better access to the means of creating such narratives (see Chapter 13). Alternatively, and more critically, it is partly this process of denying children an ontological status and agency – a view heavily critiqued by the new sociology of childhood (Qvortrup et al., 1994) – that leads to a more closed developmentalist perspective when considering younger people's learning, one that implies that they can't draw on biographical perspectives. There are notable exceptions to this. Pollard and Filer's use of the idea of 'pupil career' addresses the idea of exploring how progress at school needs to be situated in a wider perspective that encompasses family and friends, as well as a broad-based understanding of classroom interactions (Pollard & Filer, 1999). Wortham's year-long study of individuals within a classroom that explores the complex, detailed interactions between peers and teachers showing how students construct and are constituted by certain kinds of more or less productive learning identities (Wortham, 2005). Yet, the centrality of school, rather than other dimensions of children's lives, stands in contrast to sociological and cultural interpretations of how identities are formed through family or consumption (see, for example, Lareau, 2003, and Pugh, 2009, respectively).

Of course, the idea of identity is itself problematic. It tends to be used as shorthand – or, as Moje and Luke put it – as a metaphor for a range of constructs of the person, referring to, inter alia subjectivity, a person, the personal or the self, as well as to the social or psychological models of the individual (Moje & Luke, 2009). Their review notes five key metaphors: identity as difference, sense of self or subjectivity, mind or consciousness, narrative and position. They suggest that all studies of literacy learning either implicitly or explicitly draw upon one or the other of these sociological or psychological models in any conceptualisation of learning and, equally, that it is impossible to frame any research enquiry into learning without the researcher drawing on one of these models.

This epistemological dependency on an a priori notion to describe or even investigate the idea of learning identity can lead to a kind of theoretical stand-off in which one ends up finding out what one began the enquiry with in the first place. In general, much current social theory is preoccupied with the impact of changing forms of individuation and individualisation, of changing and different notions of identity in the current era. How such changes relate to ideas about learning is an important focus. Work from this perspective is interested in schools, the role of technology in learning and the role of the home and other out-of-school experiences as key sites where changing forms of individualisation are both constructed and constituted by these shifting social practices. However, such research is, by definition, troubled by the challenge of finding, describing and locating or identifying identity in learning. What are the phenomena under observation when it comes to identity? What constitutes evidence in descriptions of identity or, indeed, learning? This theme is explored in Chapter 8 by Green, Skukauskaite and Castanheira, and in Chapter 3 by Drotner. Traditionally, learning research relies on traces of identity in talk and other kinds of discourse, but what other 'evidence' might research draw on to make use of this slippery concept?

CONTEXTUALISING CONTEXTS

Whilst paying attention to contexts is often advocated by studies of learning in the sociocultural tradition, the authors collected here have probed further at this easy assumption. A larger theoretical frame exists behind this enquiry, relating to the questions just discussed about the relations between structure and agency and how we can imagine individuals in relation to identities; we conclude this subsection by revisiting these questions.

The specificity of contexts has received much attention in recent years (Cole, 1996; Duranti & Goodwin, 1992; Edwards, Biesta & Thorpe, 2009), but a central problem remains in defining the limits and nature of a context. At one level, as Edwards notes, all of life could be a 'context' but, with that perspective, how useful a concept does a 'learning context' remain (Edwards, 2009)? Whilst all action has to take place within a context, we also have to ask: Can we separate learning, and therefore learning contexts, from the everyday flow of experience? These are perhaps unanswerable and certainly difficult-to-research questions, although Green, Skukauskaite and Castanheira (Chapter 8) offer one kind of solution. A second order of questions is interested in what is particular to the context that influences the nature of the learning.

A recent review by Leander et al. has explored research around mobilities, looking at movement and spatiality in literacy research (Leander et al., 2010). This kind of approach raises questions about the role of time and scale, as well as about the idea of spatiality; that is, it uncouples places from their location and thus is interested in formulations of place as movement and as relationships. Elsewhere, Leander has explored these ideas in respect to research looking at on- and offline virtual and real worlds as a key locus embodying contradictions in spatiality (Leander & McKim, 2003). This approach suggests that we need to examine learning across a range of time and place scales to understand it better, however difficult this may be as an empirical challenge. Scholars have examined context in this uncoupled, highly spatialised fashion and have looked at learning across timescales. Jay Lemke has written about the idea of 'traversals', exploring how meaning travels across time and in relation to studies of learners (Lemke, 2000). Scale can, of course, refer to highly detailed 'building block' kinds of moments as well, as we noted earlier in the whole-life or lifecourse (and biographical) perspectives. Literacy studies have developed notions of learning events and learning episodes (Bloome et al., 2005). These effectively expand or contract the time-limited definition of context (Bloomer, 2001).

At the same time, other theorisations of contexts interest contributors to this volume. These revolve around investigating things (or objects or artefacts), people and networks. The impact of actor network theory (ANT) has helped researchers imagine the idea that objects and things bring with them to contexts agency and direction and thus they, too, play a part in influencing learning (Latour, 2007). This is also commensurate with a tradition emerging out of Vygotsky, lying at the heart of the sociocultural tradition, which has investigated the idea of 'affordances' (Wertsch, 1997). This concept has been influential in studies of the role of technology and learning, especially in how it enables researchers to examine the interplay of the learner in context.

The study of networks and how they can be theorised in relation to learning also has a long history. Current interest in social networks (Ito et al., 2010); dispersed learning (Brown & Duguid, 2000); innovation and reform (NSF Task Force, 2008); the position of school in relation to key actors, neighbourhoods, and local politics (Nespor, 1997) and, indeed, an interest in communities (Moje, 2000) are all examples of an attention to the sets of relationships pertaining to a context. Drotner (Chapter 3) takes up these themes in her contribution exploring processual methodologies.

Equally, describing people as contexts for learning can be explored in a variety of ways. Studies of the family, of parent-child interactions and/or of friendship groups and peer and youth cultures all characterise the role of other actors as part of the wider or more immediate context for learning. This concern underpins contributions here from Nixon (Chapter 10) and Sjöblom and Aronsson (Chapter 11).

Behind many of these notions of context, time, scale, spatiality, people, things and networks lie further assumptions about the interrelationship between individuals and society. We have already observed a contemporary interest in 'modern' forms of identity as part of this broader purview, but in relation to ideas about context, we need to consider the raft of theories that have attempted to rationalise this conundrum. Describing and analysing the interactions of what can best be generalised as 'people-in-context' is not a new project. The Bourdieusian *habitus* (Bourdieu, 1993)[1], the kind of 'force-field' constructed through ANT (Latour, 2007), communities of practice (Wenger, 1999), the notion of 'funds of knowledge' (Gonzales, Moll & Amanti, 2005; Cole & the Distributed Literacy Consortium, 2006) or even the Habermasian life-world, with its focus on intersubjectivity, practices and attitudes (Habermas, 1989), all refer to macro-level theories describing the production of self and learning in and through contexts. These questions animate Lemke's contribution (Chapter 4).

---

[1]   For an extended discussion of *habitus* as a learning context, see Colley (2009).

As noted in the preceding section, articulating the limits of agency without lapsing into a structural determinism has vexed theorists working within the sociocultural realm and has particularly troubled analyses of learning. Given our expanded and complex understanding of context and a use of multiple or performative constructs of identity, we would position *Learning Lives* within this matrix of ideas and within the debates that continue to unsettle work in these traditions. There is clearly no one single model to resolve these contradictions, but the studies in this volume aim to expose further the processes in which we can situate learning – and learning in context – in ways that help further our understanding of the circuits of cause and effect.

WHOSE LEARNING? (WHOSE LIFE?)

We have noted on several occasions so far a twofold methodological dilemma arising out of this synthesis. First is the acute problem of developing empirical methods to capture the difficult and subtle dimensions of identity and context. Second is the challenge of using research to validate post hoc propter hoc concepts that have been reified prior to research. Latour, for example, writes about how the social is proved through research into the social (Latour, 2007). Latour is particularly critical of how sociology produces its version of the social under the pretext of representing it, analysing this as a result of the contradictions arising from insider-outsider enquiry.

A key solution to this aspect of these dilemmas is a focus on ethnomethodological or emic perspectives (see Green, Skukauskaite & Castanheira, Chapter 8). This is important for our interests because it not only directs us to research that uses broad forms of qualitative enquiry located within an ethnographic imagination (Heath & Street, 2008), it also underscores the need for developing forms of analysis that can capture interaction – and especially that which might take place across the different dimensions of context in time and space – as is explored by Drotner in Chapter 3.

This debate also raises questions not simply about perspectives, but about power integral to the relationship between the researched and the researcher. In many of the studies collected here, this too is important because of the critical and counterintuitive ways in which we want to acknowledge those 'new' forms of learning that are often ignored, proscribed or perhaps even unrecognised by mainstream educational thinking. This challenge is taken up with authority in Chapter 9 by Brice Heath. A key common principle at work across this volume is that many kinds or modalities of learning are at work within our lives and that learners acknowledge these as meaningful, even if such learning is not defined or validated as such by more formal educational systems. This means that we have an interest in the self-definition and value systems developed by the communities and individuals explored here: see Gilje (Chapter 12) and Nelson, Hull and Young (Chapter 13). More than twenty years ago, Cohen developed the idea of 'really useful knowledge' (Cohen, 1990) to describe those kinds of knowledge that young people found meaningful and valuable within the exchange economies of various kinds of youth culture. This knowledge is to be distinguished from the kinds of knowledge deemed useful by social norms.

However, whilst we might be interested in kinds of learning and forms of knowledge produced by communities and individuals in a range of lifewide and lifelong activities, and we might also explore both the learning process involved in validating and credentialising such knowledge, we cannot ignore the fact that there are shared definitions of learning – Bruner used the term 'folklore' (Bruner, 1996) – and, of course, wider social norms that determine meanings here. People's understanding of learning and what it means to be educated is thus mediated by the repertoire available to them (Levinson, Foley & Holland, 1996).

This paradox – of valuing emic understandings and definitions of something which, by definition, carries predetermined meanings – is particularly acute in discussions about the alleged newness of learning centred in and around digital technologies. Reviews of a range of contemporary research studies continually point to the tension between characterisation of newness in learning – as a consequence of changing and different possibilities afforded by the landscape of new technologies (Jenkins et al., 2007) – and studies of how learning itself is recontextualised or recuperated[2] in this process (Sefton-Green, 2006). Whilst this debate in and of itself recapitulates the wider argument about who underwrites the values of research, it also highlights how fraught and tense is the contemporary struggle for educational legitimacy. Erstad and Sefton-Green explore these arguments in Chapter 6.

WHY *LEARNING LIVES* NOW?

This brings us to discussion of why debate about the meaning and purpose of learning is not only contested in the academic and theoretical arena but is also at the forefront of current policy concerns. A wide range of critics explore why education can well be described as being in a state of crisis (Claxton, 2008).

---

[2] See Gemma Moss' use of Bernstein making this case in respect of 'informal' out-of-school media learning (Moss, 2001).

Across most of Europe and North America, and in other developed nations, intense attention has been paid to the organisation and structure of schooling. This has been accompanied by a deep interrogation of the purposes of formal education. Many nations have invested heavily in various types of systemic school reform, although there seems to be a general decline in investments in formal education as a proportion of gross domestic product (GDP) (Dumont, Istance & Benavides, 2010). Interest in innovation and reforms has also been accompanied by a raft of standardised benchmarking, as in the use of international comparators such as the Organisation for Economic and Co-operation Development (OECD)'s PISA tests.

Commentary about this attention and the nature of these changes mainly suggests that the educational systems of wealthy countries are being transformed by the changing needs of the global knowledge economy.

OECD societies and economies have experienced a profound transformation from reliance on an industrial to a knowledge base. Global drivers increasingly bring to the fore what some call '21st century competencies'. The quantity and quality of learning thus become central, with the accompanying concern that traditional educational approaches are insufficient. (Dumont et al., 2010)

Although there is no shortage of critical interpretations of this shift (e.g. Edwards, 1997), the literature also reveals a renewed attention both to the role of new technologies within this settlement[3] (that is, equally as delivery agent, facilitator of dispersed learning and as cognitive support, amongst others) and initiatives to develop a 'new science of learning'. This perspective is developed further by Chisholm in Chapter 5.

Whether there really is a 'new science' of learning, or whether the idea is more of a rhetorical move, will unfold in the years to come. The OECD itself has focused study around what it calls '21st Century Competencies', as practiced by 'new millennium learners' (Pedró, 2006; Dumont et al., 2010; CERI, 2010). It has identified a cluster of behaviours, competencies and attributes 'of the moment', including the ability to learn together, co-operation and negotiation, self-regulation, meta-cognitive skills and learning environments that develop 'horizontal-connectedness' (Dumont et al., 2010). Some of these attributes, of course, stem from much older and more longstanding sets of values than those of the twenty-first century, but it is notable that such values carry such

---

[3] See also the raft of research and initiatives fostered by the MacArthur Foundation in the United States; http://spotlight.macfound.org/

authority in the current era. This kind of approach mixes what might best be thought of as new kinds of subjectivity (self-regulation, cooperativeness, etc.) with an expanded understanding of how learning environments might offer different kinds of learning contexts, as is explored by Rajala and his colleagues in Chapter 7. Enquiries into a new science of learning (e.g. Kalantzis & Cope, 2008) are also as focused on the production of learning selves as they exist in new kinds of discipline or knowledge. Here, then, we can see how our interest in learner identity and contexts sits at the heart of these new frames.

In Europe more than North America, policy has also been driven by the lifelong learning agenda (Biesta, 2006). A current interest, especially as relating to European Commission policy, stems from the concern, noted above, to develop a fit workforce to face the challenges of the knowledge economy. This is part of a wider position arguing for an increased focus on individuals taking responsibility for their own education and training as part of an investment in their own social capital. Nevertheless, lifelong learning, its operations, institutions and values, derives from an older tradition, most prominent in the Germanic countries, known as *bildung*. From this point of view, lifelong learning is existential rather than instrumental, developing the whole person within the 'life-world' (Habermas, 1989). We hope that the idea of *learning lives* might offer a bridge between these two traditions, focusing attention on the development of the whole-person-in-context approach but bringing with it an understanding of the wider shifts in educational policy as they relate to subjectivities.

On a final note, before we introduce the contributors to this volume, we need to note that *learning lives* is not a totalising or programmatic offer. As an edited collection, by definition it contains a plurality of views. Our aim is to bring together a set of questions investigating learner identity (or identities), an expanded understanding of contexts, an interest in exploring the meaning of a diverse range of learning for learners and an interest in the changing nature of learning in ever-shifting policy contexts. In addition, we should make it clear that this is not an attempt to psychologise the external play of relations. We do not offer studies of the construction and determining influence of mind. Not only is this collection oriented towards the social, it also is held together by an analytic ambition to disentangle complexity and the accreted layers of meaning. In an elegant turn of phrase, Dewey described a concept of 'transactions', 'a moving whole of interacting parts' (cited in Biesta, 2009, p. 62). This almost machinic metaphor (Dewey was in fact writing about organisms in biology) sums up for us a play of forces within a social field that we hope to shed light on.

THE ORGANISATION OF THIS BOOK

This book is the result of a seminar held in Oslo, in May 2009, as part of a (then) new research project.[4] The contributors to this volume have all worked with each other to produce an integrated approach investigating the meaning and purpose of the idea of learning lives. We have developed our work in relation to each other, and we follow similar structures to try to build theoretical coherence. Each chapter is rooted in a set of ideas around learning lives – issues of interdisciplinarity, whole-person-in-context, sets of learning domains and dimensions (in- and out-of-school involving the voluntary/ compulsory) and imagined futures.

We asked authors to build their work around the key concepts we have introduced here: learner identity, lifecourse trajectories, contexts, life-worlds and imagined futures. We also asked authors to offer questions for further study, both aiming at possible future research but also at how current students might want to use this work for applied purposes in schools and their own studies.

The book is organised in two main sections. Section One, Changing Approaches to Studying Learning: Identity, Policy and Social Change, includes more synthesising, conceptually oriented contributions exploring the changing approaches to studying learning (in the abstract). Section Two, From Learning to Learners: Learning Lives as They Are Lived, includes more studies of learners, as they live their lives across a range of social contexts.

The first part of Section One brings together those studies that, in the broadest sense, interrogate concepts of identity and learning. Hans Christian Arnseth and Kenneth Silseth take up the challenge of the elusiveness of the idea of identity in research into learning and focus on what it might mean to follow or trace learner identities across contexts, paying attention to change over time, as well as reflecting on how identities are imagined and 'described' in different learning contexts. They propose an attention to narratives/stories, categories and inscriptions as a way of being able to capture and make productive use of the idea of identity in learning research. This concern with the relationship between methods and concepts drives Kirsten Drotner's chapter, as she reflects on the rise and utility of processual methodologies; that is, forms of research that can capture change over time and across places, thus exploring the nature and meaning of contexts in this field. Drotner draws explicit parallels between media and education research by examining where both traditions intersect in forms of contemporary ethnography and in speculating how the digital world

---

[4]　See http://www.uv.uio.no/english/research/groups/transaction/index.html

offers a way of reconciling disciplinary traditions, as well as offering shared and common methods for describing and theorising change. As a way of extending this discussion of processual methodologies, Jay Lemke suggests that we additionally need a way of understanding the phenomenological and experiential, and he argues for a method of reconceptualising feeling that is akin to the semiotics of meaning making that we have become used to over the last twenty-five years. He suggests that the process of how we evaluate and classify both the semiotic and affective has much in common, and that we need to address research towards the affective domain both to balance the considerable amount of research into the former and to offer a more nuanced and rounded understanding of how learning takes place within a more whole-person perspective. These three contributions begin the process of opening up how we approach understanding learning within people and across time and contexts.

The next two chapters take a more policy and sociologically informed view of current changes in how we frame and organise learning. Lynne Chisholm is interested in how broad shifts in knowledge and employment are changing the parameters of traditionally held views of youth development. Traditional understandings of competence, individuality, accreditation and transitions between life courses are all under stress in 'second modernity', and Chisholm argues that, as the social structures of family, community, work and training all readjust to changing social conditions, so learning is becoming reconfigured in the digital age, at the subjective as well as the material level. Erstad and Sefton-Green pay attention to how the conceptualisation of the digital, especially that seen around the 'net-generation', has been mobilised in public discourse, alongside the idea of 'informal learning' as a way of valorising other and new ways of learning. The chapter then considers some policy responses to this challenge by looking at how school systems have responded to the perceived challenge of the digital generation. It highlights how the small Scandinavian country of Norway has appropriated and negotiated aspects of the digital vernacular in its attempts to consolidate longstanding values within the Norwegian education system.

Section Two explores learning mainly in unexpected contexts and across a range of social contexts. The section begins with three contributions that examine what might be described as an expanded sense of schooling, developing some of the themes from previous chapters by building links between school and out-of-school contexts. Antti Rajala and his colleagues from the University of Helsinki examine examples of embedded and out-of-school community-based learning to revisit pedagogical practises that explicitly and deliberately transgress conventional boundaries of space and place in schools. Judith Green, Audra Skukauskaite and Maria Castanheira then offer an historical exploration of interactional ethnography to show how such methods can illuminate the microprocesses by which all the parties in the close-knit to-and-fro of teaching and learning can develop and expand our understanding of learning as a process in which individuals communicate with each other.

Shirley Brice Heath writes about the qualities of learning offered in entrepreneurial-based enterprise projects, businesses and initiatives from around the world. She explicitly contrasts these contexts with formal schooling, pointing out what they can offer above and beyond conventional schooling, but also adding riders to such aspirations and thus positioning learning in not-school settings in relationship to what school does. This takes up the theme developed by Chisholm, as Brice Heath makes it clear that research and policy need to find ways of engaging with the kinds of learning she enumerates and analyse them in concert with, rather than in opposition to, schooling.

The next three chapters deal in detail with learning from domains that are not always characterised as such. Helen Nixon explores the discourse surrounding the educational role for parents of preschool children by examining how parents in Australia are constructed by contemporary policy discourses in ways that position them as key actors in their children's educational developments. She examines how the texts of popular parenting (including adverts for child-rearing products) work alongside the construction of play spaces and shopping malls to inscribe children and parents in pedagogic relationships. Björn Sjöblom and Karin Aronsson examine the conversation of young male gamers during computer game play in Sweden to show how such talk pays keen attention to the classification and assessment of players' learner trajectories (as Arnseth and Silseth have previously theorised) and is thus integral to the development of mastery, expertise and learner confidence and ability. Øystein Gilje examines how four young male Norwegian filmmakers construct identities for themselves as young artists and 'creatives' and how they use such ideas to mobilise potential futures for themselves. His research explores how learner identity is important in the growth of a professional self and how this relates to study at school, as well as to participation in out-of-school practices.

The final chapter in this section is also interested in artistic practices. It explores how Randy Young, a co-author based in San Francisco's Bay Area in the United States, along with Mark Nelson and Glynda Hull, reflects on his expressive communicative practices as a multimedia artist. The chapter traces how he has 'authored' a version of himself over an extensive period of time and explores how an expanded set of literacy practices may play a crucial role in developing other and different senses of the self.

CONCLUDING QUESTIONS

We believe that these chapters, taken together, begin to offer what we think of as an emergent 'learning lives' agenda. However, this is not to say that such a proposition can be taken at face value.

Chisholm, Drotner, Brice Heath, Erstad and Sefton-Green all suggest that the reconfiguration of 'classic' school-to-work transitions and the redrawing of traditional lifecourse stages have impacted on widely accepted definitions and understandings of both the processes and purposes of education in those societies that have been restructured as a consequence of neo-liberal reform. These principles have been driven forward by policies associated with the lifelong learning agenda. The argument is basically that the learner is now required to participate in a range of educational relationships that are significantly different from simply progressing through the planned routes of the education system. Furthermore, many case studies in this book and in the wider scholarly community call attention to the dimensions of subjectivity and other kinds of cultural capital configured by these kinds of relationships. It is no accident that many of the chapters in this volume highlight domestic (Nixon), affective (Lemke), informal (Sjöblom and Aronsson) and out-of-school learning experiences (Nelson, Hull and Young). Does this imply that future research will now focus on these unaccustomed and traditionally marginalised spaces? Why do analyses of contemporary, 'new' kinds of learning seem so important and yet have such difficulty in making purchase in wider public debate?

This is not to say that such approaches to education eschew study of the traditional knowledge-based domains. We did not invite scholars of such domains – the arts, science or mathematics – for example, to this project. However, as in the case study offered by Rajala and colleagues in Chapter 7, a burgeoning literature explores learning in these and other formal disciplines from outside the school (e.g. Bell et al., 2009, in relationship to science, or Lucy Green's (2008) work on informal music-making) and shows how much research is still interested in these wider non–school-based envelopes that surround and embed the content of school subjects. Does this mean that schools and schooling are no longer accepted as the exclusive sites for learning discipline-specific skills and knowledge? Is there now a different kind of acceptance that learning is an ongoing process, embedded in a wide range of experiences, across a wide range of social domains? And, if so, by whom? This may explain why chapters in this volume explore such a wide variety of places, such as shopping malls and play centres, and a diversity of formal and casual online sites as well as schools. It also raises the question about who is the audience for this kind of work and the status of its findings.

In turn, this perception about the need to explore the spread of learning contexts raises questions about our preconceptions about learning transfer and the processes by which we knit together learning from this range of experiences. For example, both chapters by Arnseth and Silseth and by Rajala and colleagues suggest that the key to analysis lies in the theorisation of individual agency-in-context. Yet, at a deeper level, many contributors are really asking the question: Who defines learning? On whose behalf and in whose interests? In Chapter 8, Green and colleagues cite the question posed by James Heap: 'What counts as social practices'? Is there a sense, as Drotner and Chisholm argue, that the digital practices of second modernity mean that our authority to answer these questions is beginning to fragment? This, in turn, suggests to us two levels of authority at work over these chapters. There is the classic challenge: how individuals assert meaning, take control and do the work of making meaning. But is there not also a challenge to the authority of who defines the frames of learning at work across these social worlds? How does everyday learning gain legitimacy as it struggles with other competing definitions?

Some of this comes down to what a number of contributors (e.g. Nixon, Erstad and Sefton-Green) describe as the 'pedagogicization of everyday life'. That is, how noneducational domains (those listed above and not usually described as such) inscribe people within teacher–learner relationships an integral part of participating in social practices. In part, drawing from the work of Foucault and his insights into how we are positioned within discourses of sexuality, and also from Germanic structural traditions (Depaepe et al., 2008), the pedagogicization of everyday life has become increasingly popular in discussions about new and other kinds of learning. It establishes the terms of a learning relationship between social actors beyond the idea of learning outcomes, the production of knowledge or the development of skills. It is useful in thinking about the way in which educational relationships appear to be creeping across other social domains. However, the concept begs the question about whether the term implies a more dystopian form of control, of a new kind of knowledge-management by institutions like the family, or whether it implies that such surveillance is the prerogative of the researcher and analyst. Is it a way of denying the agency of social actors, or a way of privileging the research gaze? In discussions about agency, who gets to 'anoint' the power of the agent?

In turn, this begs the larger question: In what sense can we suggest that learning is changing? If the discourse of what counts as learning is shifting, gaining new and different meanings, does this imply that common sense and accepted understandings of learning are also changing? How can such shifts be described? And, what does this imply for policy and research agendas? Erstad and Sefton-Green's study of one country's response to an international, global discourse begins to unpack some of the issues here. Whilst there is something counterintuitive to the notion that the processes of learning might themselves be changing (and from what? some will ask), the project at the heart of this volume asks how resituating the focus of attention on learners and their lives (empirically and conceptually) impacts on the analytical category of 'learning' itself.

REFERENCES

Alheit, P., & Dausien, B. (1999). 'Biographicity' as a basic resource in lifelong learning. Proceedings from *Conference Proceedings of the European Conference on Lifelong Learning Inside and Outside Schools*, University of Bremen.

Barton, D., & Hamilton, M. (1998). *Local literacies: Reading and writing in one community*. London: Routledge.

Bauman, Z. (2005). *Liquid life*. Cambridge: Polity Press.

Bell, P., Lewenstein, B., Shouse, A. W., & Feder, M. A. (Eds.). (2009). *Learning science in informal environments. People, places and pursuits*. Washington DC: The National Academies Press.

Biesta, G. (2006). What's the point of lifelong learning if lifelong learning has no point? On the democratic deficit of policies for lifelong learning. *European Educational Research Journal, 5*(3–4), 169–80.

Biesta, G. (2009). Pragmatism's contribution to understanding learning-in-context. In R. Edwards, G. Biesta, & M. Thorpe (Eds.), *Rethinking contexts for learning and teaching (improving learning)*. London: Routledge.

Bloome, D., Carter, S. P., Christian, B. M., Otto, S., & Shuart-Faris, N. (2005). *Discourse analysis and the study of classroom language and literacy events: A microethnographic perspective*. Mahwah, NJ: Lawrence Erlbaum.

Bloomer, M. (2001). Young lives, learning and transformation: Some theoretical considerations. *Oxford Review of Education, 27*(3), 429–49.

Bourdieu, P. (1993). *The field of cultural production : Essays on art and literature* (R. Johnson, Trans.). Cambridge: Polity Press.

Brown, J. S., & Duguid, P. (2000). *The social life of information*. Cambridge, MA: Harvard Business School Press.

Bruner, J. (1996). *The culture of education*. Cambridge, MA: Harvard University Press.

Buckingham, D., & Sefton-Green, J. (2004). Structure, agency and culture in children's media culture. In J. Tobin (Ed.), *Pikachu's global adventure: The rise and fall of Pokemon*. Durham, NC: Duke University Press.

CERI. (2010). *Are the new millennium learners making the grade? Technology use and educational performance in PISA.* Paris: OECD.

Claxton, G. (2008). *What's the point of school? Rediscovering the heart of education.* Oxford: Oneworld.

Cohen, P. (1990). *Really useful knowledge: Photography and cultural studies in the transition from school.* London: Trentham Press.

Cole, M. (1996). *Cultural psychology. A once and future discipline.* Cambridge, MA: Belknap Press.

Cole, M., & the Distributed Literacy Consortium. (2006). *The fifth dimension. An after-school program built on diversity.* New York: Russell Sage Foundation.

Colley, H. (2009). Time in learning transitions through the lifecourse: A feminist perspective. In K. Ecclestone, G. Biesta, & M. Hughes (Eds.), *Transitions and learning through the lifecourse.* London: Routledge.

Cresswell, T. (1996). *In place/out of place. Geography, ideology and transgression.* Minneapolis: University of Minnesota Press.

Depaepe, M., Herman, F., Surmont, M., Gorp, A., & Simon, F. (2008). Educational research: The educationalization of social problems. In P. Smeyers & M. Depaepe (Eds.), *Educational Research* (vol. 3, pp. 13–30). Amsterdam: Springer Netherlands.

Dumont, H., Istance, D., & Benavides, F. (Eds.). (2010). *The nature of learning: Using research to inspire practice.* Paris: OECD.

Duranti, A., & Goodwin, C. (Eds.). (1992). *Rethinking context. Language as an interactive phenomenon.* Cambridge: Cambridge University Press.

Ecclestone, K., Biesta, G., & Hughes, M. (Eds.). (2009). *Transitions and learning through the lifecourse.* London: Routledge.

Edwards, R. (1997). *Changing places?: Flexibility, lifelong learning and a learning society.* London: Routledge.

Edwards, R. (2009). Introduction: Life as a learning context? In R. Edwards, G. Biesta, & M. Thorpe (Eds.), *Rethinking contexts for learning and teaching: Communities, activities and networks.* London: Routledge.

Edwards, R., Biesta, G., & Thorpe, M. (Eds.). (2009). *Rethinking contexts for learning and teaching: Communities, activities and networks.* London: Routledge.

Fornäs, J., Lindberg, U., & Sernhede, O. (1995). *In garageland. Rock, youth and modernity.* London: Routledge.

Giddens, A. (1991). *Modernity and self-identity: Self and society in the late modern age.* Cambridge: Polity Press.

Glastra, F., Hake, B., & Schedler, P. (2004). Lifelong learning as transitional learning. *Adult Education Quarterly, 55*(4), 291–307.

Gonzalez, N., Moll, L. C., & Amanti, C. (2005). *Funds of knowledge: Theorizing practices in households and classrooms.* Mahwah, NJ: Lawrence Erlbaum Associates.

Green, L. (2008). *Music, informal learning and the school: A new classroom pedagogy.* Aldershot: Ashgate.

Habermas, J. (1989). *The theory of communicative action: Critique of functionalist reason* (vol. 2). Cambridge: Polity Press.

Heath, S. B. (1983). *Ways with words: Language, life and work in communities and classrooms.* Cambridge: Cambridge University Press.

Heath, S. B., & Street, B. (2008). *On ethnography: Approaches to language and literacy research.* London: Routledge.

Ito, M., Baumer, S., Bittanti, M., boyd, d., Cody, R., Herr-Stephenson, B., et al. (2010). *Hanging out, messing around, and geeking out: Kids living and learning with new media (John D. and Catherine T. MacArthur Foundation Series on Digital Media and Learning)*. Boston, MA: MIT Press.

Jenkins, H., Clinton, K., Purushotma, R., Robinson, A., & Weigel, M. (2007). Confronting the challenges of participatory culture: Media education for the 21st century. Retrieved May, 2012, at http://digitallearning.macfound.org/atf/cf/%7B7E45C7E0-A3E0-4B89-AC9C-E807E1B0AE4E%7D/JENKINS_WHITE_PAPER.PDF

Kalantzis, M., & Cope, B. (2008). *New learning: Elements of a science of education*. Cambridge: Cambridge University Press.

Lareau, A. (2003). *Unequal childhoods: Class, race and family life*. Berkeley: University of California Press.

Latour, B. (2007). *Reassembling the social: An introduction to actor-network-theory*. Oxford: Oxford University Press.

Leander, K., Phillips, N., & Headrick Taylor, K. (2010). The changing social spaces of learning: Mapping new mobilities. *Review of Research in Education, 34*, 329–94.

Leander, K., & McKim, K. (2003). Tracing the everyday 'sittings' of adolescents on the Internet: A strategic adaptation of ethnography across online spaces. *Education, Communication & Information, 3*(2), 211–40.

Lemke, J. L. (2000). Across scales of time: Artifacts, activities, and meanings in ecosocial systems. *Mind, Culture, and Activity, 7*(4), 273–90.

Levinson, B., Foley, D., & Holland, D. (1996). *Cultural production of the educated person: Critical ethnographies of schooling and local practice*. Albany, NY: State University of New York Press.

Livingstone, S. (2002). *Young people and new media*. London: Sage Publications.

McLeod, J., & Yates, L. (2006). *Making modern lives. Subjectivity, schooling and social change*. Albany, NY: State University of New York Press.

Moje, E. (2000). Critical issues: Circles of kinship, position, and power: Examining the community in community-based research. *Journal of Literacy Research, 32*(1), 77–112.

Moje, E., & Luke, A. (2009). Literacy and identity: Exploring the metaphor in history & contemporary research. *Reading Research Quarterly, 44*(4), 415–37.

Moss, G. (2001). On literacy and the social organisation of knowledge inside and outside school. *Language and Education, 15*(2,3), 146–62.

Nespor, J. (1997). *Tangled up in school*. Mahwah, NJ: Lawrence Erlbaum.

NSF Task Force on Cyberlearning. (2008). Fostering learning in the networked world: The cyber learning opportunity and challenge. Retrieved May 2012, at http://www.nsf.gov/pubs/2008/nsf08204/nsf08204.pdf

Pampols, C. F., & Porzio, L. (2005). Jipis, Pijos, Fiesteros. Studies on youth cultures in Spain 1960–2004. *YOUNG. Nordic Journal of Youth Research, 13*(1), 89–114.

Pedró, F. (2006). The new millennium learners: Challenging our views on ICT and learning. Retrieved at http://www.oecd.org/dataoecd/1/1/38358359.pdf

Pollard, A., & Filer, A. (1999). *The social world of pupil career: Strategic biographies through primary school*. London: Cassell and Continuum.

Pugh, A. J. (2009). *Longing and belonging: Parents, children, and consumer culture*. Berkeley: University of California Press.

Qvortrup, J., Bardy, M., Sgritta, G., & Wintersberger, H. (1994). *Childhood matters: Social theory, practice and politics.* Avebury: Avebury Press.

Rudberg, Monica, & Bjerrum Nielsen, H. (2005). Potential spaces – Subjectivities and gender in a generational perspective. *Feminism & Psychology, 15*(2), 127–48.

Scribner, S., & Cole, M. (1981). *The psychology of literacy.* Cambridge, MA: Harvard University Press.

Sefton-Green, J. (2006). Youth, technology and media cultures. In J. Green & A. Luke (Eds.), *Review of research in education 30* (pp. 279–304). Washington DC: AERA.

Sinha, C. (1999). Situated selves: Learning to be a learner. In J. Bliss, R. Saljo, & P. Light (Eds.), *Learning sites: Social and technological resources for learning* (pp. 32–48). Oxford: Pergamon Press.

Thomson, R. (2009). *Unfolding lives. Youth, gender and change.* Bristol: Policy Press.

Wenger, E. (1999). *Communities of practice: Learning, meaning, and identity.* Cambridge: Cambridge University Press.

Wertsch, J. V. (1997). *Mind as action.* New York: Oxford University Press.

Wortham, S. (2005). *Learning identity: The joint emergence of social identification and academic learning.* Cambridge: Cambridge University Press.

CHANGING APPROACHES TO STUDYING LEARNING: IDENTITY, POLICY AND SOCIAL CHANGE

Chapter 2

Tracing Learning and Identity Across Sites: Tensions, Connections and Transformations in and Between Everyday and Institutional Practices

Hans Christian Arnseth and Kenneth Silseth

Tracing learning, learning across the different settings in which learners participate, has become an important research topic during the last couple of decades. Young people are involved in a whole range of different activities across sites and over time; they play computer games with friends, discuss topics, coordinate parties or map networks on Facebook and carry out science projects at school, where they need to collect and validate information on the internet. All of these activities involve various forms of participation. Through participation in these activities, which takes places in different settings, individuals are recognised and constituted as a variety of types of persons: as the computer geek, as the best football player or as the science genius. Furthermore, many things happening in informal settings might have implications for learning school subjects, and many things happening at school are not necessarily about education, as the editors argue in the introduction to this volume. Here, we introduce a set of analytical concepts for grasping the tensions, connections and transformations that occur in participation in and across sites. Informed by a dialogic perspective on human action and meaning making, we focus on the person as a participant in various practices as our unit of analysis. Widening the analytical scope enables us to understand some of the relationships between the different activities in which young people are engaged.

While many researchers have been concerned with the impact of the social identities and skills learned in local communities on students' academic performance (Heath, 1983; Gonzâalez, Moll & Amanti, 2005; Wortham, 2006), not many have been concerned with the possible connections and/or conflicts between the identities that are constituted as relevant in the practices in which youth participate. Researchers have mainly focused on how these conflicts or connections occur within a practice and have not investigated how meanings, knowledge and social identities actually move across space and in time. In the same vein, these studies of learning and identity have not addressed the materiality of human action and meaning making. We aim to introduce analytical resources that enable us to grasp both how meanings and identities are negotiated within a practice, as well as how these meanings and identities move in space and time. In particular, we focus on how a person is constructed as a learner, and how the construction of a person as a learner is intertwined with his or her changing participation. We are interested in providing means for studying how versions of the self as learner move between situations and whether they are taken up, transformed or ignored in new situations. We use the term *learning selves* to focus on the dual nature of becoming a learner; that is to say, learning not only involves becoming a central participant, but also involves becoming a specific kind of learner. The learning self involves not only characterisations of the learner as novice – or *legitimate peripheral participant,* to use Lave and Wengers' (1991) phrase – but potentially involves all kinds of characterisations of the person that have an impact on his or her participation in and between practices. As will be outlined later in the chapter, the notion of learning selves also comprises the materiality of learning and identity construction (Fenwick & Edwards, 2010) and the materiality of the resources that are used in constituting persons as learners in specific practices.

To illustrate our approach, we use a fictitious example that is loosely based on experiences with youth participating in one of our research projects. Sunita is a fifteen-year-old girl living with her parents and two brothers outside of Oslo. Her family arrived in Norway when she was about two. She is very fond of playing board games and is a very skilled player. She often cooks with her mother and learns traditional recipes and techniques when cooking meals for the family. After school, she spends a lot of time helping her mother take care of her younger brothers. At school, she enjoys creative subjects but has some trouble with maths, and the school psychologist suspects she might have attention deficit hyperactivity disorder (ADHD). Sunita is negotiating several learning selves – selves that say something about how she and others constitute her (in)competent participation in different practices. She is learning how to cook, but simultaneously she is also learning gender – she is learning how to be a woman. The teacher encourages students to express themselves through art. This might conflict with Sunita's positioning towards her mother when cooking traditional meals, a practice where creativity is not necessarily valued. Furthermore, ADHD is a category connected to her learning self in maths, a learning self which signals problems with mastering the curriculum. The ADHD can become connected to this learning self and constitute an explanation for her problems. She can become a person with an ADHD label. However, this learning self is not necessarily relevant to all the activities in which Sunita participates. For instance, even at school, there are many situations where this learning self will not be invoked, such as when Sunita hangs out with her friends. On the other hand, the category ADHD might influence the way her parents construct Sunita's learning self at home, when she participates in leisure activities. Sunita needs to deal with the implications of these learning selves. She can appropriate them, she can transform them or she can ignore them. Nevertheless, how she orients to them has implications for her social relationships, as well as for her abilities to learn painting or cooking. In the same vein, the learning self she appropriates in specific situations has implications for her identity and how her actions are made sense of and evaluated by others. We will expand more on this example and return to Sunita throughout this chapter to exemplify our argument.

We introduce three analytical concepts or topics that we believe constitute particularly fruitful means for studying the tensions, connections and transformations that occur among practices. First, it is necessary to understand the meanings and functions of *stories and narratives* in the constructive processes involved in establishing coherence over time and across sites. Second, we must investigate learning and identity construction as *categorisation* work. Finally, it is essential to focus on how traces of knowledge, skill and identity become *inscribed* into material representations in the form of graphs, charts, exam papers or other types of artefacts, and how they move in space and time and are taken up in other situations.

Our analytical interest in studying connections between sites and practices is made relevant by what we see as important challenges facing young people, challenges mediated by recent developments in information and communication technologies (see Chisholm in Chapter 5 and Sefton-Green & Erstad in the introduction to this volume). The analytical concepts might be fruitful for capturing what is at stake for participants as they traverse these different activity settings. We argue that these concepts are particularly well-suited for studying how young people are constituted as learners; particularly how, on the one hand, links and connections are made, and, on the other, how boundaries in and between formal and informal settings for learning are established and marked (Bekerman, Burbules & Silberman-Keller, 2006; Hull & Schultz, 2002).

The outline of the chapter is as follows. First, we contextualise our argument, identifying some important changes in young people's lives that involve a renegotiation of knowledge domains and boundaries between practices. Second, we outline a dialogic approach for understanding the construction of learning selves that will prepare the ground for developing our analytical approach. Third, we introduce the analytical concepts for studying tensions and connections between practices, and, finally, we draw together the main threads in our argument and its relevance.

MULTIPLE SITES FOR LEARNING AND IDENTITY WORK

During the last couple of decades, young people's lives have become increasingly complex and diversified (Gee, Hull & Lankshear, 1996). Identity work is no longer limited to local space and time (Appadurai, 1996). On the contrary, at an early stage, young people engage with a globalised youth culture that offers multiple practices for participation – a culture that children and youth to a great extent engage with through the use of computers and the internet (Valentine & Holloway, 2002; Sefton-Green, 2006; Wortham, 2011). They play games, chat with friends or watch videos or view pictures. Some even create or remix media content and share this through social media (Lankshear & Knobel, 2006). Computers are mainly used for communication, entertainment and play. Having said that, computers are *boundary objects* that are used and understood differently depending on the practices in which they are embedded. When using computers in school, young people might need to renegotiate the meaning of the computer to be able to succeed as learners. According to Star and Griesemer (1989), boundary objects are plastic enough to adapt to local needs, and are interpreted differently by different communities, but remain robust enough to maintain integrity across sites. While computers for young people are mainly devices for play and entertainment, computers for teachers and in institutions are mainly tools for getting work done. When youth enter school, this might constitute a potential problem for them.

In a globalised youth culture, boundaries between activities and contexts become more fluid and blurred, and young people take on different identities and learn to participate in various practices. New media are becoming entangled with young people's participation in a majority of the practices in which youth engage, something that makes it difficult to perceive these practices as separated (Livingstone, 2002). For instance, with the advent of computers, a clear distinction between work and play becomes more difficult to uphold (Sefton-Green, 1998). In some activities at work or in school, creative play might constitute an important resource, as when designing a PowerPoint presentation. For young people, the challenge is to not only appropriate the genres and norms of participation in these contexts, but also to gain an understanding of the contextual framing of these activities and to be able to see potential connections or tensions between them. Of course, these are not new problems, nor are they exclusively tied to youth as such. People never stop learning new things, but we suggest that 'crossing sites' in this way is a particularly pertinent issue for young people.

Thus, we claim that it has become more challenging for young people to manage and understand the differences and similarities between the different contexts and activities they encounter, and it has become more challenging to manage their identities in and between settings (Østerud & Arnseth, 2008). For instance, when students play a 'serious game' at school, what forms of knowing do they draw on to accomplish tasks in the game, and what is the historical genesis of the resources they make use of?[1] An avid gamer might find his or her experience in navigating complex three-dimensional (3D) environments to be useful when playing the game. Conversely, his or her expertise in entertainment games might stand in the way of identifying and benefitting from intentional educational meanings in a school-based game (Silseth, 2012).

Young people also seem to swap between 'multiple activities' more rapidly and to a greater extent than before, something that in part is due to the increased availability of digital technologies (Livingstone, 2002). For instance, in educational settings, we have observed that when pupils finish doing a required task, they might quickly check their Facebook accounts until the teacher again refocuses their attention to a school task. The maintenance of social relationships is mediated by technologies, something which creates some new challenges and opportunities for young people (boyd & Ellison, 2008). Against this background, it becomes evident that it is problematic to treat formal and nonformal learning as connected to specific sites or situations. Instead, it makes more sense to treat these forms of learning as *participant orientations*, centred on the kinds of meaning and knowledge that are relevant for participants in the different situations in which they partake. These orientations are, of course, structured by the norms and rules operating in a setting, but they are not in any simple sense determined by them.

We suggest that young people face important challenges in making meta-level judgements about what they need to know and which cultural resources

---

[1] The term *serious game* signifies computer games that have some sort of educational goal built into the design. An example of such game is Global Conflicts: Palestine, in which the player takes on the role as a news reporter who is to cover the Israeli–Palestinian conflict. The goal is that, through encountering different stories told by different characters, the player will gain a better understanding of the complexity of the conflict.

to use to be able to participate in activities. In the following sections, we outline how these challenges can be identified and analysed as young people traverse a range of social settings.

A DIALOGIC APPROACH

For the purpose of developing the analytical framework that enables us to study how learning selves are constructed in and between sites, we propose a dialogic approach to learning and meaning making. In this approach, *interaction* and *context* are key concepts in the study of language, communication and cognition (Linell, 2009). When a person participates in different kinds of practices, the meanings and functions of his or her skills and identities emerge through negotiations among other people participating in and the resources available to that practice.

In this approach, every act is understood as an answer (Linell, 1998), whether it is an answer in the form of responding to other peoples' actions or to features of the environment. Language is relational – it is not simply something we own, but rather something we are shareholders in (Rommetveit, 2003), something which also makes the person using language and other semiotic tools enter into a relationship. Vološinov (1973) has argued that:

[T]he subjective psyche is to be localized somewhere between the organism and the outside world, on the borderline separating these two spheres or reality. It is here that an encounter between the organism and the outside world takes place, but the encounter is not a physical one: the organism and the outside world meet here in the sign. (p. 26)

A person's conception of the inner and outer world, and what constitutes the learning selves of that person, is located between the person and what exists in the encountered situation. Furthermore, the recognition of the learning self as something relational and situated challenges an atomistic notion of identity. A person's identity is not something given in advance of social interaction (Marková, 2003), but is something dialogically constructed in and across participation trajectories and different timescales (Holland et al., 1998; Lemke, 2007).

To grasp how meaning is made and how learning selves are constructed in particular sites, *utterance* and *voice* are two interrelated concepts of great importance. An utterance can take all sort of different shapes. It can be verbal, textual or audiovisual. It can take place verbally, in a dialogue between peers in a science classroom; it can take shape as a written article in the local school newspaper; it can manifest itself as a message on Twitter. When analysing meaning making, an important strategy, then, is to study how specific utterances are responded to and made relevant (or irrelevant) by participants in different settings. Bakhtin (1984) defined voice as 'a person's worldview and fate', but it can also be translated as referring to a specific perspective or a particular point of (world) view (Wertsch, 1991; Linell, 2009). For instance, voice has to do with specific perspectives on different topics that participants in a practice make visible when interacting. These perspectives are shaped by prior experiences and can often be contradictory; nevertheless, these perspectives continue to have an influence on how topics are understood and acted on. Voice is closely linked to utterance. An utterance has to be produced by a particular voice, which has to be located in a particular situation. Meaning making is a result of an encounter between two or more voices. According to Lemke (1995), 'We speak with the voices of our communities, and to the extent that we have individual voices, we fashion these out of the social voices already available to us, appropriating the words of others to speak a word of our own' (pp. 24–5). The constitution of learning selves involves the coordination, management and negotiation of different voices that come together in the process of meaning making, which has great importance for how a person is constituted as a learner in specific situations taking place in various practices. How a learner manages these voices has implications for how he or she is constituted as a competent or incompetent person within that particular practice.

Furthermore, the concept of voice or *multivoicedness* might enable us to capture how utterances produced in different situations – for example, students' essays on World War II in school or a young boy's comments on the global financial crisis on his private blog – consist of different perspectives and interests recruited from different practices traversed by the producer of the utterance. These perspectives and interests make up learning selves. Also, in school, the concept of voice might capture the process of meaning making between interlocutors – for example, in discussing a particular topic in a history class – as consisting of perspectives and interests that one usually associates with either in-school or out-of-school contexts. This conceptual frame enables us to grasp how utterances performed in school settings are answers to voices from both formal and informal practices. Learning selves are constructed at the intersection of these different perspectives and interests. Students will participate in situations in which they encounter a range of different voices that are not necessarily reconciled, but are, nevertheless, present and very much alive in the meaning-making process.

ANALYTICAL RESOURCES AND STRATEGIES

As we have argued, a dialogical approach emphasises the mutually constitutive relationships among humans, tools and settings. Semiotic and material artefacts are cultural resources carrying meaning potentials and potentials for action that learners might make use of for different purposes. Based on the previous discussion of dialogical principles, we want to emphasise three areas that we believe are crucial for understanding and analysing the constitution of learning selves.

Narratives and Stories

The first resource is narratives and stories. 'Telling oneself about oneself is like making up a story about who and what we are, what's happened, and why we're doing what we're doing' (Bruner, 2002, p. 64). According to Bruner (2002), narratives are crucial resources for learning, thinking and identity formation. Narratives and stories are particularly well suited for managing coherence over time, since they enable agents to connect past to present and constitute their learning selves in a way that enables them to manage the challenges of the present. When Sunita is faced with a situation in which she has difficulties solving math problems, she can construct a story of herself as a person who always has had these kinds of difficulties, something that 'explains' why she cannot engage competently in math activity. It enables her to make sense of it and provides her with a reason. Using stories thus enables her to constitute her learning self in a way that enables her to manage issues of blame and criticism. Having said that, one implication of Sunita's story – her narrative version of a learning self – is that others can dispute it. To use Billig's (1987) formulation, her narrative can be countered by forms of *particularising*, as interlocutors introduce contrasting evidence. The agent will use different voices to create stories that enable the constitution of a learning self, but these voices might stand in contrast to other voices that other people have at their disposal. For instance, Sunita's teacher might claim that, at one particular test in primary school, Sunita was, in fact, best in her class. This can again be rationalised and explained by Sunita as an exception. In this way, her learning self (or that element of it which describes her 'mastery' of mathematics) becomes a site for dispute and argument, which in principle can go on until, for all practical purposes, one voice is constituted as the 'true' story of her learning self. Our contention is that the learning self *as it emerges in dialogue* has crucial consequences for how students participate further in the educational context.

A learning self is not determined by individual agency. It is, at times, a site of struggle between different voices. For instance, when Sunita performs poorly on a math test, the teacher might confront her, telling Sunita a story about herself as someone who often doesn't pay attention in class. This story enables the teacher to treat a recent incident involving Sunita as part of a pattern. However, this might also enable the teacher to explain and account for the fact that the student is performing badly in his class and, by the same token, avoid the implication that something is wrong with his teaching. Furthermore, a school psychologist might construct stories of a history of learning difficulties by drawing on a set of associated voices. In this case, constructions of a student's learning self are even more detached from Sunita's agency, but these constructions might still have important implications and consequences for her participation trajectories in school. This is not necessarily a negative story about Sunita. On the contrary, this story might also generate extra resources and support, something that might make it easier for her to participate competently.

A crucial issue in regard to stories and narratives concerns their function as cultural tools for representing the past and projecting the future (Wertsch, 1998). Here, we are concerned with how the history of a person is represented. Narratives are generally characterised by 'being temporally organised, having a central subject, plot and narrative voice, and achieving closure around a conclusion' (Wertsch, 1998, p. 80). In contrast to categories or inscriptions, narratives present themselves as more integrated wholes. Our interest is to analyse how students *tell stories about themselves as learners*, on the one hand, and how they *respond to stories told about them as learners*, on the other. The focus is on how they manage multivoiced situations across different sites of participation. Young people's learning selves can be studied in narrative creations about the learner, the topic of the story and the agent who acts or is acted upon by others. The utterances of different agents in particular situations in and out of school form the units of analysis in the process of studying these narrative creations. An analytical strategy, then, would be to examine how the people mentioned in a story (in text or talk) – for instance peers, family members, celebrities, teachers – are described, and try to document the functions they have in the story, including how their implications are taken up and responded to by other interlocutors (Silverman, 2001).

Sunita might use voices from different places in which she participates to create stories for a particular purpose at school – the storytelling might transcend the situation where it takes place. She may be more or less in control of the stories and narratives that are mobilised in order to construct versions of her learning selves. Conversely, stories can be told about her, and, in this regard, she has particular strategies at her disposal that might enable her to counter or accept the normative implications of these stories. To scrutinise these issues is crucial for understanding how and why pupils engage in activities for longer periods of time and in time become experts, or how and why they disengage from activities in school or at home.

Categories and Categorisation

Categories and categorisation form the second set of resources that we address. Categories are crucial resources for ordering the world around us. However, as noted earlier, categories are not simply representations of the external world or containers of meaning. On the contrary, they can be conceived as cultural resources that actually *do* things – as mediational means (Wertsch, 1998). Categories are tools for understanding, describing and managing situations, persons and activities. A whole range of categories might be used to constitute learning selves, categories that have different implications for how others respond and orient to versions. Examples of such categories are girl, Norwegian, gamer, creative, bully, good student, learning disabled and so forth. Furthermore, categories are socio-historical constructs, have meaning potentials (Linell, 1998) and carry traces of how they were used in similar situations, contexts and practices.

Our task as analysts is to study categories (or clusters of categories) of learning selves and scrutinise how participants constitute and are constituted by them; that is, we study how participants use categories and how they manage their implications, but we also focus on how categories and category clusters become inscriptions that are transported into other practices (this is described in more detail in the next section). We have to study how categories are expressed in utterances and in situations of participation. Categorisations of the learning self are not simply descriptions, but rather are worked up or resisted in action through the use of different voices; that is, they are closely related to participants' rights and obligations as these are made relevant in situ.

Also, categorisations of the learning self come from somewhere. They are interested accounts created in the field of tension that exists between different voices. They are created by agents using different voices located in different practices. A category carries different implications depending on where it originates. For instance, for Sunita and her parents, it is difficult to resist the implications of an expert category, such as ADHD. Conversely, it might be difficult for teachers or school psychologists to subsume a pupil's own local categories into their frameworks. Furthermore, categories can have different normative values built into them. For instance, the category *expert* refers to a person who is good in maths or skateboarding, while beginner refers to a person who is not so good in maths or skateboarding. Now, using a category like *expert* about Sunita when she is engaged in playing board games might be a way for someone to constitute a learning self in a way that establishes her actions and activities as motivated and interested in an activity. It is a category that makes it apparent to other interlocutors how they should approach Sunita in settings in which the activity of playing board games is relevant, and it helps them understand and evaluate her actions in this activity.

As with narratives, others might constitute versions of a learning self that can have positive or negative impacts on a person's participation trajectories, but the person can accept or avoid the implications of the category. For instance, if a student like Sunita is diagnosed with the category ADHD, this might have important consequences for her learning self, for better or worse. First, ADHD is a category that might be very difficult to escape, since it is backed by a whole system of experts. Second, it is a category that might stick to her for a lifetime and make it difficult for her to succeed since other people will use that category to makes sense of and evaluate her schoolwork. On the other hand, the category might also work as a resource for Sunita in making meaning of her actions and in constituting her at-times erratic behaviour as 'normal'. And again, her fellow students and teachers might respond totally differently towards her. Instead of treating her learning self as unmotivated and uninterested in learning school subjects, they might try to help her and respond to her. In turn, this might enable her to learn something because she receives adequate and relevant help from others. In addition, she might get special tools or drugs that enable her to function better. As such, the category makes it possible to establish new ties and recruit new human and non-human actors that, together, may help her succeed better at school over time.

Inscriptions

Our third resource is inscriptions. It is important to emphasise the inherent tensions that exist in the relationships between action and mediational means (Wertsch, 1998). Humans are not entirely in control of mediational means when it comes to realising their goals and objectives. On the contrary, mediational means have a sense of agency in their own right that humans can make use of or try to resist, but cannot simply ignore. When humans use meditational means, such as language or a computer, to carry out specific action, these means will to some extent structure what it is possible to undertake. However, even if the attention to mediational means and artefacts does provide us with tools for addressing these issues, these tools do not enable us to study the processes by which artefacts are made into movable objects in their own right; that is, how objects are recruited as vehicles to transfer knowledge and how they become recruited into new practices. Such traversals are captured in some of Latour's ideas about inscriptions and non-human agents. According to Latour (1999), an inscription can be defined as:

A general term that refers to all the types of transformations through which an entity becomes materialized into a sign, an archive, a document, a piece of paper, a trace. Usually but not always inscriptions are two-dimensional, superimposable, and combinable. They are always mobile, that is, they allow new translations and articulations while keeping some types of relations intact. Hence they are also called 'immutable mobiles', a term that focuses on the movement of displacement and the contradictory requirements of the task. When immutable mobiles are cleverly aligned they produce the circulating reference. (p. 306)

In our view, an emphasis on inscriptions or what Latour calls 'immutable mobiles' is particularly useful for analysing transformations between sites. Inscriptions point to how social and cultural norms and values are embedded in artefacts, and this has an implication for the action that is carried out when employing these artefacts in specific practices. In contrast to narratives and categories, inscriptions, to a large extent, point to the importance of non-human actors. Furthermore, narratives and categories can be inscribed into artefacts and be used for specific purposes. Regarding the case of Sunita, the functions of a diagnosis such as ADHD, inscribed into a specialist report and diagnosed in accordance with a scientific system of categories, are not easily captured using a notion like meditational means, which places too much emphasis on human agency. Inscriptions point to how the learning self can be conceived of as a network of human and non-human actors. From this perspective, a learning self can expand. A whole range of stories, categories, people and so forth can be folded together and made into a version of the learning self.

Aspects of a network constituting a learning self can also dissolve and be recruited into other networks. For instance, a school psychologist's written evaluation of Sunita can be transported between sites to construct a learning self that becomes relevant and has an impact on Sunita's participation at a particular site. For instance, the evaluation form can travel between different sites in the educational system, such as between the psychologist and the teacher responsible for Sunita's education. In this case, the teacher can use specific voices inscribed into the evaluation when constructing her particular learning selves for Sunita. However, it is also possible for Sunita to negotiate these learning selves by telling stories and using categories that contrast with what is inscribed in the evaluation form that the teacher uses as a resource. Furthermore, the teacher might also actively engage with the voices inscribed into the evaluation, appropriating some and rejecting others. The psychologist's evaluation of Sunita might also be transported home to her parents. Here, the stories and categories inscribed into the evaluation might be taken up by her parents and influence how they perceive Sunita as a learner. However, they might also contrast this version of her learning self, as described by the formal educational system, by telling stories about Sunita as a good daughter who is caring for her younger brothers, helping her mother in the kitchen and always beating her father when they play board games.

In order to understand how young people are constituted as learners in specific practices, we need to study in detail how particular versions of the learning self are taken out of the social interaction and inscribed into various material tools and artefacts, trace how these inscriptions move or travel to other situations and practices and, by the same token, are translated and transformed in the process.

SUMMARY

In this chapter, we outlined the notion of *learning selves* in an attempt to address how learning across sites can be studied. The impact of identities and learning in local communities outside of school on students' performance in school has been emphasised by several scholars (Heath, 1983; Gonzâalez et al., 2005; Wortham, 2006). However, not many have been concerned with the possible connections and/or conflicts of being a learner engaged in both school and out-of-school sites. We have tried to develop some analytical resources for studying the tensions, connections and transformations among sites by taking a dialogical approach as our point of departure. We started by noticing how young people in contemporary societies are confronted with situations in which they have to manoeuvre between a variety of different sites and types of participation. This, we contend, places pressure on their identities across such practices. We have outlined how our theme of interest might be addressed in a dialogic and socio-cultural perspective, and we have pointed to three important analytical issues and strategies for capturing discursive and nondiscursive constructions of learning selves.

The first resource, narratives and stories, points to how people tell stories in order to construct themselves or others as particular kinds of learners. Stories enable people to manage coherence over time, and, in the telling of them, they bring together in new situations the different practices that people traverse. In doing so, they become crucial in understanding how learning is managed over time and place. The second concept, categories, points to how specific labels are used in the process of making parts of a person's identity relevant to a learning situation; this, in turn, impacts on how that person is constituted as a learner. Categories enable people to order the world around them, and categories have certain normative values built into them. They are crucial in understanding how people are constituted as certain persons with certain identities, and they have great influence on how that person is constituted as a learner. The third concept, inscriptions, points to the materiality of learning. Inscriptions enable us to study how versions of learning selves are inscribed into artefacts and transported over the different sites connected to a person's life trajectory. These artefacts can take the shape of documents, drawings, images and so forth, which all can be used as resources for constituting a person as a learner in settings other than where the artefacts were originally produced. In our view, these constitute potentially fruitful strategies for investigating ruptures and continuities inside and outside of schools, as institutions in society.

Finally, the agency structure dimension is inherent in the notion of learning selves. As has been emphasised, it is not solely up to the person to construct him- or herself as a learner in specific practices. Learning selves can and often are constructed by other people and mediational means. However, a crucial point is that the learning self is always to some extent negotiable, even if some learning selves are harder to negotiate than others. Whether they actually are negotiated is an empirical question. However, how the learning self is constructed and what kinds of learning selves are defined as relevant in a particular practice will have great influence on a person's participation. The notion of the learning self, and the three resources examined in this chapter, might become vital in capturing the learning lives of young people participating in the myriad of practices that contemporary societies offer.

REFERENCES

Appadurai, A. (1996). *Modernity at large: Cultural dimensions of globalization.* Minneapolis: University of Minnesota Press.

Bakhtin, M. (1984). *Problems of Dostoevsky's poetics.* Minneapolis: University of Minnesota Press.

Bekerman, Z., Burbules, N. C., & Silberman-Keller, D. (Eds.). (2006). *Learning in places: The informal educational reader.* New York: Peter Lang.

Billig, M. (1987). *Arguing and thinking: A rhetorical approach to social psychology.* Cambridge: Cambridge University Press.

boyd, d., & Ellison, N. (2008). Social network sites: Definition, history, and scholarship. *Journal of Computer-Mediated Communication, 13,* 210–30.

Bruner, J. (2002). *Making stories: Law, literature, life.* Cambridge, MA: Harvard University Press.

Fenwick, T. J., & Edwards, R. (2010). *Actor-network theory in education.* New York: Routledge.

Gee, J. P., Hull, G. A., & Lankshear, C. (1996). *The new work order: Behind the language of the new capitalism.* Boulder, CO: Westview Press.

Gonzâalez, N., Moll, L. C., & Amanti, C. (2005). *Funds of knowledge: Theorizing practice in households, communities, and classrooms.* Mahwah, NJ: L. Erlbaum Associates.

Heath, S. B. (1983). *Ways with words: Language, life, and work in communities and classrooms.* Cambridge: Cambridge University Press.

Holland, D., Lachicotte, W. J., Skinner, D., & Cain, C. (1998). *Identity and agency in cultural worlds.* Cambridge, MA: Harvard University Press.

Hull, G., & Schultz, K. (2002). *School's out!: Bridging out-of-school literacies with classroom practices.* New York: Teachers College Press.

Lankshear, C., & Knobel, M. (2006). *New literacies: Everyday practices & classroom learning.* Berkshire: Open University Press.

Latour, B. (1999). *Pandora's hope: Essays on the reality of science studies.* Cambridge, MA: Harvard University Press.

Lave, J., & Wenger, E. (1991). *Situated learning: Legitimate peripheral participation.* Cambridge: Cambridge University Press.

Lemke, J. (1995). *Textual politics: Discourse and social dynamics.* London: Taylor & Francis

Lemke, J. (2007). Identity, development, and desire: Critical discourses and contested identities. In C. R. Caldas-Coulthard & R. Iedema (Eds.), *Identity trouble: Critical discourse and contested identities* (pp. 17–42). New York: Palgrave Macmillan.

Linell, P. (1998). *Approaching dialogue: Talk, interaction and contexts in dialogical perspective.* Amsterdam: John Benjamins.

Linell, P. (2009). *Rethinking language, mind, and world dialogically: Interactional and contextual theories of human sense-making.* Charlotte, NC: Information Age Publishing.

Livingstone, S. M. (2002). *Young people and new media: Childhood and the changing media environment.* London: Sage.

Marková, I. (2003). *Dialogicality and social representations: The dynamics of mind.* Cambridge: Cambridge University Press.

Østerud, S., & Arnseth, H. C. (2008). Læring, sosialisering og identitets utvikling i nettverkssamfunnet [Learning, socialization and identity development in the network society]. In S. Østerud & E. G. Skogseth (Eds.), *Å være på nett: Kommunikasjon, identitets- og kompetanseutvikling med digitale medier [To be on the net: Communication, identity and competence development with digital media]* (pp. 13–35). Oslo: Cappelen Academic Publishing House.

Rommetveit, R. (2003). On the role of "a psychology of the second person" in studies of meaning, language, and mind. *Mind, Culture, and Activity: An International Journal, 10*(3), 205–18.

Sefton-Green, J. (1998). *Digital diversions: Youth culture in the age of multimedia.* London: UCL Press.

Sefton-Green, J. (2006). Youth, technology, and media cultures. *Review of Research in Education, 30*(1), 279–306.

Silseth, K. (2012). The multivoicedness of game play: Exploring the unfolding of a student's learning trajectory in a gaming context at school. *International Journal of Computer-Supported Collaborative Learning, 7*(1), 63–84.

Silverman, D. (2001). *Interpreting qualitative data: Methods for analysing talk, text and interaction.* London: Sage.

Star, S. L., & Griesemer, J. R. (1989). Institutional ecology, translations' and boundary objects: Amateurs and professionals in Berkeley's Museum of Vertebrate Zoology, 1907–39. *Social Studies of Science, 19*(3), 387–420.

Valentine, G., & Holloway, S. L. (2002). Cyberkids? Exploring children's identities and social networks in on-line and off-line worlds. *Annals of the Association of American Geographers, 92*(2), 302–19.

Vološinov, V. N. (1973). *Marxism and the philosophy of language.* New York: Seminar Press.

Wertsch, J. (1991). *Voices of the mind: A sociocultural approach to mediated action.* Cambridge: Harvard University Press.

Wertsch, J. (1998). *Mind as action.* New York: Oxford University Press.

Wortham, S. (2006). *Learning identity: The joint emergence of social identification and academic learning.* Cambridge: Cambridge University Press.

Wortham, S. (2011). Youth cultures and education. *Review of Research in Education, 35*(1), vii–xi.

Chapter 3

Processual Methodologies and Digital Forms of Learning

Kirsten Drotner

The concept 'learning lives' encapsulates two important research trends to do with understanding how knowledge production comes about ('learning') and to do with understanding the subjects and contexts through which this production takes shape ('lives'). As is well known, the last two decades have seen an increasing focus on the learners' end of knowledge production and on the processes through which knowledge is acquired, as witnessed, for example, by the upsurge in handbook publications (e.g. Moon, 2004; Sawyer, 2006; Bonk & Graham, 2006; Mayer & Alexander, 2010; Sefton-Green, Thomson, Jones & Bresler, 2011). Learning is a complex set of ongoing practices through which people change their understanding of themselves and the world in ways that facilitate a change of action. Equally, the focus on learning has been accompanied by a growing acknowledgement that learning can and does unfold in complex and interlocking sets of physical sites and settings – home, school, work, libraries, museums, leisure time or 'doing nothing' – and under different arrangements of organisation – formal, semi-formal, informal (Drotner, Jensen & Schrøder, 2008). Learning is intrinsic to people's lives, when viewed from both an everyday perspective and a lifecourse perspective. Taken together, then, the elements in the term 'learning lives' underscore a bottom-up perspective on the acquisition of knowledge.

What is currently beginning to materialise – and what is also the backdrop of this chapter – is the way in which digital media are entering into this already complex learning assembly and, through that very process, co-constructing that assembly (see e.g. Landow, 1997). In the developed world, digital media are rapidly becoming catalysts for new forms of knowledge production. This is not because digital technologies in and of themselves are agents of change. Rather, it is because they facilitate and demand new and more processual and social modes of shaping, sharing and storing knowledge, and because that knowledge production plays out in often-hybrid online and offline spaces. When young people comment on a YouTube clip or circulate links to favourite sites, they are having fun; yet, by the same token, they also participate in ad hoc and changing learning networks based on immediate engagements and interests. Digital media are not merely new means of distributing existing forms of knowledge, and they are not merely techno-logical glosses on existing social and physical learning arrangements. Digital media serve to transform the very fabric of knowledge production towards handling semiotic tools of meaning making rather than, say, handling mate-rial tools such as welders or sewing machines. According to socio-cultural learning theories, tools are key to learning and knowledge production (Wertsch, 1985; Cole, 1996). Following that line of thought, digital media evidently serve to orchestrate learning processes as semiotic processes of knowledge acquisition and application rather than, or in addition to, being also material forms of tool use (Drotner, 2008). Moreover, digital – and increasingly portable – media serve to further disperse and transform arenas of learning because they are not bound to specific locales or times of use. Hence, digital media facilitate and enforce new approaches to learning and literacy, approaches that are intimately bound up with changing rationales for education.

The conflicted and contested concept of the knowledge society (Stehr, 1994) is a shorthand for global discourses on the ways in which societies move towards immaterial forms of production whose vital tenets are the storage, formation, processing and communication of signs – be they figures, text, sound or images. The very mediatisation and digitisation of these processes position digital competence formation at the discursive core of the knowledge society for public and private stakeholders alike. By the same token, the once-familiar concept of literacy as the ability to handle written text (read, write) and manipulate numbers (arithmetic) is being questioned and refashioned, so that today we have a range of what may be termed 'hyphenated literacies' – digital literacy (Gilster, 1998), computer literacy (Turner, Sweany & Husman, 2000), information literacy (Bruce, 1997), new literacies (Coiro, 2007) and multiliteracies (Unsworth, 2001) to name but a few. While these intertwined strategies and practices of digitisation, media-tisation and societal transformations are the subjects of intense debate and study, much less is made of the ways in which they call on new approaches to researching learning practices.

This chapter addresses how we may study current learning practices *as they unfold*. More precisely, I wish to map what I term *processual methodologies*; that is, key methodological approaches through which we may capture learning in the making across online and offline arenas of action. I will chart the underlying traditions of these methodologies in education research and (mass) media research, respectively, in order to draw out commonalities and differences that today's researcher of digital learning practices would do well to heed.

Processual methodological approaches come in both qualitative and quantitative forms. Examples of the former are participant observation, both offline and online, video recording, associative thinking-aloud exercises and participatory design. Examples of the latter are eye tracking, data mining techniques and certain cognitive experiments. I will pay particular attention to qualitative, processual approaches for two reasons. First, while quantitative studies by nature involve more participants, they are fewer in number than qualitative studies both in education and in media research. This is very likely because qualitative approaches are simpler to adopt by the individual researcher. The research design seems easier to initiate and implement than with quantitative studies, which often require access to large-scale data sets, advanced analytical tools and even lab facilities. Second, and perhaps for the reasons just mentioned, qualitative studies are most prominent in the research literature documenting learning processes, digital or not, as is evident from the empirical documentation found in, for example, handbooks on learning. I will go on to discuss some of the key dilemmas facing the researcher adopting processual methodologies, dilemmas that are to do with defining one's research object and spelling out the relations between researcher and the researched. These dilemmas represent classical methodological issues in qualitative research, and my contention is that they bear revisiting because digital forms of learning serve to radicalise these well-rehearsed dilemmas and, I would add, even seem to offer new ways out.

ETHNOGRAPHY AS A COMMON GROUND

Ethnography is the key processual methodology impacting both education studies and media studies. Indeed, ethnography is more than a methodology, as is spelled out by British sociologists Martyn Hammersley and Paul Atkinson. They define ethnography as an interpretive research approach characterised by an epistemological commitment to explicit and holistic interpretation from a bottom-up perspective; an empirical interest in first-hand exploration of processes and practices as they take place; and an application of multiple, mainly qualitative, methodologies (Hammersley & Atkinson, 1983/1989). As a term, *ethnography* covers both a particular process of research and the resulting product. Historically, ethnography has a dual parentage in anthropology and microsociology, a parentage that goes a long way towards understanding the main tenets of the approach: the researcher's extended immersion into, and often engagement with, a particular location; the attention being paid to informants' perspectives on the world; the focus on documenting situated networks of meaning-making procedures; and the importance put on conveying the richness and complexity of all of these aspects in such a way that it makes sense not only to a specific, academic public, but to wider audiences – often including the informants themselves.

In particular, the so-called ethnography of communication (Hymes, 1962) lays a common ground for joint research developments in education and media studies to do with users' meaning-making practices. Spurred by speech-act theory (Austin, 1962) and sociolinguistics (Labov, 1972), ethnographers of communication study in situ the speech events of particular language communities; that is, socially and linguistically diverse but geographically bounded units that share the same language. In education research, these pioneering efforts point to, and are taken up by, socio-cultural literacy studies from the 1980s on, with their focus on situated and co-constructed literacy practices (see Chapters 2, 7, 8 and 9, this volume). In media studies, ethnography of communication paves the way for studies on, for example, advertising language and talk on TV and radio (Vestergaard & Schrøder, 1985; Tolson, 2005; Hutchby, 2006), challenging the hegemony of visual approaches. On a grander canvas, the tradition catalyses a wider recognition of what has been termed the 'interpretive paradigm' (Lindlof & Meyer, 1987, p. 4) and a concomitant cross-fertilisation between humanistic and social-science traditions of research.

PROCESSUAL METHODOLOGIES IN EDUCATION RESEARCH

Educational ethnography is now a well-established concept and subfield of education research; indeed, to such a degree that already at the beginning of the new millennium it was debated whether it had become a new, dominant research paradigm (Eisenhart, 2001, p. 18). With peer-reviewed journals such as *Ethnography and Education* and *Anthropology and Education Quarterly*, regular conferences and a book series, *Studies in Educational Ethnography*, the study on processes in education and learning has become an institutionalised aspect of research and of teacher education (for an overview of the Anglo-American history, see Yon, 2003). This institutionalisation has been reached in only three decades and is testimony to the scientific, didactic and policy needs to document and analyse in considerable depth how learning comes about and plays out.

While anthropologists have studied schooling as part of enculturation processes since the 1920s, and while a few anthropologists, such as American George Spindler in the 1950s, pioneered studies of the role played by educational situations in personality formation (see overview in Spindler & Spindler, 1982), educational ethnography really only took off from the late 1960s on, as part of wider social engagements and critique. Microsociologists entered the field, and now-classic studies were conducted from perspectives of social class (Hargreaves, 1967; Lacey, 1970; Willis, 1977) and gender (Delamont, 1976; Walkerdine, 1989). At the time, ethnographic approaches served as much-needed correctives to dominant cognitive and behaviourist traditions of psychology in stressing an interpretive, bottom-up and student-focused perspective on sense making, on social interaction at a micro level and on the mundane contexts of schooling. In tune with broader postmodern trends in the social sciences in general and anthropology in particular (Clifford & Marcus, 1986; Marcus & Fischer, 1986), educational ethnography from the 1990s onwards has stressed the fluctuating and contingent nature, the multiplicity of voices, not only of the empirical field under study but also of the theory and methodology applied. The processual approach came full circle.

At the same time, and beyond the ramifications of educational ethnography, interest widened in studying learning beyond the school gates. Vocational training, learning at community centres, in sports clubs, museums, and as part of the entire life course – all of these activities assumed increasing importance, in tandem with more global perspectives on learning and more economic perspectives on harnessing learning for the knowledge society. Although the United Nations Educational, Scientific and Cultural Organisation (UNESCO) from its inception has strongly supported out-of-school learning as a democratising force and as a means of social inclusion (UNESCO, 1947; Faure et al., 1972), the diversity of learning arrangements already in existence has been promoted from the 1980s on as part of a more functional rationale tied to an increasingly pervasive discourse on the knowledge society (see overview of traditions and critique in Drotner, 2008). Many of these learning activities are less circumscribed, ritualised and extensive, and, although it is a contested issue whether learning is actually different under such circumstances, the growing acknowledgement of out-of-school learning helps advance processual methodologies, which in turn reflect back on understandings of classroom arrangements of learning. For example, several studies currently focus on the ways in which joint student learning develops across online and offline sites and settings, and do so by following the formation of networked trajectories and interaction processes (see overview of studies in, for example, Ito et al., 2009; Ludvigsen et al., 2011).

Currently, scholars have a range of research positions at their disposal – from the realist to the radically relativist; that is, from positions focusing on the researchers and the objects under study as relatively fixed entities to positions deconstructing such ramifications and placing a premium on the researcher and the research process itself – and all seem more reflexive of the choices made and their implications for the research outcome (Walford, 2008). Two issues keep recurring. The first is to do with the definition and delimination of research objects: acknowledging the discursive production of subjects, what is it we study? And, facing an instability of categories, how may relations between researcher and informants be described and developed? The possible answers to these vexed questions are being broached simultaneously with the upsurge in new methodological tools. Foremost among these is visual data collection and analysis. Portable, light and relatively inexpensive digital video technologies offer means of process documentation that complement (some would say replace) written field notes on observation and reflection. Naturally, visuals are not new to anthropology and microsociology, as witnessed by the long and sophisticated tradition in visual anthropology of debating the validity claims of visual material vis-á-vis sound and writing (Crawford & Turton, 1992; Loizos, 1993). What has changed, however, is the ease with which researchers may appropriate webcams and mobile devices to record and document what is going on in the field, and this ease serves to complicate an already intricate set of voices and perspectives (Prosser, 1998; Banks, 2008). Charting the development of processual methodologies in media studies, and particularly of media ethnography, may bring us closer to an understanding of how these complications are tackled today.

PROCESSUAL METHODOLOGIES IN MEDIA RESEARCH

Just as is the case in education research, processual methodologies in media studies are primarily associated with media ethnography, a term associated with US media researcher James Lull's early work, which he undertook in the late 1970s. With a theoretical background in ethnomethodology, he and his research assistants studied more than 200 families in order to illuminate how television operated as a social resource within informants' patterned everyday procedures and normative routines. In the process, Lull defined media ethnography as an attempt to grasp 'the "native's perspective" on relevant communicative and sociocultural matters indigenous to him' (Lull, 1980, p. 199). This definition clearly resonates with key tenets of ethnography at large. At the time, it also resonated with a growing interest in media research to study audiences, rather than institutions or texts, and to define them from the outset as active and engaged in contextualised forms of meaning making. We clearly see a parallel here to trends found in education research at the time, noted earlier, to look at a micro level at learners' sense-making processes and at learning as a socially situated process of knowledge construction. From the 1980s on, the rapid uptake in the developed world of video recorders and satellite television and, from the mid-1990s, the first wave of computer and mobile devices, were all changes that made media even more seamless aspects of people's everyday lives. The processual nature of ethnographic approaches was clearly suited to capture and analyse these trends, and, today, media ethnography holds an established, if contested, position in media studies at large (see overview in Schrøder et al. 2003, pp. 71–2). Its development mirrors the route taken by educational ethnography, with a good dose of postmodern thinking influencing research in the 1990s. This did not necessarily result in better ethnographies in an empirical sense, but it certainly helped advance theoretical and methodological rigour and reflexivity.

In retrospect, a good number of qualitative studies carried out within, for example, urban, youth or feminist studies from the early 1980s on may be defined as media ethnographies, without explicitly being labeled or acknowledged as such (Fornäs et al., 1988/1995; Fuglesang, 1994; Wulff, 1995). It is worth noting that several of these studies were published within interdisciplinary fields of study that were often perceived as marginal to mainstream research at the time. On a wider canvas, the increasing interest in applying ethnography in a range of disciplines, fields and settings both within and beyond the academy testifies to a social and cultural situation in which boundary-crossings and processes of transaction and transformation are acknowledged as part and parcel of everyday life in many parts of the world – and hence become focal entry points of research.

Perhaps of even greater pertinence is the fact that the centrality of media in these ethnographic approaches serves to foreground how socio-cultural meaning-making processes are particular forms of *semiotic* action. Media are both material technologies (a TV set, a computer) and means through which signs – text, images, sound and numbers – are used to shape, share and store meaning (Carey, 1989). This dual definition brings interpretive media studies close to literacy studies that have grown out of socio-cultural education research (Drotner, 2008). For example, anthropologists Elisabeth Mertz and Richard Parmentier advocate a joint perspective on the material as well as the immaterial, or semiotic, aspects of tools, whereas the Swedish education researcher Roger Säljö stresses the importance of discursive tools (Mertz & Parmentier, 1985; Säljö, 2000). Such insights offer important common ground for conceptual and methodological developments that are needed to grasp the complexity of the current learning landscape.

DIGITAL LEARNING AND DIGITAL METHODOLOGIES

As noted earlier, the current learning landscape has become more complex in recent years because of the interrelated moves towards immaterial forms of economic production and the global digitisation of mediatised forms of communication. The proliferation during the last two decades of what I called 'hyphenated literacies' is a result of attempts in academic, policy and practice circles to chart new vistas of competence formation for the twenty-first century. That new forms of literacy – the manipulation of signs – are at the core of these attempts was spelled out within a European policy framework by the Organisation for Economic Co-operation and Development (OECD) some years ago when it launched a project to define key competences in knowledge societies. In its final report, the three most important competences were defined as (1) interactive use of tools, (2) interaction in heterogenous groups and (3) autonomous action (OECD, 2005). Evidently, digital media are crucial levers for the interactive use of tools, and, in many parts of the world, educational policies favour such uses in attempting to integrate into the school curriculum computer-assisted teaching, learning management systems and pupil evaluation of digital sources. In addition, digital media may be crucial catalysts for the formation of the other two key competences, a claim that can be substantiated by looking at digital communication practices beyond the school walls.

One of the important implications of the dispersion of discursive sites and the contestation of knowledge formation is that school no longer holds a monopoly on future-directed competence formation. Thus, several studies demonstrate that young people's out-of-school uses of digital media are more varied, more advanced and less task-oriented than are their uses at school (Livingstone & Bovill, 2001; Arafeh & Levin, 2002; Erstad, 2005; Zickuhr, 2010). Unintendedly, a good many of these engagements may also catalyse the formation of those OECD key competences that address interaction in heterogenous groups and autonomous action. Being able to interact in heterogenous groups basically involves an ability to handle confrontations with otherness – manoeuvring between familiar and foreign elements without siding with either. Being able to act autonomously involves an ability to reflect on these practices so that one is able to modify and accommodate future actions. Crucially, both of these competences will increasingly be formed in virtual communities of practice within education, work or leisure – or mixtures of these (e.g. Bonk & Graham, 2005; Osborne, Gallacher & Crossman, 2007).

Viewed from a methodological perspective, the challenges of these trends are primarily of two kinds. First, the dispersion of those physical arenas of learning that are crucial levers of digital competence formation calls for *multisited* research designs and forms of data collection that are able to grasp the transfer of learning practices from one arena to the other. Second, the integration of physical places and virtual spaces of meaning making in these learning processes calls for *multidimensional* means of grasping and analysing these processes as they play out simultaneously online and offline. As for the first of these challenges, it is no longer feasible to form one's research design by viewing out-of-school contexts of learning as marginal to the core didactic practices taking shape at school or work. Nor does it seem plausible to merely make analytical correlations of empirical studies of learning at different locations. Researchers need to chart the physical and social networks of transformation in the various communities of practice within which learning is formed and negotiated, digital or not. These needs side well with the increasing attention being paid in ethnography at large to studying the multisitedness of culture and its routes of artefacts, symbols and ideas (Marcus, 1998, pp. 79–104). As for the second challenge, the intersection of online and offline processes of meaning making and the proliferation of online learning spaces in out-of-school contexts both serve to question the focus found in traditional ethnography on bounded, physical places as the unquestioned loci of research (Leander, Phillips & Taylor, 2010). Matters are even further complicated by the rapid uptake of social media, which is a shorthand for a variety of applications and services used for widely different purposes, such as blogs, wikis and sites for social networking, meta-gaming and photo sharing. Social media ease users' means of shaping digital content and facilitate their participation in interest-based communities of sharing, connecting and commenting. In methodological terms, this trend brings us up sharply to developing means for studying semiotic production and design processes.

Taken together, the focus on digital competence formation across arenas of learning and across place and space invites researchers to develop means through which the social and semiotic hybridity of learning processes online and offline may be charted and analysed. This methodological invigoration and reflection both necessitates and allows reinterpretations of some key methodological issues to do with our definition of what we research and how we relate to what those objects are. In handling these issues, we may look to digital media as both means and ends.

ETHNOGRAPHY ON THE RUN

Many current studies of digital learning processes operate online in both an empirical and a methodological sense. The term *virtual ethnography* is applied in both of these capacities (Markham, 1998; Hine, 2000; Crichton & Kinash, 2003), whereas the term *netography* has caught on specifically in relation to marketing (Kozinets, 2006). Whatever the terms applied, the empirical processes under scrutiny materialise online – be it gamers' actions through manipulation of avatars in a game space, employees' collaboration in virtual environments or teenagers' comments and co-creation on social network sites. The methodological processes employed may involve the researcher's participation in synchronous or asynchronous online chats, disclosed or undisclosed observation of game universes or the logging of blog interactions. Naturally, for the participants, their online and offline communications and actions are interwoven, and the researcher may wish to frame a research design so as to make such interweaving processes the focus of attention. If that is the case, one starts with contacting and addressing groups of informants defined by their co-location, joint work or meeting places and goes on to study their meanderings between online and offline engagements across different arenas of action (Correll, 1995; Leander & McKim, 2003).

However, many studies of digital learning processes, be they in or outside school or work contexts, deal with the processes of communicative action between physically disparate participants. Here, the object of research is not co-located individuals, and there are no face-to-face interactions. What we have is online communication between textual representations (visual, aural, textual) of embodied identities that are often dispersed across different geographical localities. This situation immediately calls into question a fundamental tenet of traditional anthropology and ethnography – namely, the bounded physical nature of its objects of analysis and the interpersonal forms of interaction between researcher and researched as neatly delimited individuals. Rather than being an issue to be decided beforehand by one's research design, it becomes an empirical question during the empirical work at hand to delimit one's research object by charting how communicative positions are being articulated and disrupted, negotiated and possibly contested. And so, in many virtual ethnographies also of digital literacy processes, the definition of identities and of space becomes not so much multisited as mobile, not so much interaction as flow (Hine, 2000, p. 64).

Seen from the vantage point of traditional anthropology and ethnography, such studies suffer the drawback of impoverished social clues and contestable informant identifiers. Conversely, one of virtual ethnography's pioneers, British media scholar Christine Hine, cogently remarks that the researcher's analysis of online textual processes is in fact more real in an ethnographic sense than are analyses of physically bounded interactions, since it mirrors the informants' positions more closely (Hine, 2000, p. 49). So, virtual ethnographers are at pains to conduct rich analyses respecting the informants' points of view, but not with an intention to understand who they are (and if they are what they say they are) but rather to map relations and communicative interactions between discursive nodes of 'selves'. An attention to networks of people is replaced by an attention to processes of articulation and participation.

Hine's remark is of relevance in questioning easy definitions of one's objects of research when studying virtual processes – including processes of learning – and it equally addresses the issue of how we may understand the relation between researcher and informants in virtual environments. Much has been made of the ethical dilemmas involved for the researcher when studying processes online. Should he or she operate undercover, getting access to spheres and universes through 'stalking'? Should research intentions be openly declared or participation in the virtual forms of engagement actively sought? Questions such as these mirror well-known positionings of the ethnographer from being chiefly an observer to being chiefly a participant. What is different in virtual environments is that it is much easier for the researcher to unobtrusively enter 'fields' of a private or otherwise closed nature. Most researchers with empirical experience in conducting such studies advocate open 'identity' declaration (Domínguez et al., 2007).

Less light has been shed on the ethnographer's ontological stance in studying online processes. In traditional forms of ethnography, the researcher's claim to ontological veracity rests on a realist position (being able to document that 'I was there'). Naturally, this is not a viable line for the online ethnographer, who cannot easily resort to well-defined sites and settings. When studying virtual environments, one may rather claim a discursive realism ('this is what it would be to be present'). In view of this dilemma, Hine advocates what she calls an *adaptive ethnography*; that is, a mode of analysis that disbands with the holistic axiom of 'classical' ethnography in favour of a focus on, in her study, the contestations between official discourses of what the internet is like and users' particular discourses as they emerge in 'practicing' the internet. This resonates well with the analytical position taken by seasoned scholars of qualitative studies, such as British sociologist Martyn Hammersley, who argues for a 'subtle ethnography' (Hammersley, 1992) in manoeuvring between the Scylla of positivist realism, with its unquestioned focus on the objects under study, and the Charybdis of postmodern relativism, in which these objects tend to dissolve into the analytical background in favour of the researcher's position as a mouthpiece for multiple voices and contested discourses.

CO-CREATION: BEYOND PROCESSES OF COMMUNICATIVE LEARNING

The focus on semiotic learning tools, their digitisation and the multiplication of learning sites where digital literacies may be exercised – all of these changes induce close interaction between processual methodologies that have developed within learning research and media research, as we have seen. Still, the dramatic upsurge in social media calls for a consideration of the appropriateness of these methodologies when studying the learning processes that may be involved in their uses. But what makes the use of social media (and their possible learning outcomes) so different from other forms of digital communication and processes of interaction that they merit special methodological interest? In beginning to answer this question, we may look to the American media scholar Henry Jenkins' much-touted notion of participatory culture that he claims is catalysed by the use of, not least, social media (Jenkins et al., 2006). This culture is characterised by co-creation of content and co-creation of communities. Despite calls for inclusive studies encompassing both of these aspects, most empirical studies of social media production focus on the social, or contextual, aspects, whereas analyses of the actual processes of content creation play a minor role (Jenkins, 2006; but see also Ito et al., 2009; Lankshear & Knobel, 2010). Fewer studies address the semiotic, or textual, aspects of content creation (see e.g. Sefton-Green, 2005; Gilje, 2008; Perkel, 2008; Nyboe & Drotner, 2008; Erstad, 2010; overviews in Sefton-Green, 2004; Drotner & Schrøder, 2010).

In their most advanced applications, social media facilitate novel knowledge production, in which media users turn producers through joint experimentation with existing texts, images, sounds and numbers. These semiotic appropriations and 'mashups' may start as spontaneous playing around, which is often the case in out-of-school contexts. They may also be harnessed for more systematic training of semiotic innovation through specific programmes. Central to both of these types of learning is the focus on making something new through semiotic recombination. How may we study these emergent properties of joint semiotic production processes? One route taken is charting users' semiotic interactions at an interface level while at the same time having them think aloud as they go about their experiments. This simultaneous combination of semiotic and social documentation goes some way towards charting emergent production processes for the individual. But, such an approach is difficult to apply when studying joint processes of learning when, for example, a group of young people remix a sound track or tag images for immediate circulation via photo-sharing sites. Design-based research has been developed as a methodology (and some would claim a theory) of intervention for framing design processes such as these while, at the same time, studying their learning outcomes. The term *design experiments* was introduced in 1992 by Ann Brown (1992) as a way of systematising educational designs based on principles derived from prior research. Currently, design-based research is applied more widely to denote intervention into learning processes in order to further innovation (Design-Based Research Collective, 2003). So, although the formative aspect is still part of the methodology, it is more focused on framing and charting emergent learning processes through, for example, probes and modelling. Still focused on learning outcomes, the approach remains loyal to a cognitivist and predictive perspective, which is less amenable to the socio-cultural theories of learning underlying much recent research into digital cultures of production.

Here, a Scandinavian participatory design tradition offers a welcome alternative. Based on welfarist notions of democratic participation and inclusion, and on professionals in service of a common societal good, the tradition has evolved from the 1970s on and increasingly so in tandem with studies of human–computer interaction (overview in Bjerknes & Bratteteig, 1995). Currently, a good number of scholars study and facilitate users' own semiotic actions through provision of what the Swedish design researcher Jonas Löwgren terms *crossmedia infrastructures, expressive tools* and *tribe values* (Löwgren, 2010). In methodological terms, probes and low-fidelity prototypes are developed and tested through iterative processes that are reminiscent of action research and where the researcher 'sets the stage, provides the props and hires the actors' (Löwgren 2010, p. 33). This function is clearly similar to a teacher scaffolding a learning process, and participatory design research shares with situated learning approaches a vision of users/learners as the key actors of the process, jointly shaping their own perceptions and practices.

This shared vision points to much-needed professional convergences in attempting to map current empirical convergences at the intersection of digital media and learning. The vision equally points to ways in which the practices of semiotic and social co-construction enabled by social media radicalise the challenges of methodological reflexivity. For, in addition to the situated and circumscribed nature of the users'/learners' co-construction, the co-construction of users and researchers-cum-designers must be taken into consideration as analytical backdrop and ethical basis. The dual process of shaping meaning in action – between users and between users and researchers/designers – makes for what we may term *second-order reflexivities*: can the researcher's perspective be untangled from the designer-in-action? Can the researcher-cum-designer's perspective be separated from the informants' perspectives? Does everybody involved really share the same intentions? Are there ethical limitations that the researcher should observe in the co-construction of we-ness? In answering questions such as these, we need to specify the overall ramifications of power in entering these processes in the first place.

Digital Media Learning Research: Convergence or Divergence?

This chapter has charted the methodological chances and challenges brought about by the combined dynamics of digitisation and changing societal objectives of competence formation. Focus has been on the needs for processual methodologies that are at once agile, robust and reflexive. The dual developments of such methodologies have been charted within education and media studies, respectively, with particular emphasis being paid to qualitative approaches. Last, but not least, the chapter has discussed joint methodological challenges in terms of defining our objects of study and the relations between researcher and researched. It has been argued that the upsurge in so-called social media serve to radicalise a number of these challenges, especially because of the potential conflation of user-producer-designer-researcher in dynamic interplays of co-creation.

In order to address these challenges and dilemmas, we need to draw more systematically on traditions of literacy studies, digital media studies and learning sciences at large. This need, in turn, calls for sustained interdisciplinary collaboration across disciplinary boundaries and practices of work. But, in pursuing these aims, we should be also aware that these traditions harbour different power relations and objectives of voice, differences that need to be considered as legitimate entry points to processes of collaboration. In order to cross boundaries, we need to acknowledge limits and limitations.

REFERENCES

Arafeh, S., & Levin, D. (2002). *The digital disconnect: The widening gap between Internet-savvy students and their schools.* The Pew Internet and American Life Project, 2002. Retrieved from http://www.pewinternet.org/Reports/2002/The-Digital-Disconnect-The-widening-gap-between-Internetsavvy-students-and-their-schools.aspx
Austin, J. (1962). *How to do things with words.* Oxford: Oxford University Press.

Banks, M. (2008). *Using visual data in qualitative research.* London: Sage.

Bjerknes, G., & Bratteteig, T. (1995). User participation and democracy: A discussion of Scandinavian research on system development. *Scandinavian Journal of Information Systems, 7*(1), 73–98.

Bonk, C. J., & Graham, C. R. (2006). *The handbook of blended learning: Global perspectives, local designs.* San Francisco: Pfeiffer.

Brown, A. (1992). Design experiments: Theoretical and methodological challenges in creating complex interventions in classroom settings. *The Journal of the Learning Sciences 2*(2), 141–178.

Bruce, C. (1997). *The seven faces of information literacy.* Blackwood: Auslib Press.

Carey, J. W. (1989). *Communication as culture: Essays on media and society.* Boston, MA: Unwin Hyman.

Clifford, J., & Marcus, G. (Eds.). (1986). *Writing culture: The poetics and politics of ethnography.* Berkeley: University of California Press.

Coiro, J., Knobel, M., Lankshear, C., et al. (2007). *Handbook of research on new literacies.* New York: Lawrence Erlbaum.

Cole, M. (1996). *Cultural psychology: A once and future discipline.* Cambridge, MA: Belknap Press of Harvard University Press.

Correll, S. (1995). The ethnography of an electronic bar: The lesbian café. *Journal of Contemporary Ethnography, 24*(3), 270–98.

Crawford, P. I., & Turton, D. (Eds.). (1992). *Film as ethnography.* Manchester: Manchester University Press.

Crichton, S., & Kinash, S. (2003). Virtual ethnography: Interactive interviewing online as method. *Canadian Journal of Learning and Technology, 29*(2). Retrieved from http://www.cjlt.ca/index.php/cjlt/article/view/40/37

Delamont, S. (1976). *Interaction in the classroom.* London: Methuen.

Design-Based Research Collective. (2003). Design-based research: An emerging paradigm for educational inquiry. *Educational Researcher, 32*(1), 5–8. Retrieved from http://www.aera.net/uploadedFiles/Journals_and_Publications/Journals/Educational_Researcher/3201/3201_DesignCollective.pdf

Domínguez, D., Beaulieu, A., Estalella, A., Gómez, E., Schnettler, B., & Read, R. (2007). Virtual ethnography. *Forum: Qualitative Social Research/Sozialforschung, 8*(3), Special issue.

Drotner, K. (2008). Boundaries and bridges: Digital storytelling in education studies and media studies. In K. Lundby (Ed.), *Digital storytelling, mediatized stories: Self-representations in new media* (pp. 61–81). New York: Peter Lang.

Drotner, K., Jensen, H. S., & Schrøder, K. S. (Eds.). (2008). *Informal learning and digital media.* Cambridge: Cambridge Scholars' Publishing.

Drotner, K., & Schrøder, K. C. (Eds.). (2010). *Digital content creation: Creativity, competence, critique.* New York: Peter Lang.

Eisenhart, M. (2001). Educational ethnography past, present, and future: Ideas to think with. *Educational Researcher, 30*(8), 16–27.

Erstad, O. (2005). *Digital kompetanse i skolen: En innføring* [Digital competence at school: An introduction]. Oslo: University Publishers.

Erstad, O. (2010). Content in motion: Remixing and learning with digital media. In K. Drotner & K. C. Schrøder (Eds.), *Digital content creation: Creativity, competence, critique* (pp. 57–73). New York: Peter Lang.

Faure, E., Herrera, F., Kaddoura, A.-R., et al. (1972). *Learning to be: The world of education today and tomorrow*. Paris: UNESCO.

Fornäs, J., Lindberg, U., & Sernhede, O. (1988/1995). *In garageland: Rock, youth and modernity*. London: Routledge.

Fuglesang, M. (1994). Veils and videos: Female youth culture on the Kenyan coast. *Stockholm studies in social anthropology, 32*. (Dissertation). Dept. of Social Anthropology, Stockholm University.

Gilje, Ø. (2008). Googling movies: Digital media production and the culture of appropriation. In K. Drotner, H. S. Jensen, & K. C. Schrøder (Eds.), *Informal learning and digital media* (pp. 29–48). Cambridge: Cambridge Scholars Publishing.

Gilster, P. (1998). *Digital literacy*. Indianapolis, IN: Wiley Publishing.

Hammersley, M. (1992). Ethnography and realism. In M. Hammersley (Ed.), *What's wrong with ethnography? Methodological explorations* (pp. 43–56). London, New York: Routledge.

Hammersley, M., & Atkinson, P. (1983/1989). *Ethnography: Principles in practice*. London, New York: Routledge.

Hargreaves, D. H. (1967). *Social relations in the secondary school*. London: Routledge and Kegan Paul.

Hine, C. (2000). *Virtual ethnography*. London: Sage.

Hutchby, I. (2006). *Media talk: Conversation analysis and the study of broadcasting*. Maidenhead: Open University Press.

Hymes, D. (1962). The ethnography of speaking. In T. Gladwin, & W. Sturtevant (Eds.), *Anthropology and human behavior* (pp. 15–53). Washington, DC: Anthropological Society of Washington.

Ito, M., Baumer, S., Bittanti, M., & Boyd, D. (2009). *Hanging out, messing around, and geeking out: Kids living and learning with new media*. Cambridge, MA: MIT Press.

Jenkins, H., Purushotma, R., Weigel, M., & Clinton, K. (2006). *Confronting the challenges of participatory culture: Media education for the 21st century. Building the field of digital media and learning*. Chicago: The John D. and Catherine T. MacArthur Foundation. http://digitallearning.macfound.org/atf/cf/%7B7E45C7E0-A3E0-4B89-AC9C-E807E1B0AE4E%7D/JENKINS_WHITE_PAPER.PDF

Kozinets, R. V. (2006). Netnography 2.0. In E. Russell, & R. W. Belk (Eds.), *Handbook of qualitative research methods in marketing* (pp. 129–142). Ed. Russell W. Belk. Cheltenham, UN and Northampton, MA: Edward Elgar Publishing.

Labov, W. (1972). *Sociolinguistic patterns*. Oxford: Blackwell.

Lacey, C. (1970). *Hightown grammar*. Manchester: Manchester University Press.

Landow, G. P. (1997). *Hypertext 2.0: The convergence of contemporary critical theory and technology*. Baltimore: The Johns Hopkins University Press.

Lankshear, C., & Knobel, M. (Eds.). (2010). *DIY media: Creating, sharing and learning with new technologies*. New York: Peter Lang.

Leander, K. M., & McKim, K. K. (2003). Tracing the everyday 'sitings' of adolescents on the Internet: A strategic adaptation of ethnography across online and offline spaces. *Education, Communication & Information 3*,(2), 211–240.

Leander, K. M., Phillips, N. C. & Taylor, K. H. (2010). The changing social spaces of learning: Mapping new mobilities. *Review of Research in Education, 34*, 329–394.

Lindlof, T. R., & Meyer, T. P. (1987). Mediated communication as ways of seeing, acting, and constructing culture: The tools and foundations of qualitative research. In

T. R. Lindlof (Ed.), *Natural audiences: Qualitative research of media uses and effects* (pp. 1–30). Norwood, NJ: Ablex.

Livingstone, S., & Bovill, M. (Eds.). (2001). *Children and their changing media environment: A European comparative study.* New York: Lawrence Erlbaum.

Loizos, P. (1993). *Innovation in ethnographic film.* Chicago: University of Chicago Press.

Ludvigsen, S., Lund, A., Rasmussen, I., & Säljö, R. (2011). *Learning across sites: New tools, infrastructures and practices.* London: Routledge.

Lull, J. (1980). The social uses of television. *Human Communication Research, 6*(3), 195–209.

Löwgren, J. (2010). Designing for collaborative crossmedia creation. In K. Drotner & K. C. Schrøder (Eds.), *Digital content creation: Creativity, competence, critique* (pp. 17–35). New York: Peter Lang, 2010.

Marcus, G., & Fischer, M. (1986). *Anthropology as cultural critique: An experimental moment in the social sciences.* Chicago: University of Chicago Press.

Marcus, G. (1998). *Ethnography through thick and thin.* Princeton, NJ: Princeton University Press.

Markham, A. (1998). *Life online: Researching real experience in virtual space.* Walnut Creek, CA: AltaMira Press.

Mayer, R. E., & Alexander, P. A. (Eds.). (2010). *Handbook of research on learning and instruction.* London: Routledge.

Mertz, E., & Parmentier, R. J. (1985). *Semiotic mediation: Sociocultural and psychological perspectives.* Orlando, FL: Academic Press.

Moon, J. A. (2004). *A handbook of reflective and experiential learning: Theory and practice.* London: Routledge.

Nyboe, L., & Drotner, K. (2008). Identity, aesthetics and digital narration. In K. Lundby (Ed.), *Digital storytelling, mediatized stories: Self-representations in new media* (pp. 161–176). New York: Peter Lang.

Osborne, M., Gallacher, J., & Crossan, B. (Eds.). (2007). *Researching widening access to lifelong learning: Issues and approaches in international research.* London: Routledge.

Perkel, D. (2008). Copy and paste literacy? Literacy practices in the production of a Myspace profile. In K. Drotner, H. S. Jensen, & K. C. Schrøder (Eds.), *Informal learning and digital media* (pp. 203–224). Cambridge: Cambridge Scholars Publishing.

Prosser, J. (1998). *Image-based research: A sourcebook for qualitative researchers.* London: Routledge.

Säljö, R. (2000). *Lärande i praktiken: Ett sociokulturellt perspektiv* [Learning in practice: A socio-cultural perspective]. Stockholm: Prisma.

Sawyer, R. K. (Ed.). (2006). *The Cambridge handbook of the learning sciences.* Cambridge: Cambridge University Press.

Sefton-Green, J., Thomson, P., Jones, K., & Bresler, L. (Eds.). (2011). *The Routledge international handbook of creative learning.* London: Routledge.

Sefton-Green, J. (2005). Timelines, timeframes and special effects: Software and creative media production. *Education, Communication & Information, 5,* 99–110.

Sefton-Green, J. (2004). *Literature review in informal learning with technology outside school.* Bristol: Futurelab. http://www.futurelab.org.uk/download/pdfs/research/lit_reviews/Outside_Learning_Review.pdf.

Spindler, G., & Spindler, L. (1982). *Doing the ethnography of education: Educational anthropology in action.* New York: Holt Rinehart and Winston.

Stehr, N. (1994). *Knowledge societies*. London: Sage.

Tolson, A. (2005). *Media talk: Spoken discourse on TV and radio*. Edinburgh: University Press.

Turner, G. M., Sweany, N. W., & Husman, J. (2000). Development of the computer interface literacy measure. *Journal of Educational Computing Research, 22*(1), 37–54.

UNESCO. (1947). *Fundamental education: Common ground for all peoples*. Paris: UNESCO.

Unsworth, L. (2001). *Teaching multiliteracies across the curriculum: Changing contexts of text and image in classroom practice*. Buckingham: Open University Press.

Vestergaard, T., & Schrøder, K. C. (1985). *The language of advertising*. Oxford: Wiley-Blackwell.

Walford, G. (Ed.). (2008). *How to do educational ethnography*. London: Tufnell Press.

Walkerdine, V., & the Girls and Mathematics Unit. (1989). *Counting girls out: Girls and mathematics*. London: Virago.

Wertsch, J. (1985). *Mind as action*. New York: Oxford University Press.

Willis, P. (1977). *Learning to labour: How working class kids get working class jobs*. Farnborough: Saxon House.

Wulff, H. (1995). Inter-racial friendship: Consuming youth styles, ethnicity and teenage femininity in South London. In V. Amit-Talai, & H. Wulff (Eds.), *Youth cultures: A cross-cultural perspective* (pp. 63–80). London, New York: Routledge.

Yon, D. A. (2003). Highlights and overview of the history of educational ethnography. *Annual Review of Anthropology, 32*, 411–429.

Zickuhr, K. (2010). *Generations 2010*. Washington, DC: Pew Research Centre. Retrieved from http://www.pewinternet.org/~/media//Files/Reports/2010/PIP_Generations_and_Tech10.pdf

Chapter 4

Thinking About Feeling: Affect Across Literacies and Lives

Jay L. Lemke

Our notion of *literacy* has grown significantly over recent decades. It has moved from the traditional meaning, limited to comprehension of 'serious' formal print texts, to a redress of the original bias towards reading alone and so to placing more emphasis on the ability to write such texts. The notion of literacy has evolved even further, from an almost exclusive focus on literary and academic literacy to a recognition that, in some significant part, we are shaped by all of what we read and write, much of which consists of more personal texts and more popular genres. Most recently, the idea of literacy has grown from an exclusive emphasis on print and verbal literacy to acknowledging the multisemiotic, multimodal nature of the media that are important to our lives and our identities.

As we can see from the chapters in this volume, our uses of literacy have become co-extensive with living our lives: across places and times, across media and the roles we play in diverse activities, across the different communities in which we participate. We are always making meaning; we are always drawing on or pushing off from the conventions and intertexts of public and private media; we are always mediating the meanings of our lives with semiotic objects, durable or transient, that are or behave in many respects like texts.

How can we study this extended spectrum of literacies as a system of practices and strategies strung out along the trajectories of our days, weeks and lives? I think we have so far come to agree that we have to study it *ethnographically*, insofar as we need to know the contexts of use of literacy practices and how they link to one another across time and space. We also need to study it *discursively* and *semiotically*, insofar as every literate practice deploys cultural resources that can be analysed into systems of alternatives and contrasts, typical syntagms and recognizable genres. I would now like to suggest a third dimension: we need to study the literacies of our lives *phenomenologically* and *experientially*, trying to understand how our use of media *feels* to us as creators and interpreters, as participants and as analysts.

Academic studies of literacy practices usually focus on the construction or construal of meaning alone, but it seems clear that the connections of identity to meaning, which are so central to our concerns, are significantly mediated by feelings. Whether we speak of *feeling, affect* or *emotion*, such phenomena are constructed and experienced along with meanings across multiple time-scales and multiple media, along the trajectories of our lives. I believe that meaning and feeling are inextricable. No meanings are made devoid of feeling; the experience of our feelings makes sense to us in terms of available meanings. Every literate practice is always also an affective experience, and how we feel about an event, meaning or action plays a critical role in co-determining our next action, the next meaning.

But our scholarly and intellectual traditions have for so long sought the complete disjunction of reason and emotion that it has become very difficult to find the common ground and meeting points of their contemporary successors, cognition and affect, or, in the terms I prefer, *meaning* and *feeling*. I would like to suggest here two small steps towards overcoming this diffi-culty. The first proposes that we reconceptualise feelings in ways that let us see them more nearly in the same terms we have come to see meaning-making processes over the last two decades, thus making them easier to integrate with more familiar semiotic modes of media analysis. The second recognises that the media and messages we identify with (or disidentify from), both as producers and as consumers, depend critically on *evaluations* that we make, both semiotically and affectively. Evaluative practices provide a key meeting point in the analysis of meaning-with-feeling.

ILINX IN AN INTERACTIVE GAME

For a few years now, I have been fascinated with high-end multimedia digital (aka computer or video) games. Players of these games are doing very sophis-ticated literacy activities, integrating in real time textual, visual and auditory information from a computer program and often also from other players that (and who) react in turn to our responses to their moves. A complex dynamic cycle is thus produced in which each next display of text, image, video and sound depends critically on our response to the last one, and not simply in a turn-taking mode, but in a continuous interaction that simulates activity in normal life. This dynamics is organised on and across multiple timescales from fractions of a second (quick hand-eye reaction times are required in many cases) to episodes lasting a few to many minutes, to the whole story arc of the game, which may take dozens or hundreds of hours to play through. In the course of these events, players may develop and evolve different identities, both as their in-game characters and as their player-selves, and they are certainly learning a lot (for excellent accounts and analyses, see Gee, 2007).

But why do so many, especially school-aged people, play such games? Because they are *fun*. And what does *fun* mean? It can, in fact, mean dying-in-character; it can mean feeling panicked by threats and events paced beyond your capacity. It can be frightening and tiring. But it also packs in emotional rewards: for winning out after having failed on previous attempts, for developing supportive relationships with other players or game characters, for the sheer joy of running or flying in a beautiful new world. One of these rewards is the joy of *ilinx* (Caillois, 1961), a category of emotional pleasure that comes from the sense of vertigo, as you might feel in a drop on a roller-coaster. Dependent in games on the phenomenon of telepresence, in which we feel physically present in the virtual world of a game with well-coordinated visual responses to our active input, *ilinx* appears in games mostly in the form of jumping and flying or swooping around – as, for example, in the virtual realisation of the imagined aerial soccer known as Quidditch in digital games based on the *Harry Potter* books and films.

In this case, it is experientially clear that feelings matter to the meanings made in the game world. In particular, the joy of swooping plays a big part in how you play the game (i.e. the Quidditch game-within-a-game) as much so as your calculated sense of good moves and strategy. Far more generally, how we feel at the time we make a choice in an immersive game depends both on how we feel (e.g. pressed for time, at leisure; frustrated, empowered) and how we want to feel (thrilled, dizzy, proud, victorious, noble, wicked), as well as on our rational calculations of strategic goals and means. Indeed, the feeling qualities of the goals and means themselves matter in a way that is experientially inextricable from their more narrowly rational, cognitive or meaning-system functions and values.

What is also especially clear from analysing game media experience is that this interdependence of meaning and feeling, rational calculus and affective loading is greatly amplified over time as each feeling-dependent choice leads to the next program output and other players' responses, then our own subsequent choices and so on. Our trajectory through the space of possible game-plays (and more obviously through the virtual place-space within the gameworld) depends, in the long run, cumulatively and increasingly on the feelings we've had along the way, as well as on the meanings we've made.

You cannot analyse the trajectory over time in gameplay – where the player went, what he or she did, how his or her in-game or as-player identity developed – unless you look not simply at the meaning affordances and meanings made, but also at the feelings imagined and feelings experienced. Desire is both reasoned (these means to those ends) and felt. Choice is the outcome of evaluation, and evaluation is the construction of a meaning about a feeling.

A SEMANTICS OF FEELING AND EVALUATION

What I have said implies, so far as a research method is concerned, some sort of virtual ethnography of in-game activity, with player self-reports (reports made in real time can be difficult; however, retrospective reports made while viewing replays also present issues) about meanings made and feelings experienced (and anticipated or imagined) across multiple timescales. But it also implies that we make use of a reasonably well-developed semantics and semiotics of possible feelings and evaluations and how they are expressed or cued verbally, visually and acoustically.

The linguistic semantics of evaluations is thus far moderately well-developed (Lemke, 1998; Martin & White, 2005); that for feelings, much less so. If we limit ourselves to evaluations of propositions, states of affairs, scenes or scenarios, then there are, in fact, semantically only about a half-dozen possible kinds of evaluation (Lemke, 1998). While surprising at first sight, the basic linguistic facts have been known for a long time (Greenbaum, 1969). We evaluate states of affairs for their probability (including truth as a limiting case), usuality (ordinary or surprising), desirability (good or bad), normativity (appropriate or transgressive), significance (important or trivial), comprehensibility (mysterious or obvious) and seriousness (serious or humorous). The corresponding feelings are evident: anticipation, surprise, desire, virtuousness, importance, mysteriousness and humor, along with their opposites, variants by degree and subspecies. All evaluations and all feelings are also matters of degree, not categorical all-or-nothing meanings. All evaluations and all feelings are also bipolar, with opposite extremes of positive (attraction) contrasting with their corresponding negative (repulsion) forms.

If we move beyond the evaluation of states of affairs to evaluations of people and things, the situation is more complex (see Martin & White, 2005, on appraisals), but the conclusions seem to remain valid. The act or process of evaluation is both a semiotic practice, usually a linguistic one, and also an affective process or experience. Language, or other signs, present our feelings and allow us to link them semantically to whatever else we can put into words (objects, situations, possibilities, ideas, facts and fancies). So, methodologically, a focus on evaluations as grounds of choices in action, and on the feelings tied to those evaluations, both experienced and imagined (or desired), seems essential.

RECONCEPTUALISING FEELING

One reason we have not already had a strong focus on the role of feelings in the deployment of literate practices is that our intellectual traditions have made it extremely difficult to understand how to integrate an account of feelings with an account of meaning making. According to our traditional view, feelings are internal, personal, subjective, psychological-physiological, and, if we are critically honest about it, childish, feminine, dangerous and unscientific. Feelings, it is said, are antithetical to reason.

In the last two decades or so, most of us who consider ourselves analysts of socio-cultural practices and meaning making have adopted a substantially revised view of cognition. We now see cognition (or, as I would rather say, *meaning making*) as not entirely internal, but as a process that takes places in interaction with the environment, with people and things, signs and tools and artefacts. It is distributed; it normally occurs in rich complex settings, even if we can also learn to do it in relative isolation by a kind of internalisation of the more normal distributed process. We also do not see it as entirely endogenous, but rather as a deployment of resources provided to us socially by a community and described as a part of the culture of that community, both the resources and the norms and typical practices for using them. Meaning making is social and cultural, even if it also involves each participant's body in any particular instance.

But, while we have made these changes of conceptualisation with regard to meaning as a process, we have not as yet done so with regard to feeling. Are feelings not also social, cultural, situated and distributed? Do feelings not also arise in and through our interactions with the social and material environment? Are there not feelings that only arise when we are in interaction with other people? And that, therefore, arise in a system that goes beyond our singular selves? Is our personal repertoire of feelings truly a biological universal? Or, is it not actually the case that, while there are certainly phylogenetic antecedents for many emotions, the particular experienced forms they take – and most definitely the circumstances that elicit them and the norms of when they are appropriate – vary greatly across cultures and communities? Even more telling, anthropology informs us that there are named and familiar emotions in other cultures that have no correspondence in our own and are indeed difficult for us to imagine or grasp (Lutz, 1988).

While we traditionally conceptualise cognition as an active process under our control (hence its ideologically masculine associations), feelings, conversely, are imagined to be merely experienced passively and not under our control (hence ideologically feminine). But is it so? Meaning making can indeed occur by an active construction, but it is also quite frequently something that just happens. A thought occurs to us. An interpretation 'presents itself'. A meaning is simply obvious (or canonical, automatised). And, more important for our argument here, feeling can also be something that we *do*. We can close off or close down our feelings, and we can deliberately open ourselves up to a feeling, reactively perceiving some situation, some person, some phenomenon. We can deliberately tune in to something, actively, more intensely or subtly feeling it. This is not a practice that is taught or encouraged in our dominant culture, in large part because of the myth that feeling more acutely necessarily implies or risks being less rational in our interactions with the environment.

Not so, of course, in many other cultures, and in some traditions in the West. And, more recently, in work such as that of Damasio and others, it has come to be seen that rational processes of choice, necessary to all reasoning chains, need to be based on values, evaluations and feelings. When those parts of the brain that supply feeling are damaged, then those that do rational sequential argumentation, even if undamaged, no longer function properly and break down precisely at the points where choices must be made and branch points passed in the reasoning process (Damasio, 1994).

Far from inhibiting or distracting adaptive meaning making, feelings support reasonings and make them possible. Intuitions ground our imagining new, rational possibilities and alternatives, which may later be argued without explicit reference to feelings and values (Poincare, 2001). A better understanding of how feelings ground and co-constitute meaning making, and so all literate, semiotic practice, may well allow us to find ways in which the cultivation of more acute feeling will lead to better, more adaptive ways of making sense of the world and one another.

To do that, I believe, we need to examine more closely activities such as evaluations and do so with a revised view of feeling that sees it as more active, situated, distributed, socially constituted and culturally specific.

We also need, I think, in moving away from the older tradition of a small number of core or biologically based and therefore universal emotions (Tomkins, 1995; Darwin, 1998), to ask ourselves just how many named emotions, affects or feelings there are in our language(s) and in our cultures and communities. A socio-cultural view of feeling also implies that there must be a history of feelings, that the repertoire must have changed over historical time. If we are going to get a better semantics of feelings, we can start with lexicography. Obviously, we will need to look also at the grammar of feeling expressions, and, eventually, we will need a more multisemiotic model that includes visual, musical and other modalities. We can begin by listing the repertoire of feeling names accumulated over centuries in any given language.

In my own explorations in this area so far, I have compiled a list of many dozens of distinct, named feelings in modern English. Some are traditionally considered 'emotions' and others are not. Some of these many others might be termed 'affects', and some are clearly very physiological in nature. I am not going to try to present a full taxonomy here, but just consider a few points. If we begin with the linguistic form: 'I feel . . .' and supply a descriptor term for a way we might be feeling, we could have:

> I feel sleepy, hungry, nauseous, energised, . . .
> I feel angry, afraid, happy, disgusted, jealous, . . .
> I feel noble, expectant, hesitant, proud, mystified, lonely, . . .

The first group are clearly feelings, but not usually recognised as emotions because they seem too strictly physiological. I would class them as 'bodily feelings'. The second group are the traditional emotions, and one feature they share is that they all presume (except maybe *happy*) an external trigger or object; we are angry at someone, afraid of something or the like. The last (and largest, as it turns out) group tend to be evaluations of the self or self-of-the-moment and might be termed simply 'affects'. All are varieties of feelings.

I want to close this section with one more important observation. The semantics or lexicography of named feelings offers us a practical way to bridge between the analysis of feelings and that of evaluations and meaning making more generally. But it is not by any means to be taken as exhaustive of the range of actual feeling states – even culturally common feeling states – as actually experienced by people in some time and place, or as representable in any medium.

Viewing two exhibitions of portraiture recently, one photographic (Richard Avedon) and one in the medium of etchings (Rembrandt), I was immediately struck by how difficult it can be to name what the person portrayed is feeling. It is very clear that, in many of these works, a strong and definite feeling is portrayed. But no words come to mind to name or easily describe it. Some sense of empathy may allow us to gain a nonverbal intuition of the feeling, but, clearly, many feeling states, even those which are salient to a visual artist and which trigger a sense of recognition in viewers, fall outside the verbal repertoire which is often, I think, mistaken for an adequate accounting of feelings or emotions.

LITERACY, IDENTITY, TRAVERSAL

In this argument, I am not concerned simply with how we conceptualise feelings or with their semantics. I am concerned with how feelings interact with meanings as we live our lives across places and times, being and becoming the persons we are moment to moment and across longer timescales.

As we have expanded our view of literacy, so, too, have we been expanding our concept of *identity* from a near-synonym of *personality*, to an index of position within the structure of social subgroupings, to a claimed sense of self, to a performed practice that affiliates us to some people, things and ideas around us and disaffiliates us from others. Our identity-in-the moment need not coherently cumulate into a single longer term identity. Identities can be multiplex, strategic, logically inconsistent or incommensurable, and call for quite different conceptualisations when considered at different timescales (Lemke, 2008).

Some aspects of our identities are constantly changing and developing, while others may persist more stably over time. One key factor influencing identity development and identity performance is our (more fluid or more stable) identifications with people, groups, symbols, media and objects. Identity performances, whether by display or by enacting an identification, are also felt. They critically involve evaluations, and those evaluations may occur on multiple dimensions, so that, for example, we may feel a sense of belonging even to a group we are not altogether happy with, or we may find ourselves surprised by how much we like something we don't morally approve of. We can identify strongly with something at the same time that we hate it or fear it. The excluded middle of reason's logic does not apply in the domain of feelings and feeling-based evaluations, in part because we can feel in many different ways about the same thing. Indeed, it is this richness and contradictoriness or perversity of actual identifications that artists and literary writers find absent in sociological accounts of our humanity.

A core concern that many of us have is with tracking how our engagement with media through literate practices contributes to the development of our identities and how our identity habits and performances influence this engagement. We may see literacy practices as tools for the development and display of identities. We may wonder how changes in media affordances allow us to make new kinds of identifications (e.g. with distributed, virtual communities; with remote individual others; with imaginary places, times and characters). These concerns tend to make us especially aware that we live our lives across time and place, across situations, settings and activities, and we notice how media and communication provide some of the means by which we construct continuities (and discontinuities) of meaning and self along our traversals.

I use the term *traversal* (Lemke, 2002) specifically to describe a trajectory through space and time, real or virtual or both, that crosses boundaries of place, setting, activity, genre and the like. Given that we mean, feel and act differently in different settings and situations, in different places, with different people and possibilities, it is a genuine question of concern just how we construe continuities for ourselves and everything else across events and moments. I want to suggest that feelings are the glue that makes this possible. This may be something of an overstatement, in that our accounts of intertextuality already show us much about how we use meanings to construct such continuities and discontinuities. We can also clearly see that the persistence of material artefacts and landscapes plays an important role in enabling us to carry over continuities of action from one event and time to another. Indeed, this is a key element of many online gameworlds, where the arrangement of the world persists from one login to the next except insofar as someone else has made a change there or the program clock has advanced the state of things, much as natural processes do in our ordinary experience.

But I want to suggest that how we feel about places (our homes, our personal offices, our familiar neighbourhoods real and virtual) and the things and people persistently found in them, and how we feel about meaning relationships across texts, are fundamental to the specific kinds of continuities we make. What is important to us? What is salient? What matters? What is desirable? What is judged to be normal versus novel? What possible relationships that we can imagine do we feel to be more probable or less so? What connections and continuities are allowed, required or forbidden in our sense of the norms of our communities? In all these ways, the feelings we have about and the evaluations we make of the possibilities for constructing continuities are fundamental to which of those possibilities we actually enact.

We do this in every moment, construing multiple continuities and discontinuities with immediately and more remotely past moments and events. We also project ahead and anticipate, imagine and desire future events, whether in the next few seconds or the next several years. We develop habits in how we do so, and those habits may persist or change, but, generally, on longer timescales than do those on which we make our immediate meaning-and-feeling connections and projections. Some of these habits we model on what others are doing around us, what we might call a *habitus* (Bourdieu, 1990) for making meaning-and-feeling continuities. As Bourdieu notes, such a habitus tends to be common within social groups having similar life chances and life obstacles, similar social, economic and political life trajectories (Bourdieu, 1984).

So, in research on new media literacies, social networking and identity development, we may expect to find similar habits regarding ways of making meaning and experiencing feeling within particular age groups and social class fractions, with variation by gender and by ethnic cultural background. But, we may also find similarities and differences according to our experiences with different media and our participation histories in various online communities and cultures.

FEELING AND LEARNING

If I have not spoken here very explicitly about learning and education, it is because I see learning as an aspect of living, an aspect of development. We cannot *not* learn because, in every activity of life, every event of life, some elements will be carried forward and put into close relation with imagined or enacted activities of a few moments, or even a few years, later. Everything that we do, everything that happens to us, potentially alters our later choices and actions. Determining which of those potential learnings actually do significantly change our future is, again, very much a function of how we feel about them, how we evaluate them for their desirability, probability, usuality, importance, normativity, comprehensibility and seriousness.

That our feelings matter to learning, understood as the retroactively retraceable influences on our present of constructed continuities from our past, is pretty obvious. Obvious to us, to students, to teachers, to parents. But ignored in educational policy, in curriculum and in most official theories of learning and pedagogy. Good teachers know very well how feelings matter in the classroom, but they are encouraged to consider this a somehow illegitimate part of the process of education. Like the mathematician or the scientist who states a proof or provides an experimental result with no reference made to the intuitions that led to success, no account of the trajectory of feelings and tacit evaluations along the way, so do educational systems simply recount learning outcomes with no honesty about the felt lives that did and did not lead to them.

There is something morally and humanly wrong about an educational system that refuses to take into account what students do or do not want to learn, what they enjoy and do not enjoy, what interests them and what does not and, above all, how they feel about the process of learning and more generally about their lives in school. The exclusion of all consideration about how students feel allows a false legitimation of the claimed right of some to say what all should learn. It also works to constitute the fundamental contradiction of formal education: that students have a right to a compulsory education and of its practical corollary – that very little of what is taught in schools does in fact have any significant influence in most people's lives years later. Indeed, we know perfectly well that most of what is taught (and is then misjudged to have been 'learnt' on some examination) is quite forgotten or wholly misremembered even a few months later.

The illusion of education that we maintain in our society also requires that formal schooling be wholly separated from the rest of students' lives and the rest of social activity. We imagine that we can cut the cord of continuity, ignore the traversals of learners' lives. The curriculum pays no attention to what the students do in the hallways and on the street corners, what they do at home and with their friends or even what they do in some other classroom an hour later. It cuts learning in school off from adult activity in every other aspect of social and community life. How can it not fail to be felt and judged irrelevant and pointless most of the time by most students? How can it not, simply, fail?

As a result, if you observe students' literacy activities outside school, you find them more varied, more sophisticated and, not surprisingly, more specialised than what you observe in school. Students who will write two pages of boring prose for a school assignment will write twenty pages of heartfelt and desperately creative prose to post online in a fan-fiction community which shares their passion for some fictional universe. Students who are expected to do mindless calculations of context-free and interest-free problems with outdated calculating technologies in school may show considerable insight in reasoning their way to the practical solution of a technological problem that matters in their own lives. School-based literacy practices are recognisably related to the practices of literate adult lives at some level of abstract similarity that can only be perceived by adults who know both and are trained to see the similarity.

Our failure to include feeling in our accounts of the nature of learning and living leads to a fundamental distortion and dysfunction in our institutional practices of education. As researchers, we have a basic responsibility to show how feeling plays its part in literacy practices, identity development and all meaning-making activity. And to do so with feeling!

SUMMARY

A Coda on Communication

I want to briefly mention one other implication of this reintegration of affect into our views of meaning making and into our own research practices.

We regard it as a basic obligation of research practice to communicate our research findings, interpretations and potential implications to our peers and to wider communities. But the genres of research, writing and publication that have evolved in the last century or so emphasise only that we do so with clarity and precision, with well-organised logical argumentation, with citation of data and sources, but not with feeling. The result is communication that is mostly boring and dull, affectively flat and uncompelling to any but those few specialist colleagues with a real need to plough through our prose (my own included).

This is not simply a matter of talent at writing. We are very much locked in by the conventions of the genre and very much let off the hook by the low expectations of our specialist readers. Many of us can write more engagingly, or speak more passionately and personally in other settings, even about our research. Many more could certainly learn to do so, if it were felt that this is an essential part of being a good researcher.

Moreover, as a research community, we are finally recognising that prose alone, whether placid or purple, simply cannot convey as effectively what audio recordings or videos, carefully edited, could enable us to say and our various communities to learn from. The emotional affordances of these rich media are more easily let loose, if also more difficult to control. Perhaps in response, we have severely limited our use of them to simply illustrating key points in our data. We do not normally produce movies or multimedia expositions of our work. We do not normally put our own faces, as researchers and analysts, on the screen alongside or in montage with those we aim our cameras at. We do not usually point a camera at our processes of research themselves, thus eliding the 'I' once again in this new medium as we traditionally did in the old one.

If feeling, affect and emotion are essential to our accounts of how people live their lives, then are they not equally essential to how we present those accounts?

REFERENCES

Bourdieu, P. (1984). *Distinction: A social critique of the judgment of taste*. Cambridge, MA: Harvard University Press.

Bourdieu, P. (1990). *The logic of practice*. Stanford, CA: Stanford University Press.

Caillois, R. (1961). *Man, play, and games* (M. Barash, Trans.). New York: Free Press of Glencoe.

Damasio, A. (1994). *Descartes' error: Emotion, reason, and the human brain*. New York: HarperCollins.

Darwin, C. (1998). *The expression of the emotions in man and animals*. New York: Oxford University Press. (Original work published in 1872).

Gee, J. P. (2007). *What video games have to teach us about learning and literacy* (2nd ed.). New York: Palgrave/Macmillan.

Greenbaum, S. (1969). *Studies in English adverbial usage*. Coral Gables, FL: University of Miami Press.

Lemke, J. L. (1998). Resources for attitudinal meaning: Evaluative orientations in text semantics. *Functions of Language, 5*(1), 33–56.

Lemke, J. L. (2002). Discursive technologies and the social organization of meaning. *Folia Linguistica, 35*(1–2), 79–96.

Lemke, J. L. (2008). Identity, development, and desire: Critical questions. In C. Caldas-Coulthard & R. Iedema (Eds.), *Identity trouble: Critical discourse and contestations of identification* (pp. 17–42). London: Macmillan Palgrave.

Lutz, C. (1988). *Unnatural emotions: Everyday sentiments on a Micronesian atoll and their challenge to western theory*. Chicago: University of Chicago Press.

Martin, J. R., & White, P. R. R. (2005). *The language of evaluation: The appraisal framework*. New York: Palgrave Macmillan.

Poincare, H. (2001). Intuition and logic in mathematics. In S. J. Gould (Ed.), *The value of science: Essential writings of Henri Poincare*. New York: Random House/Modern Library.

Tomkins, S. (1995). *Exploring affect*. Cambridge: Cambridge University Press.

Chapter 5

Learning Lives in Second Modernity

Lynne Chisholm

This chapter considers the ways in which long-established boundaries between categories of knowledge are shifting and loosening and the implications of these changes for learning lives (cf. Chisholm, 2007, 2008a, b). The ways in which propositional and experiential knowledge intersect and are used in everyday life are implicated in these changes. They also resonate with the theoretical capture of more differentiated understandings of what counts as learning, the ways in which people (of all ages) can learn and how learning outcomes can be identified and recognised. We can speak here of a recontextualisation of learning itself, which is generated by the transition to an increasingly globalised second modernity.

The phrase 'learning lives' embodies a dual connotation. First, the life course can be seen in terms of continuous learning of different kinds and in different contexts: everyone has a learning life. What counts as and is recognised as learning – whether by the self or one's environment – is nevertheless historically and culturally specific. In given times and spaces, only some kinds of lives will have been defined as importantly signified by learning. Second, the term refers to the conditions under which and the ways in which subjects learn to live – as and with themselves, and in the communities and societies in which they live or might live in the future.

This chapter explores these connotations and their interconnections, in order to extend our conceptual understanding of learning in second modernity. It begins from the conviction that the fluid worlds of second modernity (Beck, Giddens & Lash, 1994; Bauman, 2000) do indeed lead to changes that are not simply those of degree, but more pertinently those of kind – that is, contemporary social formations are beginning to cross a threshold that will ultimately be understood to have been epochal in quality. The refiguring of time and space in learning lives is a key element in describing and making sense of these developments (Adam, 1994, 1995; Edwards & Usher, 2003; Ecclestone, Biesta & Hughes, 2010).

This discussion also consciously chooses to use the term 'learning' rather than 'education' and 'training', terms which, in English, generally refer to formalised, institutional and systemic characteristics and outcomes. The term 'learning' privileges agency and process, enabling a more organic conceptual connection between subject and social context. It is equally but one side of the relational couple 'teaching and learning', which expresses pedagogic relations between individual and collective subjects – and thus, by and large, relations of social power and authority in which the 'teaching' side of the couple is usually in the more privileged position. But, here, too, the stability of this dichotomy of structural opposition is beginning to weaken in favour of more differentiated, symmetrical and recursive pedagogic relations.

Young people are specifically positioned in these changes: they are prime learning subjects, or perhaps more pointedly, constructed as pedagogical objects. In all societies, young people learn to know, to do, to be and to live together (cf. UNESCO, 1996, pp. 22–3 ['The Delors Report']). However, it was only in first modernity that mass systems of initial education and training were developed, thus bringing together legitimised curricula, pedagogy, assessment and certification as highly standardised and formalised structures for and processes of learning. Today, these arrangements appear self-evident, but only because we are accustomed to their presence and because their continuing relevance in second modernity is generally assumed (but see du Bois-Reymond, 2004; Diepstraten, du Bois-Reymond & Vinken, 2006). Learning thus became synonymous with schooling, whereas in terms of time (specified periods of the life course) and space (specialised formal settings) both learning and schooling became activities and locations for children and young people through to the moment at which they 'graduated' to adulthood in the form of labour market entry and family building.

These alliances and conjunctions are neither natural nor inevitable: they are social constructions, just as are life phases within the social life course. Current theoretical perspectives go further: they posit that youth is no longer to be understood simply or primarily as a phase of life, but as a social condition that represents itself in culturally differentiated ways (Van de Velde, 2008). Transitions and their problematisation have dominated youth research in the past two decades (du Bois-Reymond & Chisholm, 2006; Furlong, Woodman & Wyn, 2011), not only in terms of their timing within the life course (i.e. prolongation of the youth phase) but also with regard to their internal spatial structuring (i.e. fragmentation and nonlinearity of youth transitions).

Such changes lead to problematising the very concept of adulthood (Blatterer, 2007a, b, c; Horowitz & Bromnick, 2007; Chisholm, 2012), so that the question of 'transition *to what*' gains salience. Normative liberalisation means that most young people in Europe enjoy considerable autonomy in their personal and private lives: they do not have to wait so long for permission or approbation from parents, community and the state. Simultaneously, they have to wait much longer to achieve material independence. Furthermore, the notion that such independence is equivalent to stability and security in the longer term is becoming implausible – at least in some social contexts and for some social groups (Brannen & Nilsen, 2002; Leccardi, 2005; Woodman, 2011). If adulthood no longer *specifically* signifies either personal autonomy or material independence, what does it signify at all, and why would young people wish to make the 'transition to adulthood' or even have a clear sense of what the difference would be in comparison with 'being young'?

With respect to learning lives, such blurring of categories and boundaries between life phases is highly relevant. Learning as a distinct and primary activity has, bis dato, become ever more closely associated with being young, not only in terms of social roles and institutional provision (as outlined earlier) but also in connection with definitions of suitable learning subjects. In normative developmental terms, young people are understood to learn more easily and more rapidly, their intellects and their attitudes are seen to be more malleable and responsive to guidance. The universal human capacity to learn is self-evident, and the very young learn a great deal extraordinarily quickly, but there is no persuasive evidence to show that the human capacity to learn declines *in principle* as people grow older. There is certainly an everyday *assumption* that this is so. Most studies that ask adults, especially older adults, about learning per se and participation in organised learning elicit such views on the part of some of their respondents, most particularly those who are asked to explain why they have not participated in organised learning for some time or have little wish to do so now or in the future (see Crowther, Maclachlan & Tett [2010] for a current study; see Illeris [2003a, b] and Jarvis [2008] for fundamental analyses). It seems that active participation in learning as an activity recognised to be such – by oneself and by one's social environment – is a question of opportunity, practice and confidence: the more one participates, the more one continues to do so and to recognise the outcomes of doing so.

As the boundaries between youth and adulthood become more fluid and ambiguous, so do conceptions of suitable learning subjects diversify and elongate through the life course (see Blatterer, 2010; Illeris, 2009). This ought to mean that, in future, learning lives do not conclude when one becomes an adult and has learned what one needs to learn for living one's life. Concomitantly, young people will not necessarily be primarily defined as learning subjects, nor will their activities necessarily be seen to be dominated by learning lives defined by formal education and training. There is every reason to suppose that young people themselves are already well aware of the disjunction between social attributions and personal realities with respect to their everyday understandings and practices that implicate learning as an array of diverse activities in youth time and space.

At least three core dimensions of contemporary change are likely to lead to a gradual reshaping of learning lives in second modernity: digital technologies and their implications for the organisation and the configuration of learning; identities and subjectivities in fluid worlds and their implications for the meanings and purposes of learning; and restructuring of the relations between education and work in the context of economic and demographic change.

Each of these dimensions impinges on the ways in which time and space are and may be legitimately envisioned and negotiated with respect to learning throughout and across life.

ORGANISING AND CONFIGURING LEARNING IN DIGITALISED WORLDS

Virtual learning environments have become a real possibility only within the past decade, as hypertext technology and satellite communications have brought the digital galaxy into everyday life at rapidly declining cost to educational systems, workplaces, public and commercial services and individual homes. Social inequalities continue to exert an impact on access per se, but social differences in the quality of access (broadband penetration, direct access in the household) together with, most importantly, the quality of use (range of use patterns, active vs. passive use modalities) continue to delineate digital divides.

Teachers and trainers continue to underexploit the potential of virtual learning modalities, as anyone who works in almost any mainstream educational institution knows only too well. This is not primarily a question of whether schools and campuses are equipped and (incongruously) 'wired' for wireless local area networks (WLANs), although we should not underestimate the effects of these barriers on holding back the tide of pressure to extend didactic imaginations.

The core problem lies in a widespread incapacity to discover and explore the pedagogic potential of digital worlds; again, technical incapacity to use the tools is not the main issue, but rather blinkered vision and resistance to change. It is probably not accidental that the tools universities have embraced most rapidly are those which permit plagiarism checks, whilst concerns about collaborative learning tools are widespread, on the grounds that these make it difficult to adjudicate the quality of individual contributions. The predominant tenor is the demonisation of the different, the new and the unknown, grounded in mourning the world of learning we are – so it seems – about to lose irrevocably, together with all the civilised virtues that go along with being 'learned' in the classical sense, a term that, in English, evokes the image of someone who has read many books and can talk sagely about their contents. This has to count as a rather partial view of literacy and knowledge production, whereas digital technologies render broader modalities of learning and knowledge creation altogether more visible – including those that do not use written text as the relay medium.

Digital learning worlds dismantle the shackles of time and space constraints, enabling communication and exchange between individuals and groups that otherwise could not possibly learn together or form an ongoing community of practice. The sheer organisation of learning no longer needs permanent, purpose-built edifices – applied to the higher education sector, this could effectively imply a return to the original concept of *universitas*; that is, a transitory community of scholars that meets to discuss ideas and practices in a place of their own choosing. Learning lives might so become mobile in ways quite different from those now possible, and these learning lives need not relate directly or inevitably to life phase – after all, it is only too possible to adopt a series of avatar identities that disguise the shackles of the flesh.

A generational gap has opened up between those who professionally teach and those who learn – insofar as these roles and identities are linked directly to age and life stage – and this gap is equally embodied in the institutionalised organisation of teaching and learning. This is not simply a competence gap. It comprises disjunctions within processes of knowledge acquisition and use between those whose learning lives were configured in the Gutenberg galaxy and those who are configuring – and in some cases reconfiguring – their learning lives in the digital galaxy. These disjunctions comprise differential confluences not only between materiality and immateriality but also between individuality and collaboration. These disjunctions may indeed risk a pervasive colonisation of subjectivities and personal worlds, yet transformations in young people's *everyday* learning lives – that is, what they experience in and how they use multifaceted learning environments of all kinds – can be neither denied nor ignored.

The configuration of digital learning worlds is based on mixed – blended – modalities of acquisition, transmission, participation and engagement. It is the *relations between* these modalities that comprise the creative force for personal and competence development, for the capacity to gain and apply critical reflection and to achieve a sense of autonomy and independence with respect to shaping and piloting a learning life. Such configurations are no 'freer' than they were until now – the tensions between structure and agency in constructing learning lives do not weaken – but they do become more complex, since they incorporate, rather than exclude and negate, more differentiated forms of teaching and learning.

Parallelism is the more usual order of the day: young people are already living in new configurations, but the legitimacy of existing configurations continues to hold sway. Conventional paper certificates and qualifications gained in educational and training institutions, the material representation of the pedagogic device of the Gutenberg galaxy, are the unchallenged currency of socially successful learning lives – but every employer knows that the really valuable currency is that for which these insignia do not vouch; namely, the communicative, personal, social and transformative capacities and competences that derive from collaborative interaction, explorative practice and innovative composition.

Probably more young people know this than is comfortable for those whose job it is to educate and train them. The 'great education and training robbery' (Brown, Lauder & Ashton, 2011) has certainly induced their scepticism about the genuine value of institutionalised learning and its accreditation: it is something they must get through as well as they can, but it does not capture their hearts and minds. Digital learning worlds are no solution in themselves, but what they can do is to open up alternative ways to perceive and construct learning lives. And this is, above all, of no little significance for those young people who live in the social backwaters and on the edges: they may never have held a violin in their hands, or even a guitar, but they know it is perfectly possible to make good music in the virtual studio.

MEANINGS AND PURPOSES OF LEARNING
IN FLUID WORLDS

In fluid worlds that offer multiple opportunities for choosing – and discarding or reconfiguring – sets of identities, the idea that formalised and institutionalised learning plays a key role in conveying and regulating the identities young people may legitimately adopt loses relevance and credibility. Classical theories of identity development (as in Erikson, 1994) assume that young people must acquire a single, stable identity; this is a prime task to be accomplished in puberty (i.e. in early adolescence); all else leads to identity confusion and potential psychic instability. The idea that multilayered and transitory identities might be equally positive, or indeed be regarded as 'normal', runs against the established theoretical grain. Translated into temporal and spatial terms, such traditions of thought build on stasis and immobility: subjects develop singular identities at specified moments in the life course, and these are prestructured by their physical location in a given culture, language community and society.

If identity is about 'who I am', then subjectivity is about 'how I relate to myself in social context'. This equally expresses the distinction between learning as a purely individual activity and learning as a social process. First modernity placed individuality in the forefront, in the largely ideological context of individual achievement in educational and social meritocracies. Such individualised subjectivities are certainly capable of cooperation with each other and do so in two ways: either in hierarchically organised communities that impose synchrony (as on production lines or in fast-food restaurants) or in symmetrical groupings whose rationale is competition (as in sales and marketing departments or sports events). Genuine teamwork and collaborative achievement, in which the sum becomes more than the contributing parts, and in which individual achievement is neither necessarily nor in practice definable, seem only to come to the fore in situations of extreme risk and threat, such as during wars and natural catastrophes. In modern representative democracies, the 'will of the people' disintegrates as the proportion of those casting a vote falls and the number of parties fielding candidates rises. Individual rights may reign supreme in principle, but, in practice, their exercise makes no predictable difference.

In second modernity's polities and economies, subjectivities face the challenge of reconstruction between individuality and sociability, since both democracy and productivity come to rely on new forms of collective engagement that are both more symmetrical in principle and more ephemeral in practice. Time and space are implicated in these processes, as identities become open to reconstitution across the life course and across the cultural geographies of mobility and migration. Identity work as a core dimension of learning becomes a continuous personal project that is not confined to the youth phase; subjectivities become sufficiently flexible to enable integration with diverse and changing reference communities.

These processes of change do not and cannot affect everyone to the same extent, in the same way and at the same pace: social location is inevitably crucial to specification and differentiation, configuring the confluence of associated chances and risks. In societies marked by deepening polarisations, openness and contingency bring many new risks and few new chances for those already or potentially vulnerable to marginalisation and exclusion.

Yet, plurality across time and space lends differentiated learning practices greater salience: diversified identities and subjectivities demand diversified learning environments and processes. Public demand in many European countries for more individualised approaches to teaching/learning and for greater differentiation of schooling provision exemplify this shift. Commitment to educational equality in the form of unified secondary schooling no longer necessarily implies a single model for all. Schools in many countries, including those that already have unified secondary systems, are increasingly encouraged to develop a distinctive profile and may explicitly serve a specific community (applying a specific educational philosophy, paying particular attention to specific interests and activities or based on the values of a specific faith). Parents, too, place increasing importance on choosing the schools they judge best suited to their children – and they are likely to integrate their children into the decision-making process. Where educational systems restrict such choice, parents increasingly find ways to secure it (moving house so that they fall into the catchment area of the neighbourhood school they have selected, sending their child to a fee-paying school or joining together with like-minded parents to found a new or supplementary school).

The determination to assure the best possible life prospects for one's offspring is a major driver, but this should not be translated as mere narrow instrumentalism to maximise achievement and credentials in the interest of employment, career and social distinction. Parents take a variety of factors into account, not least their children's characters and interests, as well as their own social values and community traditions. The caveat is that socially disadvantaged families are much less likely to deploy such strategies, partly because they do not have the economic resources to do so but also because they may not have the personal and social resources (knowledge, confidence, networks) to act accordingly (Ball, Bowe & Gewirtz, 1996; Bernal, 2005; Sliwka & Istance, 2006; Butler & van Zenten, 2007). Significant sections of the population find themselves living in pluralised, fluid worlds, but their life circumstances render them as the flotsam and jetsam of a fast-flowing stream carrying them forwards on its own terms alone.

Where identities are reworkable and subjectivities are adaptable, then the youth phase no longer bears the unique load of their uniform and stable formation. Exploration and experimentation are no longer activities with the definable end-purpose of transition to adulthood, whether prespecified or self-determined, but rather they constitute infinite ends in themselves. The commodification of youth culture (fashion, music, dance, sports, events and swarms) serves to underline this open-endedness, offering rapidly changing and multifarious stances and styles that, for bystanders from older generations, come to take on an almost arbitrary quality. Yet, the stage is not populated by anonymous youth actors: individual uniqueness produces itself in personalised digital mobile devices, in Facebook-style social networks and in multiple virtual identities that permit and encourage restyling of age, gender and ethnicity.

In such life-worlds, initial institutionalised learning (schools, colleges, universities etc.) loses relative salience. It continues to affirm and significantly to co-determine life chances in adulthood, but sites for identity work multiply and, in turn, raise the salience of nonformal and informal learning processes. As adulthood itself blurs, adults are less salient examples of what lies (or should lie) ahead: it is less clear what they can 'teach' young people, and the purpose of 'learning' from them seems less obvious. For those who are personally and socially well-equipped to fashion self-directed life journeys, this can readily be judged as a positive step towards the emancipation of human subjectivity. Those who do not have sufficient resources at their disposition may be at risk of anomie and purposeless drift.

Purposive learning in the sense of a self-determined, goal-directed activity seems to be the only solution that modernity offers to develop and distribute personal and social resources more effectively and widely – but it does not all have to take place in institutionalised, formal education and training environments. Nonformal and informal learning settings, processes and outcomes introduce greater fluidity into learning to be (identity formation) and learning to live together (subjectivity and social relations). Learning in fluid worlds does not imply the loss of its meaning and purpose, but rather the temporal and spatial broadening of its fields of action and modes of operation. Personal and social development becomes more closely interwoven with knowledge acquisition and competence development, taking on a more holistic character altogether. In a certain sense, this reformulates the Enlightenment concept of education (the German *Bildung*) and speaks to generating active engagement with information and enquiry across the full range of human experience.

Concomitantly, the meaning and purpose of formal learning modalities lose focus precisely because schooling and higher education have become *too narrowly* focused on competitive and demonstrable achievement, and this, in the very first instance, in order to secure the best possible foothold in the labour market and career stakes. Young people today know they must run the education and qualification gauntlet and that poor performance will leave them with little time and space for exploration and experimentation with anything very much in their lives. Meaning and purpose in their wider sense are more readily found and created in other times and spaces of life. On reflection, it is evident that this is nothing new: since the introduction of mass schooling systems no more than about 150 years ago in Europe, the majority of young people have not spent more years in formal education and training than they were obliged to do, and many of them did not leave schools with high-level credentials and a solid sense of personal worth. Why should this kind of learning be experienced as meaningful and purposeful? The framing conditions of growing up in fluid worlds seem, however, to be leading to a more generalised loss of meaning and purpose, since making connections between schooling and the rest of everyday life, in the present or in the future, seems tenuous and opaque, even for the educationally successful and socially well-placed (Leccardi, 2005 and, more broadly, Rosa & Scheuerman, 2009).

EDUCATION AND WORK RELATIONS IN AGEING WORLDS

Europe's ageing societies and the consequences for economic and social life thematically richly populate the policy and research literature (for example, Lutz, O'Neill & Scherbov, 2003; Lutz, Sanderson & Scherbov, 2008; Blome, Keck & Alber, 2009; European Commission, 2009). The past half-century has seen declining birth rates and rising life expectancies, with migration into Europe rising, but insufficiently to offset mid-term population decline (European Commission/Eurostat, 2011). Populations will not fall everywhere in Europe, but the average age of populations everywhere is on the rise. The proportion of those aged under twenty-five will continue to decline, whereas those aged over sixty-five will rise significantly.

Replacing and renewing knowledge and competence on the labour market used largely to be achieved by recruiting new entrants into existing and new occupations, who (continue to) learn on the job from the more experienced, whilst bringing fresh knowledge and ideas. Rapid technological and organisational change, together with declining labour market entry cohorts (also due to delayed and falling recruitment by employers), means that this is not an adequate model for future employer policy and practice. The consequences have been more widely discussed and prescribed with respect to the older than the younger, and primarily in the following terms: the real age at retirement (not simply the age at which people can or must formally retire onto a pension) should rise; a higher proportion of the adult population (especially those over fifty) should be labour force active; and participation rates in continuing general and vocational education and training must increase (especially amongst older and low-qualified employees). In general, and regardless of age, more people should acquire higher level education and qualification, and they should upgrade and renew these regularly.

Learning thus becomes a continuous activity throughout life, and it increasingly takes place in parallel with working and family life. In parallel, economy and society have an interest in making use of the full range of knowledge and competence that people can and do develop and possess – howsoever they have acquired and demonstrated what they know and can do. This accounts for the explosion of interest in nonformal and informal learning and its recognition, including in the youth sector (e.g. Marsick & Watkins, 2001; Belzer, 2004; Chisholm & Hoskins with Glahn, 2005; Hager & Halliday, 2009; Werquin, 2010). The risks associated with these developments, not only for the distinctiveness and relative autonomy of nonformal education and pedagogy but also for the instrumental colonisation of subjectivity per se, have been well rehearsed in the literature (Sennett, 1998; Field, 2006; see also Crowther, 2004).

The shift towards lifelong and lifewide learning paradigms in ageing societies poses intriguing questions for learning itself and for teaching–learning relations. First modernity coupled learning closely with age (the young need to learn, and they are better at it) and hence with life phase (learning is for young people). It built formal teaching–learning relations on a pedagogic hierarchy that mirrors parent–child power and status relations; in the workplace, similar principles apply, expressed through organograms and professional hierarchies. When renewing work-related knowledge and competence applies to everyone, conceptualising and practising appropriate teaching–learning relations *for and between* adults becomes a key pedagogic issue. In short, adults cannot be treated like children – decoded, this means that effective adult learning is founded in symmetrical relations that place relevance, respect and self-direction at the centre. This inevitably leads to asking why effective youth learning does not equally conform to such principles – and whether it is necessary or even desirable to bracket learning so closely with such a short period in the life course.

The oppositional dichotomy between teaching and learning is a metaphor for the structured power and status relations between older and younger; gender and age are the oldest parameters by which human societies have structured divisions of labour and social positions. Age represents the distinction between those who know and can do, and those who do not know and cannot do. The traditional superiority of age over youth rests on the value accorded to experiential knowledge and practised skill: those who have lived longer have had more time to acquire and use these cognitive and practical resources, and to do so in a wider range of contexts. Formal education and training is not a prerequisite for their transmission; it merely institutionalises the process and legitimates it by issuing credentials. The exigencies of the working world in second modernity rediscover the existence and the potential of nonformal and informal learning between the more experienced and the less experienced, but do not amend the hierarchical terms of the pedagogic discourse.

From another perspective, however, second modernity weakens the oppositional dichotomy between teaching and learning since the conditions and demands of working life are no longer predicated on the one-way transmission of knowledge and competence between the more experienced and the less experienced. Rapid change and complex working processes result in experience taking on a more fractured, fragmented and contingent quality. Relevant experience is now not simply a matter of time to amass it, but equally of access to relevant spaces in which to acquire it. The spaces in which today's young people are learning what they need to know to make a working life (digital communication media; mobility and migration) were just not available to those born twenty to thirty years earlier. This implies that relevant experience is less age-related, as such, and more generation-related: life time counts less than the social time that shapes collective circumstances and experience.

This dimension of contemporary change attracts much attention, but it poses imponderables for which there are no sound answers. In ageing societies, whose knowledge and competence is seen to be more valuable and useful? That of the young, because innovation is (always) at a premium and there will be ever fewer young people in the coming decades? Or that of the old, because they will be ever more numerous and can exert more influence on social values? In ageing societies with shrinking labour markets and extended, precarious entry trajectories, will the life course as a whole undergo further structural reconfiguration? Is it possible that 'youth' as a life phase will indeed reach into the fourth decade of lifespans that can expect to approach their centennial? Or, will age itself lose some of its personal and social relevance, given more degrees of normative freedom for age-related divisions of labour, roles and lifestyles?

SUMMARY

Learning Lives in Compression and Expression

Abstract analysis of contemporary education system and process can readily conclude that they are largely defined by prescriptive linear pathways and structured internal divisions that lead to predictable outcomes. Concrete analysis of real learning lives repeatedly uncovers much more varied stories about how people manage, with differing degrees of success, to navigate obstacles and build their own bridges, so that outcomes are much broader in their meaning and purpose. The unbridgeable gap between abstract analysis and lived experience notwithstanding, everyone does build and experience a learning life.

An effective and meaningful public sphere in polity and society for second modernity depends inter alia on creating new kinds of times and spaces for active and autonomous learning for democracy (cf. Annette, 2009). These have to be rooted in social, self-directed and peer-based contexts and methods because these qualities mirror those that should be the outcome of such learning processes. They must also take their initial cue from local communities, so that relevance and belonging set the framework for learning in the realities of everyday lives.

Under first modernity, only some kinds of learning lives were recognised as importantly signified by learning. Specifically, those with recognised learning lives have been those whose learning has been formally accredited on paper, having spent time in the legitimate learning space of education and training institutions. In particular, those whose learning lives have been a prominent dimension of their curriculum vitae were – and still are – those who acquired highly valued knowledge to the highest level of achievement. These are the veritable *learnéd*, equipped not only with profound expertise but also with the civilisation and character that such intense learning is held to bring. Indeed, traditional *learnéd professions*, such as the clergy and academics, were so closely defined by learning as the aim and substance of their craft that they appeared to represent the epitome of continuous learning as an ennobling activity.

But these were – and still are – the chosen few. For the most part, learning has been something that came to dominate all lives only for a specific period, once and for all. First modernity's young people all came to have recognised learning lives, but only within specific and regulated parameters of time and space. As the economic relevance of formal qualifications rose, so did the personal and social significance of learning lives gain momentum – and most particularly of all for those young people with curtailed and less successful formal learning lives. In today's labour markets, good formal qualifications are a necessary, but frequently no longer sufficient, entry ticket.

Young people now find themselves extending their curriculum vitae to include a broader range of learning experiences and their outcomes in a differentiated and highly individualised portfolio. Such developments can be seen as highly problematic, not only because they raise the competitive stakes for evaluating the worth of an incipient learning life, but also because they open up young lives to intense evaluative scrutiny at each and every turn – as some of those whose lives are openly available on Facebook have already discovered to their cost. At the same time, these developments can open doors to building new kinds of learning lives that can find new forms of recognition in both professional and social life.

There can be little doubt that all young people today must construct a *formalised* learning life under hardening conditions: pressure to achieve across a broad range and under compression of time and space; to learn under self-direction but in the context of increasing external monitoring of progress; and to cope with multiple methods for learning, both conventional and, increasingly, virtual. In contrast, where and how can time and space for learning as expression be found and used well? Young people themselves give us at least part of a workable answer, in that they show us examples of nonsurveilled learning niches that they create for themselves and imbue with personal meaning, countering McLaren's (1999) schooling as a ritual performance in the public sphere with learning as a hedonistic pursuit in the private sphere. This may not result in productive resistance, but it has legitimacy as a constructive facet of informalised learning lives in Europe's second modernity.

REFERENCES

Adam, B. (1994). *Time and social theory*. Cambridge: Polity Press.
Adam, B. (1995). *Timewatch: The social analysis of time*. Cambridge: Polity Press.
Annette, J. (2009). 'Active learning for active citizenship' – democratic citizenship and lifelong learning. *Education, Citizenship and Social Justice*, 4(2), 149–60.
Ball, S. J., Bowe, R., & Gewirtz, S. (1996). School choice, social class and distinction: The realization of social advantage in education. *Journal of Education Policy*, 11(1), 89–112.
Bauman, Z. (2000). *Liquid modernity*. Cambridge: Polity Press.
Beck, U., Giddens, A., & Lash, S. (1994). *Reflexive modernisation. Politics, aesthetics and tradition in the modern order*. Stanford, CA: Stanford University Press.
Belzer, A. (2004). Not like normal school: The role of prior learning contexts in adult learning. *Adult Education Quarterly*, 55, 41–59.
Bernal, J. L. (2005). Parental choice, social class and market forces: The consequences of privatization of public services in education. *Journal of Education Policy*, 20(6), 779–92.
Blatterer, H. (2007a). *Coming of age in times of uncertainty*. Oxford/New York: Berghahn Books.
Blatterer, H. (2007b). Contemporary adulthood: Reconceptualising an uncontested category. *Current Sociology*, 55(6), 771–92.
Blatterer, H. (2007c). Adulthood: The contemporary redefinition of a social category. *Sociological Research Online*, 12(4), 3. Retrieved January 9, 2012, from http://www.socresonline.org.uk/12/4/3.html

Blatterer, H. (2010). The changing semantics of youth and adulthood. *Cultural Sociology*, 4(1), 63–79.

Blome, A., Keck, W., & Alber, J. (2009). *Family and the welfare state in Europe: Intergenerational relations in ageing societies*. Cheltenham: Edward Elgar.

Brannen, J., & Nilsen, A. (2002). Young people's time perspectives: From youth to adulthood. *Sociology*, 36(3), 513–37.

Brown, P., Lauder, H., & Ashton, D. (2011). *The global auction: The broken promises of education, jobs and incomes*. Oxford/New York: Oxford University Press.

Butler, T., & van Zenten, A. (2007). Parental choice: A European perspective [Introduction]. *Journal of Education Policy*, 22(1), 1–5 (special issue).

Chisholm, L. (2007). Lifelong learning: Citizens and governance. In F. C. Gulbenkian (Ed.), *Educação, inovação e desenvolvimento* [Education, innovation and development] (pp. 167–78). Lisbon: Fundação Calouste Gulbenkian.

Chisholm, L. (2008a). Generations of knowledge, knowledge of generations and the generation of knowledge. In R. Rauty (Ed.), *Youth, control, citizenship, social reproduction* (pp. 159–70). Salerno: Rubbettino.

Chisholm, L. (2008b). Re-contextualising learning in second modernity. *Research in Post-Compulsory Education*, 13(2), 139–47.

Chisholm, L. (2012). The life-course as hyper-text. In L. Chisholm & V. Deliyanni-Kouimitzis (Eds.), *Changing landscapes of childhood and youth in Europe*. Newcastle-upon-Tyne: Cambridge Scholars Publishing.

Chisholm, L., & Hoskins, B., with Glahn, C. (Eds.). (2005). *Trading up: Potential and performance in non-formal learning*. Strasbourg: Council of Europe Publications.

Crowther, J. (2004). 'In and against' lifelong learning: Flexibility and the corrosion of character. *International Journal of Lifelong Education*, 23(2), 125–36.

Crowther, J., MacLachlan, K., & Tett, L. (2010). Adult literacy, learning identities and pedagogic practice. *International Journal of Lifelong Education*, 29(6), 651–64.

Diepstraten, I., du Bois-Reymond, M., & Vinken, H. (2006). Trendsetting learning biographies: Concepts of navigating through late-modern life and learning. *Journal of Youth Studies*, 9(2), 175–93.

du Bois-Reymond, M. (2004). Youth – Learning – Europe. Ménage à trois? *Young*, 12(3), 187–204.

du Bois-Reymond, M., & Chisholm, L. (Eds.). (2006). *The modernization of youth transitions in Europe*. New Perspectives on Childhood and Adolescent Development 113. Hoboken, NJ: Jossey-Bass.

Ecclestone, K., Biesta, G., & Hughes, M. (Eds.). (2010). *Transitions and learning through the life-course*. Abingdon, Oxon: Routledge.

Edwards, R., & Usher, R. (Eds.). (2003). *Space, curriculum and learning*. Charlotte, NC: Information Age Publishing.

Erikson, E. H. (1994). *Identity: Youth and crisis*. New York: W.W. Norton and Co.

European Commission/Eurostat. (2011). *Demography report 2010: Older, more numerous and diverse Europeans*. Commission Staff Working Document (Directorate-General for Employment, Social Affairs and Inclusion, Unit D.4 and Eurostat, Unit F.1). Luxembourg: Publications Office of the European Union. Retrieved January 9, 2012, from http://ec.europa.eu/social/main.jsp?langId=en&catId=502&newsId=1007&furtherNews=yes

European Commission. (2009). *Dealing with the impact of an ageing population in the EU (2009 Ageing Report)*. Communication from the Commission to the European Parliament, the Council, the European Economic and Social Committee and the Committee of the Regions, COM(2009) 180 final, Brussels, 29.4.2009. Retrieved January 9, 2012, from http://eur-lex.europa.eu/LexUriServ/LexUriServ.do?uri= COM:2009:0180:FIN:EN:PDF

Field, J. (2006). *Lifelong learning and the new educational order* (Rev. ed.). Stoke-on-Trent: Trentham Books.

Furlong, A., Woodman, D., & Wyn, J. (2011). Changing times, changing perspectives: Reconciling 'transition' and 'cultural' perspectives on youth and young adulthood. *Journal of Sociology*, 47(4), 355–70.

Hager, P., & Halliday, J. (2009). *Recovering informal learning: Wisdom, judgement and community*. Dordrecht: Springer.

Horowitz, A. D., & Bromnick, R. D. (2007). "Contestable adulthood": Variability and disparity in markers for negotiating the transition to adulthood. *Youth & Society*, 39 (2), 209–31.

Illeris, K. (2003a). Towards a contemporary and comprehensive theory of learning. *International Journal of Lifelong Education*, 22(4), 396–406.

Illeris, K. (2003b). Adult education as experienced by the learners. *International Journal of Lifelong Education*, 22(1), 13–23.

Illeris, K. (2009). Transfer of learning in the learning society: How can the barriers between different learning spaces be surmounted, and how can the gap between learning inside and outside schools be bridged? *International Journal of Lifelong Education*, 28(2), 137–48.

Jarvis, P. (2008). *Lifelong learning and the learning society* (3 volumes). Abingdon, Oxon/ New York: Routledge.

Leccardi, C. (2005). Facing uncertainty: Temporality and biographies in the new century. *Young*, 13(2), 123–46.

Lutz, W., O'Neill, B. C., & Scherbov, S. (2003). Europe's population at a turning point. *Science*, 299(5615), 1991–2.

Lutz, W., Sanderson, W., & Scherbov, S. (2008). The coming acceleration of global population ageing. *Nature*, 451(7), 716–9.

Marsick, V. J., & Watkins, K. E. (2001). Informal and incidental learning. *New Directions for Adult and Continuing Education*, 89(Spring), 25–34.

McLaren, P. (1999). *Schooling as a ritual performance. Towards a political economy of educational symbols and gestures* (3rd Rev. ed.). Lanham, MA: Rowman & Littlefield.

Rosa, H., & Scheuermann, W. E. (Eds.). (2009). *High-speed society. Social acceleration, power and modernity*. University Park, PA: Pennsylvania State University Press.

Sennett, R. (1998). *The corrosion of character: The personal consequences of work in the new capitalism*. New York: W.W. Norton.

Sliwka, A., & Istance, D. (2006). Parental and stakeholder 'voice' in schools and systems. *European Journal of Education*, 41(1), 29–43.

UNESCO (1996) *Learning : The treasure within*. Report to UNESCO of the International Commission on Education for the Twenty-First Century ('The Delors report'). Paris: UNESCO.

Van de Velde, C. (2008). *Devenir adulte: Sociologie comparée de la jeunesse en Europe.* Paris: PUF.

Werquin, P. (2010). *Recognising non-formal and informal learning. Outcomes, policies and practices.* Paris: OECD.

Woodman, D. (2011). Young people and the future. Multiple temporal orientations shaped in interaction with significant others. *Young, 19*(2), 111–28.

Chapter 6

Digital Disconnect? The 'Digital Learner' and the School

Ola Erstad and Julian Sefton-Green

The changing role of media in our societies, and especially the impact of digital technologies since the mid 1990s, has implications for where and how learning might happen, whether on- or offline, situated and distributed. On one level, being a learner has always implied operating within and across different spaces and places, as described by the contested notion of transfer (Perkins & Salamon, 1992; Beach, 1999) dominating both popular and academic ideas of understanding. Still, current opportunities to move across 'sites of learning' means that understanding how one context for learning relates to another has become a key concern in conceptualising learning and knowledge in the twenty-first century (Edwards, Biesta & Thorpe, 2009, Leander, Phillips & Taylor, 2010).

If we imagine learning as lifewide, life-deep and lifelong, how (as well as where) do we 'locate' the learner? And in what ways do young people experience themselves as learners? Typically, in educational research, we locate the learner within certain institutional settings like schools and in classrooms. In this chapter, we intend to raise some questions about how we conceptualise who the learner is, where learning is taking place and with what purpose. We will be concentrating on the task of locating learners as they appear in the intersection between school and other learning contexts. We address how digital learners are being conceptualised in public discourse and how education systems address the challenges of digital technologies as they are used by young people.

The chapter draws on our shared experiences, backed up by a substantive research literature that has explored a significant disjuncture between learning in and out of school, especially that experienced through the uses of popular media technologies. We have both been involved in projects that have sought to ameliorate and even 'overcome' this disjuncture. However, in reality, it has been the construction of this disjuncture as an opposition, as an epistemological rupture and as a way of framing learning that has preoccupied us. One ambition here, then, is to think through ways that this 'disjuncture' has been framed and what (if any) might be ways forward to overcoming this potentially divisive binary opposition.

The first section focuses on the construction of the learner in the literature devoted to the so-called 'Net Generation'. It argues that a range of theoretical perspectives and policy initiatives have combined to redefine learning as a particular kind of contemporary social process, repositioning subjectivity – the learner – at times awkwardly as both surfeit and deficit, across a dichotomy of in- and out-of-school. The argument then considers two parallel responses to this challenge. It first offers analyses from the growing literature about informal learning and how this might provide a certain kind of theoretical response to 'traditional' or schooled ways of learning. We then consider in general how schooling systems have responded to this characterisation and move to presenting some examples from developments in Norway, to highlight differences in the ways that the culture of an education system can impact on the use of digital technologies. We conclude by trying to move beyond this 'dichotomy' by focusing on the position of the learner within and across contexts of learning.

RESEARCHING THE DIGITAL LEARNER: THE NET GENERATION HYPOTHESIS

During the last twenty-five years, we have seen a wide range of commentators, journalists, academics, politicians and other kinds of cultural critics argue that a sea change has occurred in the nature of learning, particularly for young people due to their use of digital technology, specifically the internet. From as long ago as Seymour Papert's claim, at the beginning of the 1980s, that the school as we know it, with its classes, specific subjects and exams, would be obsolete in a few years due to the impact of the computer (Papert, 1980), similar statements have been made about the impact of computers at home and the growth of the internet during the mid-1990s (see discussion in Giacquinta, Bauer & Levin, 1994, and, more recently, with the development of Web 2.0 technologies, Palfrey & Gasser, 2008). Such conceptions about the role of digital technologies to change the ways we learn have now become a kind of common sense – a 'fact' that permeates virtually all discussions about youth, education and contemporary society. This generational change has also been popularised by the idea of digital *natives* and *immigrants* (Prensky, 2006), although this formulation has been criticised as being partial and skewed (Thomas, 2011).

New Literacies

Net Generation habits have frequently been characterised as a kind of 'literacy' (Sefton-Green, Nixon & Erstad, 2009; Coiro et al., 2008), for two reasons. First, the computer and video game is, in effect, a form of 'text', used in its broadest sense as encompassing visual, interactive and other kinds of multimodality (Jewitt & Kress, 2003). On one level, how the Net Generation engages with these changing texts defines their distinctiveness, and it is true that much interest in the changing nature of learning has been led by advocates of the new literacies movement. Second, the idea of literacy is used as a way of summing up competence in a new domain, as in emotional literacy, computer literacy, visual literacy and so on. Other scholars, however, have debated the validity of the use of the concept of literacy as a way of understanding insights in all of these domains (Buckingham et al., 2005). Nevertheless, understanding Net Generation activities and learning as a kind of literacy clearly strikes a popular chord as a way of summing up the sea change in capabilities, one that is comparable to the importance of the introduction of print literacy in the development of modern societies (Luke, 1989). The questions remain, however, about how such developments challenge the literacy practices in schools, which are, of course, mainly based on print.

Speculations About the Self and Subjectivity

As a space, the internet has become increasingly central as an alternative location for a broad set of practices that extend, complement or supplement everyday or learning practices in schools. It is, of course, the idea that persistent interaction with digital technologies has changed fundamental aspects of how young people create, interact with others and develop themselves that lies at the heart of the Net Generation hypothesis. Some of the earliest speculation about the effects of online and contemporary computer interactions are some of the most ambitious in conceptual terms and most difficult to prove empirically. Sherry Turkle led the way by exploring how the use of virtual avatars and a corresponding capacity to 'play' with identities has led to a change in the formation of subjectivities – how we imagine our selves (Turkle, 1985, 1997). It is this perceived nature of the *differences* between this model of self-formation and traditional ones that has led to the current dilemma as schools, teachers and parents seem to struggle to come to terms with a gap between what is expected in terms of guiding and teaching the young and what they are presented with on a day-to-day basis. At the same time, it is obvious that young people today have many similarities with earlier generations, in the sense that certain aspects of being young seem 'constant': for example, the role of friends, a sense of belonging, of developing sexuality and the importance of school as a place both for formal education and for socialising.

Seeking the Social

Two aspects to the impact of the social seem relevant here. First, we have the idea that digital technology facilitates access to a wide range of public, civic, community, interest and friendship groupings. Young people, it is argued, can interact online and can act in any of these fora with independence and authority. A series of studies has explored all of these discrete areas, examining the extent to which the online life does or does not afford these new opportunities and how (and who by) they are taken up (Loader, 2007; Ito et al., 2010). Second, there is the idea that such processes support qualitatively different notions of collective and collaborative activity, especially those that relate to learning. Scholars of computer gaming, as well as of online life, have noted that inhabiting rule-bound virtual worlds encourages discrete kinds of social behaviour that has ramifications for education, such as working in teams on focused and dedicated tasks and being able to work at ones' own pace and within one's own timeframes. Again, a number of scholars have noted how such behaviours are quite specifically at odds with dominant forms of teaching and learning within the curriculum, with its individualised modes of study and assessment (see, for example, Shaffer, 2008). Some scholars argue that social interaction using digital media evokes certain forms of empowerment and agency. For example, being able to act with others on- and offline using different digital tools changes the agency or power of the young person as a social actor and, subsequently, his or her civic engagement (Cassell et al., 2006; Loader, 2007).

Skills and Competencies Across the Life Course

Significant attention in much of the literature concerning the Net Generation is focused on a set of behaviours that are learnt through computer-based interactions and that can be described as a new skill set. In general, the range of new skills learnt in this way break down into *user* and *producer* types and exist on a sliding scale. User skills can be both mental and physical, covering, for example, information retrieval and manipulation or increased hand–eye coordination. Producer skills range from the ability to customise to making expressive media (O'Hear & Sefton-Green, 2004). The spread of these abilities and the different ways that young people learn them through various forms of self- or peer teaching (Willett & Sefton-Green, 2002) is contested and unequal, with scant sociological evidence for their reach and penetration and with case study examples often standing in for more general habits. Attention to the power of auto-didacticism and its various trial-and-error methods has important implications for formal education (Sefton-Green, 2004), but this must not stand in the way of a level-headed evaluation of what David Buckingham (2008) has called the 'banality' of much new media use. The discussion of the range of skills and competences demonstrated in new media use ranges from the capacity to manipulate computers, programs, icons and other formal features of digital technologies to learning the rules, conventions and genres of chat rooms, games and so on – the more cultural side to these activities. Much attention has been paid to the mastery of text and its seemingly organic transmutations through different language shapes and forms in chat and other online interactions (see, for example, Pahl & Rowsell, 2006 or Snyder, 1998, 2002). The producer skill set has ranged from study of adaption and customisation to more complex cultural activities like digital storytelling[1], pursuing special interests in film and audio (see Gilje, Chapter 12, this volume) and, of course, websites or blogs (Stern, 2004).

The increased focus on user-generated content production and how it is said to stimulate new practices of reading and writing is one example of activities embracing the digital learner. Young people can, to a much larger degree than before, create multimodal products that they can share with others (Drotner & Schrøder, 2010). In the emerging participatory media culture (Jenkins, 2006), digital media has increasingly blurred the distinction between production and consumption, as shown by Mizuko Ito (2005) in the peer-to-peer exchange surrounding Japanese animation media mixes.

In summary, we suggest that, although it is unclear precisely how to measure the growth of a Net Generation, there is a generally agreed-upon body of international research that documents a series of changing behaviours and competences by some young people as a result of their use of digital technologies. We do not know how equal, far-reaching or widespread such changes are, but a series of identified behaviours that offer authentic and challenging learning experiences has been enumerated. These coalesce around a different kind of learning self – different from the forms of subjectivity validated by current school arrangements – who can act with authority across a series of domains and who is accustomed to forms of collaboration, genuine challenge, experimentation, risk-taking, curiosity and expressivity.

---

[1] For example http://www.intermedia.uio.no/mediatized/

THE RELEVANCE OF INFORMAL LEARNING

In addition to notions of the Net Generation as a descriptor of generational transition, another important category in this debate has been the conceptualisation of 'informal learning' in relation to young people's use of digital technologies and the rhetorical use of such studies of learning to challenge the interrelationship between home and school.

During the last three decades, studies of informal learning have been growing. It is difficult to offer a comprehensive sociological understanding of why this might be so, but we should consider such work as both a strategic opposition to formal ways of learning, as well as a theoretical response to an interest in the ways young people develop practices using digital technologies that are self-initiated and self-motivated.

Scholars of childhood and youth have contributed distinctly to the study of informal learning. A particular focus has been on the role of markets and the changing place of children and young people as actors within a changing, commercialised environment (Kline, Dyer-Witheford & Peuter, 2003). Scholars have noted how induction into forms of commercially mediated play offers forms of 'structuration' that impact on notions of changing subjectivity (Buckingham & Sefton-Green, 2004). Studies of the role of commercial companies exploring the new home markets opened up by digital technologies (Kenway & Bullen, 2001; Buckingham & Scanlon, 2002) not only develop this theme but obviously explore the role and nature of what informal learning might mean in these changing domestic contexts.

Informal learning, however useful and helpful in reigniting debates about curriculum structures, learning progressions or pedagogic relationships (Sefton-Green, 2004), is, of course, a notoriously slippery and ultimately undefinable concept (Bekerman, Burbules & Silberman-Keller, 2006). It can be used to describe the quality of the pedagogic relationship, its casual or organised/ disorganised structure, its individually paced nature, a lack of formal accreditation or even the kind of language used. In the context of the Net Generation, it is often used to describe a way of working (referring to multitasking or just-in-time learning) or *gameification* (i.e. both drawing on the complex intellectual nature of game playing [Gee, 2004] *and* the understanding of game-play as a way of characterising other kind of social interactions [Beck & Wade, 2004]). It describes a kind of digital habitus, a way of being with the technology that both depends on and contributes to vigorous meaningful and authentic learning trajectories. It is furthermore very much a domestic habitus, with most studies exploring its nature with peers in home or peer-culture environments (e.g. see Sjöblom & Aronsson, Chapter 11, this volume).

Although it might be paradoxical, a number of initiatives attempt to capture informal learning and institutionalise it. On the one hand, there is a tradition of scholarship that explores the cultural and out-of-school literacies of young people (see e.g. Hull & Schultz, 2002) that, although it doesn't use the terminology of informal learning, explores how young people make meaning with texts out of school and try to bring such processes into the school curriculum. At the same time, studies of out-of school learning and after-school clubs and other kinds of nonformal learning environments (Herr-Stephenson et al., 2011) examine how modes of informal learning may be recuperated and mobilised within other kind of curriculum structures and alongside more formal pedagogies.

Both of these approaches come together in studies on informal science and maths learning that examine embedded and day-to-day kinds of scientific knowledge and then try to understand how more formal but nonschool educational environments, such as museums, develop such understanding in ways that might complement or support the classical science curriculum. In their report on learning science in informal environments, Bell and colleagues (2009) present different 'strands' of science learning that expand the perspectives of how young people are engaged in science issues. By using an ethnographic approach to studying different families, the authors show how science-specific issues are part of young people's everyday life practices. This is done by studying young people as part of participation trajectories and how these relate to school-based science education.

A key principle underpinning much research into informal learning is that of a paradigm shift – or at least degrees of difference – between old and new ways of learning. Either through a compound of learning theories or through a new literacies approach, or even through study of the interpolating function of the market, there is considerable uniformity in the notion that learning informally – outside the school – is in some way in serious competition with schooling. This presents a series of significant implications for how schools address, engage and empower young people.

EDUCATIONAL RESPONSES TO TWENTY-FIRST-CENTURY CHALLENGES

Responses of educational systems around the world towards the developments of a digital generation and the increased role of informal learning are, to say the least, ambivalent. There are numerous examples of so-called, innovative practices using new digital technologies within educational settings from around the world (Kozma, 2003; Voogt & Knezek, 2008). Still, education as a system has not changed according to the expectations raised by both policy makers and researchers (Livingstone, 2011). There are no simple reasons for this. Our point, however, is that these developments have created a disconnect between innovative cases and expectations, on the one hand, and education as a system, on the other, one that hinders a more holistic approach to important educational issues today and for the future, especially those focused on how digital learners relate to knowledge across different contexts (Selwyn, 2011a).

The question then becomes how to handle this mismatch between what is highlighted by policy makers and researchers as the new brave world of digital technologies through numerous 'best practices' and 'early adopters', and the conditions under which most teachers and students are operating in schools. Neil Selwyn has described this as 'educational technology and media research focused firmly on the *state-of-the-art* rather than the *state-of-the-actual*' arguing for 'accounts of the ordinary rather than the extra-ordinary aspects of how digital media and technology are being used and not being used' (Selwyn, 2011b, pp. 211–12).

We highlight three aspects of educational responses to twenty-first-century challenges, pointing towards some of the systemic challenges of connecting with the technological issues at stake for education systems today.

School as Oppositional Culture

One approach has been to 'estrange' the everyday culture and informal learning of young people. Historically, this has been characterised as a 'moral panic' by the public towards new media (Springhall, 1998). Furthermore, critical voices, like Neil Postman's (1993, 1996) have, for decades, warned about the cultural impact of popular media culture, a position often taken up by teachers to fight the commercialised media culture of young people. The focus has been on cultural values rather than on learning and literacy. This opposition towards the digital media practices of young people can also be seen in public debates about the negative aspects of these practices, such as bullying, access to violent and pornographic content, copy-and-paste plagiarism and so forth.

Also, the increased focus on basic science, technology, engineering and mathematics (STEM) skills defines certain ways of using digital technologies. These ways are quite different from the use of digital technologies in what is termed *soft skills*, such as collaboration and creation. These skill sets are often defined in opposition to each other, leaving the soft skills in the margins, together with the everyday practices of students. If by chance they are made relevant in school practices, it is as part of marginal subjects like media studies or as part of arts projects (Erstad, 2010).

Supporting Established Practices

When digital technologies are used to support established practices, they are embedded into established educational practices and change nothing fundamental about how school-based learning activities are performed. Teachers dealing with these new technologies find ways that support their comfort zones. In this way, digital technologies often simply become advanced and expensive typewriters, calculating machines and information sources, and regular classroom activities, featuring a teacher in front of the class and students following teacher instruction, remain unchanged. One example is the implementation of whiteboards in many classrooms around the world or the use of virtual learning environments that often simply support existing practices (Higgins, Beauchamp & Miller, 2007; Weiss, Nolan, Hunsinger & Trifonas, 2006).

In Terms of Standardisation

As a system, education is very much about standardising learning, yet the informal media experiences of young people are more about individual interests and the collective processes of creation and collaboration. Consequently, new initiatives are easily interpreted in terms of how they fit into the system of standardisation that regulates educational practices. The daily routines of schools are regulated through such mechanisms as the school bell, the layout of classrooms, or through the use of age-specific textbooks. The most important mechanism of standardisation, though, is the assessment system. New technologies in learning pose a number of challenges here, and a recent initiative, 'Assessment and Teaching of 21st Century Skills' (http://atc21s.org/), analyses the systemic challenge of changing the assessment system in order to create school development and learning environments for digital learners in the twenty-first century (Griffin, McGaw & Care, 2012).

These three elements point to some of the challenges that reinforce a disconnect between innovative cases and systemic change, and between digital practices in and out of school. Let us now look at one country case in which certain recent developments might indicate a way forward.

CREATING SYSTEMIC SUPPORT FOR DIGITAL LEARNERS ACROSS SCHOOLS AND COMMUNITIES: NORWAY

As described earlier, state education systems typically ignore, proscribe or attempt to recuperate the kinds of knowledge, learning and experiences going on in young peoples lives. In Norway, however, as in other Nordic countries, the 'digital vernacular' (Brown, 2006) has made a unique connection with traditional views on out-of-school learning, even though the last decade has seen a strong move towards teacher-centred classroom practices and more tests of student outcomes, mainly due to average performance levels on the PISA tests. The in-school implementation of digital technologies, however, resonates more with longstanding traditions of project work in Norwegian schools (Erstad 2005) and an orientation towards student engagement in and out of school since the technology provides means of information access, communication and mobility.[2]

Historically, Norwegian education is part of the *Nordic educational model* (Telhaug, Medias & Aasen, 2006), which goes back to the 1930s and is firmly rooted in social-democratic educational policies that provide equal opportunities for all within public schools and almost no alternative private schools. In addition, the Nordic countries are characterised by high access to state-funded digital technologies. This has also been proclaimed as an alternative model ('the welfare model') for innovation, development and technology to the market-oriented approach, as exemplified by Silicon Valley technology organisations (Castells & Himanen, 2002). Many US researchers of technology and learning tend to focus on digital learners outside of school and to define public schools as a problem; while Norwegian researchers, to a greater extent, see an interest in the role of public schools in supporting all digital learners by creating resources.

We will highlight three aspects of recent developments in the Norwegian education system that relate to ways of overcoming the binary oppositions between in- and out-of-school uses of digital technologies. As in other countries, the implementation and educational use of digital technologies in schools has gone through several waves or phases. The first wave is characterised by a focus on the technology itself and on implementation, often sidetracking educational issues altogether. The second wave has focused more on the educational use of digital technologies in practice and the resource equity needed in learning environments as part of school development. Most countries are still focusing on strategies for handling this second wave of challenges. Some recent initiatives in Norway indicate a movement towards a third wave that might signal a way of overcoming the disconnects and mismatches discussed above.

---

[2] Similar developments have evolved in places like Singapore, as part of their Masterplan on industrial communication technology (ICT) in education, described as 'seamless learning'. However, the education systems have quite different historic roots, which makes the framing of digital technologies in education different.

Digital Competence in the National Curriculum

The national curriculum of Norway consists of a general part and a part that specifies aims and content areas for different subject areas on different levels. The national curriculum of 2006 is of special importance since it defines the ability 'to use digital tools' as one of five core skills running through all subjects and levels of schooling (the others being reading, writing, numeracy and oral skills) as a systemwide reform. The term 'digital competence' is used to describe this basic skill. This development has created a totally new commitment within the whole education system towards using digital technologies in all subjects and on all levels. The emphasis on digital competence as one of the core competencies of learning in the twenty-first century makes it critical to understand how digital practices at school connect with media practices outside of school. As such, it gives teachers the legitimacy to blend school activities with skills and competencies gained from outside of schools, such as using computer games or digital storytelling in schools (Erstad & Silseth, 2008). The learner is, as such, not defined solely within the space of the classroom but in connection with experiences gained from other spaces in everyday life.

Reevaluating *Bildung* for a Digital Culture

In recent years, the German term *Bildung* has regained an important position as a reformist agenda for Norwegian education in a digital culture. The term goes back to Humbolt and his ideals of academic scholarship, but is now reinterpreted as the challenge of what it means to be learned. As such, it represents an alternative route to the one proclaimed by cultural pessimists like Neil Postman. The Norwegian educational philosopher Lars Lovlie (2003) writes about the internet as the new interface for a 'meetings of minds' and for what it means to become literate.[3] Further, key concerns are raised about the overall challenges of being part of digital culture. What does it mean to function optimally in a media culture and a knowledge society? What does it mean to be informed enough to make decisions of importance for oneself as a citizen and for society as a whole, as occurs, for example, when elections become digitalised and political debate takes place online? In a Norwegian context, broad issues of citizenship become important for the implications of education in a digital culture.

---

[3] Similar ideas can be found in writings by the Swedish literature scientist Jan Thavenius (1995).

Emphasising Relevance and Authenticity

In addition to these two aspects of the national curriculum creating the foundations for committing all schools to work on using digital technologies, there are examples of important policy initiatives in which the digital disconnect is addressed directly. One example is the recent White Paper No. 22 (2010–2011), 'Motivation-Coping-Possibilities' (*Motivasjon-Mestring-Muligheter*), which focuses on changing lower secondary education in Norway. In it, students' lack of motivation is defined as the major challenge for succeeding at school. It has been suggested that many students at this level experience schooling as disconnected from other domains in their lives, lacking in relevance and in variation and being too theoretical (Kunnskapsdepartementet, 2011). Teachers face the dual demand of fulfilling curriculum requirements of knowledge provision while, at the same time, creating motivation. Several researchers have pointed out that bringing young people's experiences from outside of school into the classroom may strengthen motivation (Nordahl, Mausethagen & Kostøl, 2009). It is not obvious, however, how teachers can do this and whether it will enhance learning in school. The key concepts running through this document are *relevance* and *authenticity* as key to increasing motivation for learning. In this sense, the White Paper highlights key values in the Norwegian education system that seek to engage all students and increase their potential.

In highlighting these three aspects of developments in Norway, we are not saying that they are unique, nor that Norway is a model for others to follow since these developments are linked to historic roots in the Norwegian education system. Still, these three aspects are all parts of an important movement in overcoming the gap between digital practices in and out of school and in providing for digital learners in contemporary culture. These developments in Norway lead us to a more fundamental question of defining the purpose of public schools in the twenty-first century.

SUMMARY

One Step Beyond

In this chapter, we have examined how the literature describing the Net Generation has constructed an idea about new and different kinds of learning, although such views are not uncontested. We have seen how the idea of informal learning has been proposed as a theoretical way of legitimising the 'newness' of such learning. However, drawing on the case of Norway, it becomes evident that questions about access, equity and learning quality are fundamental to ways of providing for the digital learner. A systemwide approach is needed to embrace the macro and micro factors of development (Erstad, 2009), as the concepts of 'digital competence' and 'digital *bildung*' exemplify, thus connecting the digital learner and school development with practices both in and out of school.

By way of summary, we propose the following three approaches as different ways of forging a connection between different learning spaces for the digital learner.

Reinforcing

This approach sees in- and out-of-school relationships as complementing each other and as working as supplements and extensions to each other. However, each domain follows its own logic and preserves a nonporous boundary; an example of this occurs when parents buy software to stimulate reading and writing skills in young children, in order to prepare them for later schooling. Another such example of reinforcement occurs when technologies are used as part of homework, either for performing assignments given by the teacher or in preparing for assessments. The learner is still the subject of formal schooling, but the pedagogical gaze has simply been extended beyond the school walls into the home and young people's leisure cultures.

Replacing

Another, more controversial approach that we might conceive is that the home or other community setting in some way replaces the school as a location for learning. Schools are devalued and discredited as relevant institutions for learning and education in the twenty-first century. The Net Generation/Digital Generation literature has located and defined several forms of meaningful, socially valuable learning that takes place in these locations. Most important for this chapter's discussion are those ways that young people develop competencies of importance for living in the twenty-first century, which schools do not provide. This is also justified in policy and practice through some of the implications of the work we have described as digital *bildung*. This creates perceptions of other contexts for learning that would replace the school as we know it.

Reinventing

The third approach both describes the opposition and disconnect between in- and out-of-school use of digital technologies and focuses on some way of reframing or reinterpreting such an interrelationship. This would imply a need to see the school as one of several contexts for learning: important in certain ways by bringing different students together and providing guided knowledge building, but a context that also must be linked to other practices and activities that young people are involved in using digital technologies, both on- and offline. The learner here is continuously being re-located in the terms of our discussion.

The aim of this chapter was to explore how the digital learner has been located across different settings and how different spaces have been framed as learning contexts in policy and research discourse.

The risk of such an approach, despite all the richness it can offer to the analysis of young people and their changing technologically mediated experiences, is that 'learning' replaces 'learners'. We are not suggesting that we need to individualise and romanticise persons, but that we need a way of moving beyond discursive oppositions to understand how individuals may mediate and rationalise such models of learning in the synthesis of living their lives.

Bruner's notion of what he called 'folk-pedagogies' (Bruner, 1996) – commonly held ways of conceptualising mind and learning – could clearly be applied to the typologies we have offered in this paper. The frames we use now to think of children and young people are irredeemably modulated by conceptions of home, school, informality and transformed learning, however contingent and careful many of us would like to be. The Net Generation is a new character in this changing folk landscape. The digital vernacular may well offer an inflection, a trend in what is a continuous struggle for legitimacy in an ongoing debate about the purpose, value and operation of learning and schools.

However, reducing the formal/informal or the digital to a play of discourses ignores the real effect such ideas have in making or cutting off real opportunities for young people in contemporary societies – an argument we hope we have explained in our study of policy and development using a single-country perspective. In that sense, we want the broad perspectives we have offered in this chapter to open up ways of moving beyond the simple binaries that have so often been used in this discussion as a way of artificially polarising differences that, for the individuals concerned, have little or no meaning.

REFERENCES

Beach, K. (1999). Consequential transitions: A sociocultural expedition beyond transfer in education. *Review of Research in Education, 24,* 101–39.

Beck, J. C., & Wade, M. (2004). *Got game: How the gamer generation is reshaping business forever.* Cambridge, MA: Harvard Business School Press.

Bell, P., Lewenstein, B., Shouse, A. W., & Feder, M. A. (Eds.). (2009). *Learning science in informal environments. People, places and pursuits.* Washington, DC: The National Academies Press.

Bekerman, Z., Burbules, N. C., & Silberman-Keller, D. (Eds.). (2006). *Learning in places. The informal education reader.* New York: Peter Lang.

Brown, J. S. (2006). New learning environments for the 21st century: Exploring the edge. *Change, September/October,* 18–24.

Bruner, J. (1996). *The culture of education.* Cambridge, MA: Harvard University Press.

Buckingham, D. (2008). *Youth, identity, and digital media (John D. and Catherine T. MacArthur Foundation Series on Digital Media and Learning).* Boston, MA: The MIT Press.

Buckingham, D., Banaji, S., Burn, A., Carr, D., Cranmer, S., & Willett, R. (2005). The media literacy of children and young people. Retrieved from http://www.ofcom. org.uk/advice/media_literacy/medlitpub/medlitpubrss/ml_children.pdf

Buckingham, D., & Scanlon, M. (2002). *Education, entertainment and learning in the home.* Buckingham: Open University Press.

Buckingham, D., & Sefton-Green, J. (2004). Structure, agency and pedagogy in children's media culture. In J. Tobin (Ed.), *Pikachu's global adventure: The rise and fall of Pokemon.* Durham, NC: Duke University Press.

Cassell, J., Huffaker, D., Tversky, D., & Ferriman, K. (2006). The language of online leadership: Gender and youth engagement on the Internet. *Developmental Psychology, 42*(3), 436–449.

Castells, M., & Himanen, P. (2002). *The information society and the welfare state: The Finnish model.* New York: Oxford University Press.

Coiro, J., Knobel, M., Lankshear, C., & Leu, D. J. (Eds.). (2008). *Handbook of research on new literacies.* New York: Lawrence Erlbaum.

Drotner, K., & Schrøder, K. C. (Eds.). (2010). *Digital content creation. Perceptions, practices & perspectives.* New York: Peter Lang Publishing.

Edwards, R., Biesta, G., & Thorpe, M. (Eds.). (2009). *Rethinking contexts for learning and teaching. Communities, activities and networks.* London: Routledge.

Erstad, O. (2005). Expanding possibilities: Project work using ICT. *Human Technology. An Interdisciplinary Journal on Humans in ICT Environments, 1*(2), 109–264. Retrieved from http://www.humantechnology.jyu.fi

Erstad, O. (2009). Addressing the complexity of impact – A multilevel approach towards ICT in education. In F. Scheuermann & F. Pedro (Eds.), *Assessing the effects of ICT in education.* Luxembourg: Publications Office of the European Union.

Erstad, O. (2010). Media literacy and education: The past, present and future. In S. Kotilainen & S.-B. Arnolds-Granlund (Eds.), *Media literacy education – Nordic perspectives.* Gothenburg: Nordicom University of Gothenburg.

Erstad, O., & Silseth, K. (2008). Agency in digital storytelling – Challenging the educational context. In K. Lundby (Ed.) *Digital storytelling, mediatized stories: Self-representations in new media*. New York: Peter Lang Publishing.

Gee, J. P. (2004). *What video games have to teach us about learning and literacy*. London: Palgrave Macmillan.

Giacquinta, J. B., Bauer, J. A., & Levin, J. E. (1994). *Beyond technology's promise: An examination of children's educational computing at home*. Cambridge: Cambridge University Press.

Herr-Stephenson, B., Rhoten, D., Perkel, D., & Sims, C. (2011). *Digital media and technology in afterschool programs, libraries, and museums*. Cambridge, MA: The MIT Press.

Higgins, S., Beauchamp, G., & Miller, D. (2007). Reviewing the literature on interactive whiteboards. *Learning, Media and Technology, 32*(3), 213–225.

Hull, G., & Shultz, K. (Eds.). (2002). *School's out! Bridging out-of-school literacy with classroom practice*. New York: Teachers College Press.

Ito, M. (2005). Technologies of the childhood imagination: Yugioh, media mixes, and everyday cultural production. In J. J. N. Karaganis (Ed.), *Structures of participation in digital culture*. Durham, NC: Duke University Press.

Ito, M., Baumer, S., Bittanti, M., Boyd, D., Cody, R., Herr-Stephenson, B., et al. (2010). *Hanging out, messing around, and geeking out*. Cambridge, MA: The MIT Press.

Griffin, P., McGaw, B., & Care, E. (Eds.). (2012). *Assessment and teaching of 21st century skills*. New York: Springer Science + Business Media.

Jenkins, H. (2006). *Convergence culture. Where old and new media collide*. New York: New York University Press.

Jewitt, C., & Kress, G. (2003). *Multimodal literacy*. New York: Peter Lang Pub Ing.

Kenway, J., & Bullen, E. (2001). *Consuming children: Education – entertainment – advertising*. Buckingham: Open University Press.

Kline, S., Dyer-Witheford, N., & Peuter, G. D. (2003). *Digital play: The interaction of technology, culture and marketing*. Montreal: McGill-Queen's University Press.

Kozma, R. B. (Ed.). (2003). *Technology, innovation and educational change. A global perspective. A report of the Second Information Technology in Education Study Module 2*. Eugene, OR: The International Society for Technology in Education.

Kunnskapsdepartementet. (2011). *Motivasjon-mestring-muligheter (Motivation-coping-possibilities)*. White Paper No. 22 (2010–2011). Oslo.

Leander, K., Phillips, N. C., & Taylor, K. H. (2010). The changing social spaces of learning: Mapping new mobilities. *Review of Research in Education, 34*, 329–394.

Livingstone, S. (2011). Critical reflections on the benefits of ICT in education. *Oxford Review of Education, 38*(1), 9–24.

Loader, B. D. (2007). *Young citizens in the digital age: Political engagement, young people and new media*. London: Routledge.

Lovlie, L. (2003). The promise of bildung. In L. Lovlie, K. P. Mortensen, & S. E. Nordenbo (Eds.), *Educating humanity. Bildung in postmodernity*. London: Blackwell Publishing.

Luke, C. (1989). *Pedagogy, printing and Protestantism: The discourse on childhood (SUNY Series, the Philosophy of Education)*. New York: State University of New York Press.

Nordahl, T., Mausethagen, S., & Kostøl, A. K. (2009). *Skoler med liten og stor forekomst av atferdsproblemer. En kvantitativ og kvalitativ analyse av forskjeller og likheter mellom skolene* (Schools with minor and major behavioural problems. A quantitative and qualitative analysis of differences and similarities between the schools). Elverum, Norway: University College of Hedmark.

O'Hear, S., & Sefton-Green, J. (2004). Creative 'communities': How technology mediates social worlds. In D. Miell & K. Littleton (Eds.), *Collaborative creativity: Contemporary perspectives*. London: Free Association Press.

Pahl, K., & Rowsell, J. (2006). *Travel notes from the new literacy studies: Instances of practice*. Multilingual Matters Ltd.

Palfrey, J., & Gasser, U. (2008). *Born digital: Understanding the first generation of digital natives*. New York: Basic Books.

Papert, S. A. (1980). *Mindstorms: Children, computers, and powerful ideas*. New York: Basic Books.

Perkins, D., & Salomon, G. (1992). Transfer of learning. In *International encyclopaedia of education* (2nd ed.). Oxford: Pergamon Press.

Postman, N. (1993). *Technopoly: The surrender of culture to technology*. New York: Vintage Books.

Postman, N. (1996). *The end of education: Redefining the value of school*. New York: Vintage Books.

Prensky, M. (2006). *Don't bother me Mom – I'm learning!* St. Paul MN: Paragon House Publishers.

Sefton-Green, J. (2004). Initiation rites: A small boy in a Poke-world. In J. Tobin (Ed.), *Pikachu's global adventure: The rise and fall of Pokemon*. Durham, NC: Duke University Press.

Sefton-Green, J., Nixon, H., & Erstad, O. (2009) Reviewing approaches and perspectives on 'digital literacy'. *Pedagogies: An International Journal, 4*(2), 107–25.

Selwyn, N. (2011a). *Schools and schooling in the digital age*. London: Routledge.

Selwyn, N. (2011b). Technology, media and education: Telling the whole story. *Learning, Media and Technology, 36*(3), 211–13.

Shaffer, D. (2008). *How computer games help children learn*. New York: Palgrave Macmillan.

Snyder, I. (1998). *Page to screen: Taking literacy into the electronic era*. London: Routledge.

Snyder, I. (2002). *Silicon literacies: Communication, innovation and education in the electronic age*. London: Routledge.

Springhall, J. (1998). *Youth, popular culture and moral panics. Penny gaffs to gangsta-rap, 1830–1996*. New York: St. Martin's Press.

Stern, S. (2004). Expression of identity online: Prominent features and gender differences in adolescents' WWW home pages. *Journal of Broadcasting and Electronic Media, 48*(2).

Telhaug, A. O., Medias, O. A., & Aasen, P. (2006). The Nordic model in education: Education as part of the political system in the last 50 years. *Scandinavian Journal of Educational Research, 50*(3), 245–83.

Thavenius, J. (1995). *Den motsägelsefulla bildningen (The contradictory bildung)*. Stockholm: Brutus Östlings Bokförlag Symposion.

Thomas, M. (2011). *Deconstructing digital natives. Young people, technology and the new literacies*. New York: Routledge.

Turkle, S. (1985). *Second self: Computers and the human spirit*. New York: Pocket Books.

Turkle, S. (1997). *Life on the screen: Identity in the age of the Internet*. New York: Simon & Schuster Inc.

Voogt, J., & Knezek, G. (Eds.). (2008). *International handbook of information technology in primary and secondary education*. New York: Springer Science + Business Media.

Weiss, J., Nolan, J., Hunsinger, J., & Trifonas, P. (Eds.). (2006). *The international handbook of virtual learning environment*. Dordrecht: Springer.

Willett, R., & Sefton-Green, J. (2002). Living and learning in chatrooms (or does informal learning have anything to teach us?). *Education et Sociétiés, 2*, 57–77.

SECTION TWO

FROM LEARNING TO LEARNERS: LEARNING
LIVES AS THEY ARE LIVED

Chapter 7

Expanding the Chronotopes of Schooling for the Promotion of Students' Agency

Antti Rajala, Jaakko Hilppö, Lasse Lipponen and
Kristiina Kumpulainen

> (In other courses) we sit and read, there are textbooks and note-taking, a fast pace in everything. There is one book per course . . . Mostly you just sit in the classroom, write and listen.
>
> (Student interview, the *Bicycles on the Move!* project)

Conventionally, as the above extract shows, space and time at school are often strictly controlled and circumscribed to specific times and places (Leander, 2002; Vadeboncoeur, 2005; Brown & Renshaw, 2006). Similarly, the dominant discursive space of schooling is dictated to a large degree by curricula, textbooks and teacher talk (Mehan, 1979; Leander, 2002; Engeström, 2008b). Thus, little room is left for students' agency, including those experiences that learners bring to school from other contexts, such as their homes, playgrounds, after-school clubs, libraries, science centres and museums. Accordingly, school learning mostly stays relatively disconnected from learners' other worlds, as formal education arguably fails to value and build on the cultural resources of learners and the communities of which they are part – their expertise, knowledge and artefacts (Engeström, Engeström & Suntio, 2002; González, Moll & Amanti, 2005).

Furthermore, the space-time configuration of schooling rarely provides students with diverse or rich possibilities for becoming engaged and involved. The learning practices in these situations are often reduced to the acquisition of new knowledge and skills, and students' agency and identities are not fostered (Bloome et al., 2009). In particular, conventional schooling is failing to provide students with agentic experiences (Tyack & Cuban, 1997; Hubbard, Mehan, & Stein, 2006). One indication of this lack of agentic experiences is that, despite the successes of the Finnish education system in international assessments (OECD, 2010), a recent survey reported that a third of Finnish secondary school students did not know how to take part in decision making at school and, when they did take part, their opinions were not taken into account in school development (National Institute for Health and Welfare, 2011). Furthermore, in international comparisons, Finnish students are ranked highly in societal knowledge and competence, but they are not taking part in politics or public affairs in general (Schulz et al., 2010). Yet, if we want to educate agentic learners who are prepared to tackle the challenges that they face in their everyday lives and in future adulthood, we need to arrange situations in which they are positioned as doing something important and valuable of their own volition.

Thus, there is clearly a need to develop pedagogical approaches that employ novel space-time configurations that promote students' agency. Even though significant new pedagogical breakthroughs have been made to develop schooling within the last fifty years (see, for example, Daniels, 2008), only a few studies connect schools' space-time and students' agency (see also Brown & Renshaw, 2006).

In this chapter, we examine an innovative learning project in a Finnish upper secondary school (students aged 16–19), namely, *Bicycles on the Move!* Our purpose is to understand what opportunities this project and its peda-gogical principles provided for students and their teachers to transform and refine the conventional space-time dimensions of their schooling. In examin-ing the social construction of a new space-time matrix, we use the notion of a *chronotope* (Bakhtin, 1981, 1986; Lemke, 2004; Bloome et al., 2009). In partic-ular, we ask: What kind of a chronotope does the *Bicycles on the Move!* project manifest? What implications does this chronotope have for providing oppor-tunities to promote students' agency?

In the following sections, we first briefly define the concept of chrono-tope and how we have used it as a tool for making sense of the school's space-time configuration. We then present our chronotopic analysis of the *Bicycles on the Move!* project and demonstrate the implications that this chronotope has for students' agency. The chapter ends by reflecting on a pedagogy that expands the configuration of the school's space-time and is thus, we argue, more responsive to the learning requirements of this century.

INVESTIGATING THE CHRONOTOPES OF SCHOOLING

The ability to *see time*, to *read time*, in the spatial whole of the world and, on the other hand, to perceive the filling of space not as an immobile background, a given that is completed once and for all, but as an emerging whole, an event, this is the ability to read in everything *signs that show time in its course*, beginning with nature and ending with human customs and ideas ...

(Bakhtin, 1986, p. 25, italics original)

Contrary to the still prevalent everyday understanding, the categories of time and space are not separate and independent (Lemke, 2004). Instead, time and space are deeply interconnected and also socially constructed in discourse and everyday activities (Bloome et al., 2009). The interconnection of time and space can be understood by the concept of a chronotope. This concept can be traced back to the work of Bakhtin (1981), who defines the spatio-temporal matrix as being produced, shaped and reshaped by the discourses of participants as they relate to spaces and times beyond here and now. Thus, the construct of a chronotope focuses attention on how people – for instance, teachers and students – understand and conceptualise their collective and individual movement through time and space (Brown & Renshaw, 2006; Bloome et al., 2009).

Jay Lemke (2004, p. x) defines chronotopes as follows: 'The typical patterns of organization of and across activities in space and time are described by chronotopes. Chronotopes are defining features of a culture or a subculture, and of communities of practice. Chronotopes inform our design choices in shaping social-institutional spaces for particular uses'. In subcultures, such as classrooms, chronotopes are often messy, complicated, incomplete, multiple and competing, and may vary across different situations within the same classroom (Bloome et al., 2009). Moreover, David Bloome et al. (2009) make a distinction between individually held chronotopes, shared chronotopes and publicly held chronotopes. *Publicly held chronotopes* are located in the public event and accessible to participants. An *individually held chronotope* is one held by a person him- or herself alone. *Shared chronotopes* are also often taken up by individuals, but in addition, they are shared and, thus, require intersubjectivity. Following the interpretation of Lemke (2004) and Bloome et al. (2009), we analyse chronotopes as public patterns of organisation, both of and across activities in space and time.

BICYCLES ON THE MOVE!: A SITUATED EXAMPLE OF AN EXPANSIVE CHRONOTOPE

The *Bicycles on the Move!* project is being run at the Etelä-Tapiola Upper Secondary School in the City of Espoo, Finland. The project, currently running for the third time, was first implemented during the 2009/10 school

FIGURE 7.1 Interactive virtual map used in *Bicycles on the Move!* © National Land
Survey of Finland (MML), permission number 53/MML/11

year and has been a huge success, arousing interest in the media even internationally. Two teachers, Mikael Sorri and Pentti Heikkinen, started the project
in order to take learning into 'authentic environments'. The project aims to
increase students' cooperation with different social actors in order to develop
their sense of citizenship and agency. During the project, students collaborate
with city authorities and influence the decision making of the city council
concerning cycling.

Bicycles on the Move! was inspired and supported by two nationally
operated projects, *On the Move!* (*Liikkeelle!* in Finnish) and *Location
Learning* (*PaikkaOppi* in Finnish), funded by the Finnish National Board of
Education. The larger projects provided teachers and students with, among
other things, the *Link* learning environment, which features an interactive
virtual map that is used in the *Bicycles on the Move!* project (see Figure 7.1).
As part of the course activities, students add to the map photographs of
their cycling experiences, details of places where cycling conditions need
improvement and suggestions for new or alternative cycling routes.
These photographs then provide opportunities for sharing experiences and
observations when they are discussed collectively in the classroom. Link also
serves as a forum for social networking among students, teachers and various
experts.

Within schools and classrooms there exist not only institutionally estab-lished chronotopes, but also new, emerging forms of chronotopes (Lemke, 2004). However, new chronotopes do not simply replace the old ones; instead, conventional and novel chronotopes live side by side in contemp-orary schooling and may create conflicts and disturbances in the flow of activity (Leander, 2002). In fact, the teachers of *Bicycles on the Move!* reported that the year-long timespan of the project conflicted with the course-per-period–based way of organising teaching in the school. This manifested, for example, as difficulties with allocating times for meetings with the students.

In what follows, we examine the chronotope of the *Bicycles on the Move!* project. In line with Leander (2002), we use the notion of conventional schooling here in a general sense; that is, as an analytical backdrop to high-light the distinctively novel features of the *Bicycles on the Move!* chronotope. Based on our ethnographic understanding of the project, we have purpose-fully selected certain key aspects of the project for chronotopic analysis. We argue that accountability, meaning making and relationships and develop-mental aspects are essential for understanding how chronotopes are talked into being in schools. They also exemplify how we have empirically inves-tigated the chronotope of the project. Here, we use the idea of a chronotope more like a heuristic tool, not as an empirically tested and rigorous research approach.

First, concerning students' accountability, there are spatial and temporal dimensions to the audiences and the criteria for students' contributions (Brown & Renshaw, 2006). We analyse the introduction of a typical learning task of the project and illustrate how the audiences to which the students were made accountable were situated in space and time. We also analyse the spatial and temporal connections of the criteria for students' contributions.

Second, meaning making in school also has a spatio-temporal dimension (Kumpulainen & Lipponen, 2010). In our analysis of classroom interaction and teacher interviews, we show how the resources utilised in the project were located in and across space and time. We additionally examine whether and how the project fostered interpersonal relationships with stakeholders within and outside of school.

Finally, we analyse the developmental aspect of chronotopes. Bakhtin (1986) addresses how people and their lifeworlds mutually influence each other. That is, chronotopes differ in the extent to which people, their life-worlds or both are seen as either static or in a process of (mutual) change (Bakhtin, 1986). To capture the developmental aspect of the chronotope of *Bicycles on the Move!*, we identified those passages from student and teacher interviews in which the interviewees talked about change as they experienced it. In order to identify indications of transformations in the local environment initiated by the classroom community, we analysed various documents relating to the project, such as a public talk, newspaper articles and a television program.

In all, through these analyses, we argue that the chronotope of the *Bicycles on the Move!* project involves features that distance it from chronotopes typical of conventional schooling. It represents what we call the *expansive chronotope*. Here, we are inspired by Yrjö Engeström's theory of expansive learning (Engeström, 1987; Engeström, Puonti & Seppänen, 2003) and Randi Engle's research concerning expansive framing in classroom interaction (Engle, 2006; Engle, Nguyen & Mendelson, 2011).

Expanding Students' Accountability Across Space and Time

Our first example (see Excerpt 1) illuminates how the chronotope of the *Bicycles on the Move!* project extended the students' accountability as active agents across space and time. The teacher introduces the students to an assignment relating to construction of a new pedestrian and bicycle path near the school as part of a city plan. The students were going to take photographs of the surrounding area to illustrate the advantages and disadvantages for cyclists.

EXCERPT 1

TEACHER: The most urgent issue would be . . . right now they [the city authorities] are really starting to ponder and think about . . . whether Tapiolan Raitti is a functional main route for cyclists or whether it should be arranged in some other way . . . It is likely that we'll get an audience with the big bosses in January, so before that we should have something of an idea and we should have already checked every corner there and we should have an idea. So would you possibly feel up to going through those corners, especially from the Sokos Hotel heading East, and think about it? What would be a functional route?

In the example, the teacher holds the students accountable to a high-stakes audience by reminding them of the importance of their observations; they are going to meet a top city official who could be interested in the students' observations as the construction project is currently being planned. In the *Bicycles on the Move!* project, the students were generally made accountable not only to their teachers, but also to a broader audience, such as city officials, who they met during the project, newspaper readers when co-authoring opinion pieces with their teachers or current and future citizens living in the area (Brown & Renshaw, 2006; Gresalfi et al., 2009).

The example further illustrates that, instead of the students being accountable for providing the right answer to the teacher with respect to the criteria of a subject domain, their observations were going to be assessed from the point of view of their feasibility, considering the current local political situation. Indeed, the students' observations would not only function as 'raw data' for city planning but would also be used later when jointly formulating a thoughtful and critical contribution to the discussion about the new route. Hence, not just any observation or opinion would count, but the students would have to take into account whether what they proposed would be functional and doable from the perspective of city officials. Furthermore, the feasibility of contributions was temporally determined and connected to the unfolding here-and-now of local political decision making. For example, for their opinions to be heard, it was not wise to focus on matters that were neither currently on the local political agenda nor likely to be in the near future.

On the whole, this example highlights two connected ways showing how the expansive chronotope in the *Bicycles on the Move!* project temporally and spatially expanded the conventional school chronotopes (Gresalfi et al., 2009). First, the students were held accountable to a wider audience of current and future stakeholders. Second, the students were held accountable for producing thoughtful opinions and views that would feasibly contribute to current public debates concerning cycling. Thus, the feasibility of the students' contributions was connected to activity systems outside of school. Both of these extensions were also reflected in terms of how meanings were negotiated within the expansive chronotope and what counted as knowledge and knowing.

Making Meaning and Establishing Relationships by Connecting to Surrounding Communities

The second example (see Excerpt 2) illustrates the intercontextual and connected nature of the meaning-making processes typical of the expansive chronotope. In the example, the teachers and students are jointly exploring different ideas for projects for the whole course. The example begins with one of the teachers (Teacher 1) inviting one of the students to elaborate on her thinking in public.

Excerpt 2

TEACHER 1: Have you had any insight into what you could do so far? Have you even thought about this?

STUDENT: I have thought about it, umm, about Ring Road I, it's being built, there are big construction projects going on. Maybe something about that now.

TEACHER 1: Do you mean there at Leppävaara?

STUDENT: Yeah, yeah, that's right. There is the motorway intersection and then, um, the tunnel. If that could be something?

TEACHER 1: Yes, yes, what about cycling or whatever?

STUDENT: Yes, exactly, public transportation or, I mean, pedestrian and bicycle traffic solutions.

TEACHER 1: Yeah, yeah, it would be a good idea to look at that and the plans around it.

TEACHER 2: Really brilliant idea, I already looked into it last summer, and I have already sent some e-mails about it but it doesn't really mean that nothing should be done about it.

The example demonstrates how the dialogue in itself provides a bridge across past, present and future learning contexts in a way that allows students to weave their experiences and worlds together (Kumpulainen & Lipponen, 2010; Kumpulainen et al., 2010). In the example, reference is made to the student's and teachers' experiences and observations of a specific location, namely, a motorway intersection near the school. Interestingly, these observations are juxtaposed with the local political decision-making process and with past actions taken by one of the teachers. In the dialogue, contexts are presented as malleable to civic action mediated by democratic decision-making processes.

Throughout the course, the teachers emphasised the importance of the students' mundane observations on the surrounding environment. In this respect, the technological mediation provided by the interactive virtual map and photographs contributed considerably to the expanding space-time reconfigurations (see also Hakkarainen, Ritella & Seitamaa-Hakkarainen, 2011). The pedagogical intention of the teachers was to cultivate the students' understanding and appreciation of how small things and actions in their everyday lives could make a difference. As a result, the students' funds of knowledge were extensively brought in, acknowledged and built upon. International comparison played a part in the students' meaning-making processes, for example, when the classroom community discussed a

YouTube video about Copenhagen's cycling conditions presented by one of the students.

In addition, the course provided students with opportunities to develop interpersonal relationships and to learn with and from others. Whereas, in more conventional settings, the expert community is mainly positioned as being distant and disconnected from students' lives and school activities, in the expansive chronotope, the students established personal and meaningful contacts with the expert community. This was evidenced in classroom discussions in which a city official was referred to as 'our old friend'. Other cycling activists also came to the school to talk with the students about taking cycling issues to city officials and, in general, to share their experiences and insights. Moreover, international relationships were established during the project. For example, the classroom community made a trip to the Netherlands to investigate cycling culture and compare observations made in the Netherlands and Finland.

In summary, in the expansive chronotope, meaning making was connected across settings, communities and time. In particular, cultural resources and students' prior experiences stemming from multiple contexts were utilised and built on in the dialogue. Students also forged and maintained contacts with various stakeholders both locally and internationally.

Orienting to Transforming the Local Environment

Our third example (see Figure 7.2) demonstrates how the students, together with their teachers, managed to contribute to the local political debate concerning cycling by questioning assumptions and decisions about local cycling conditions. The impact of the classroom community is evidenced by several newspaper articles published about the project and the project's appearance on TV. Although some of these concerned the innovative pedagogical approach, the newspapers also wrote about the students' observations and opinions pertaining to cycling. In our example, a local newspaper headline reports that the students had discovered that the cycling routes in the City of Espoo were in poor condition. According to the teachers, a city official responsible for cycling conditions had even become upset about this headline, demonstrating that students' questioning was indeed taken as a serious contribution.

Although the project involved an orientation to transforming the local environment, this type of societal change is necessarily slow and happens in small steps, often through a complex decision-making process. The students also acknowledged this: 'I think this is a kind of a future-oriented project so

FIGURE 7.2 A local newspaper headline stating that upper secondary school students found that the cycle routes in Espoo are in a miserable condition

that . . . the things will not happen right now, but instead we try to influence some plans and everything possible . . . like how would it be in thirty years time'. (Student group interview)

Although showing evidence of actual, sustained transformation of the local environment is beyond the scope of this chapter, it is notable that the course involved an orientation towards transforming the local environment. In fact, the teachers and students clearly made considerable effort to pursue this goal.

Moreover, the students reported that trying to make a change to cycling conditions also changed them to some extent. As a consequence of the course, the students had started to pay attention to their living environments in a new way, and they now took more notice of deficiencies in cycling conditions even when out walking. Importantly, this new way of seeing the world also involved a critical aspect, as the students reported an emergent critical view of their surroundings. A bump or a crack in the road was no longer just a bump or a crack, but something that should and could be fixed by taking action. Thus, the students learned to see their surroundings not as being static and unchangeable but, instead, as being contingent and situated in historical time. In a sense, they developed what Bakhtin (1986) calls the ability to see time in space.

In all, the expansive chronotope, as reflected in this example, involves an orientation similar to what Anna Stetsenko (2008) has called the 'transformative activist stance'. From this stance, merely adapting to one's environment is not enough; instead, one tries to change the environment. At the same time, this effort alters the actor who contributes to the change process. While within the more conventional school chronotope, neither the participants nor the environment undergo any significant transformation (Bloome et al., 2009), in the expansive chronotope, the surrounding environment is perceived as historical and political and, hence, transformable. Furthermore, the participants are understood to have opportunities to promote this change and also to change themselves in the process. Thus, the participants and the world are not seen as static, but as co-emergent (see also Bakhtin, 1986; Bloome et al., 2009).

IMPLICATIONS FOR STUDENTS' AGENCY

Until now, we have focused on illuminating the social construction of the expansive chronotope within the context of the *Bicycles on the Move!* project. In this section, we discuss the expansive chronotope in the light of its implications for students' agency. We focus in particular on three distinct kinds of agency – relational, conceptual and transformative – made available for the students by the features of this chronotope.

Fostering Relational Agency

As discussed earlier, in the expansive chronotope, the students were provided with opportunities to build and connect to a network of relevant others in order to ask for help, seek opinions or take joint action. These relevant others included their peers, other students in local and global settings and cycling activists, as well as policy makers. Thus, the expansive chronotope provided supportive grounds for what Edwards, among others, has called 'relational agency' (Edwards & D'Arcy, 2004; Edwards & Mackenzie, 2005). Indeed, as Edwards and Mackenzie (2005, p. 294) explain, relational agency 'involves a capacity to offer support and to ask for support from others . . . one's capacity to engage with the world is enhanced by doing so alongside others'.

Relational agency also involves 'a capacity to engage with the dispositions of others in order to interpret and act on the object of our actions in enhanced ways' (Edwards & D'Arcy, 2004, p. 147). *Bicycles on the Move!* was also likely to foster students' relational agency, since meeting city officials and decision makers afforded opportunities for learning to understand their views. This sensitivity to the ongoing political decision-making process was manifested in the demand for feasibility of the students' contributions. In order to be achievable, contributions had to be functional and timely from the perspective of the local political decision-making process. Yet, these relations to decision makers were not always harmonious, as was indicated by the city planner who became upset about the newspaper article about the *Bicycles on the Move!* project.

Fostering Conceptual Agency

The expansive chronotope also fostered students' conceptual agency. This entails actions depending on students' choices of the types of material or conceptual resources to be appropriated, adapted or modified for a specific purpose in the learning activity, as evidenced in students' transfer of knowledge and skills across contexts and time zones (Engle, 2006; Greeno, 2006; Engle et al., 2011; Kumpulainen & Lipponen, in press). Through acknowledging and building on the students' everyday observations and experiences, the teachers supported the students in thinking with, rather than about, their experiences (Kumpulainen, Vasama & Kangassalo, 2003). In addition, multiple cultural resources were used in collective meaning making, including various kinds of expert voices. However, rather than treating these as authoritative voices (Bakhtin, 1981; Scott, Mortimer & Aguiar, 2006), which could be appropriated as such, the classroom community constructed counterarguments in juxtaposing these expert voices against each other and against students' own experiences and observations. Thus, the expansive chronotope was likely to provide students with skills and capabilities for exploring and navigating across many kinds of past experiences and cultural resources and for flexibly utilising these as resources in ongoing involvement towards fulfilling future goals (Emirbayer & Mische, 1998).

The expansive chronotope provided the students with multiple and diverse positions of authority. Knowledge and knowing were therefore not only associated with the teacher, the curriculum or outside experts, but rather with everyone participating in the *Bicycles on the Move!* project. In other words, within this chronotope, students were seen by themselves and by others as knowledgeable and committed participants whose identities were variable, multivocal and interactive (Holland et al., 1998). This multiplicity, or what Bakhtin (1981) calls *heteroglossia*, is in contrast to conventional schooling that often marginalises students who are not at ease with authoritative school discourses and standardised ways of knowing (González et al., 2005; Thomson & Hall, 2008).

Fostering Transformative Agency

The third form of agency made possible in the expansive chronotope was transformative agency. The students exercised transformative agency in breaking away from traditional 'taken-for-granted' practices (Engeström, 2008a; Rainio, 2008) and taking initiatives to influence local cycling conditions and contributing to public political debate about cycling issues (Engeström, 2008a; Lipponen & Kumpulainen, 2011). In a sense, they were starting to question and problematise ideas about traffic arrangements that had been taken for granted (Engle & Conant, 2002; Engeström, 2008a) and, hence, launched expansive learning (Engeström, 1987).

In general, experiences of transforming social practices are especially relevant in educational settings, since, as Stetsenko (2008) argues, through transformative agency

people come to know themselves and their world as well as ultimately come to be human *in and through* (not in addition to) the processes of collaboratively transforming the world in view of their goals. This means that all human activities (including psychological processes and the self) are instantiations of *contributions* to collaborative transformative practices. . . .

(Stetsenko, 2008, p. 471, italics original)

The everyday lives of upper secondary school students, younger children or adults are often imbued with more or less contradictory demands and situations that do not present a clear course of action; these contradictions arise from multiple motives embedded in and engendered by their historically evolving communities and objects (Engeström, 2008a). Taking part in the expansive chronotope provides students with the opportunity to learn to see their lifeworlds and their embedded practices as being changeable. This is an important transformation on the part of the learner and educationally valuable in itself, since imagining alternative futures is at the heart of agency (Emirbayer & Mische, 1998; Rainio, 2010).

PEDAGOGY FOR EXPANDING THE CHRONOTOPES OF SCHOOLING

Conventional pedagogies that produce restricted educational space-time configurations do not resonate with students' learning lives in the twenty-first century. The *learning lives* perspective, entailing an understanding of learning as situated in and relevant to students' lifeworlds and life trajectories, highlights the importance of promoting students' agency in the context of the school. In this chapter, we have illuminated how the limitations of conventional pedagogies were overcome – at least partially and momentarily – as time and space were reconfigured and expanded in an innovative upper secondary school classroom community. In the following passages, we elaborate on our findings in order to outline a draft for a new pedagogy that we argue will promote the social construction of the expansive chronotope in educational settings.

At the core of this novel pedagogy is the aim to transform social practices. Enacting this orientation, whether inside the educational system or outside it, requires agency on the part of the teachers, not just the children (Edwards & D'Arcy, 2004; Lipponen & Kumpulainen, 2011). In particular, pursuing this transformative stance may involve taking a course of action that is not shared or valued by others and that, at first, brings forth contradictions and stirs up negative emotions (see also Brown & Renshaw, 2000). However, questioning current practices and seeing alternative possible futures is an important way to develop social practices, resolve contradictions and launch expansive learning (Engeström, 1987). Likewise, transforming practices by taking into account and reconciling the perspectives of other stakeholders potentially fosters students' and teachers' relational agency (Edwards & D'Arcy, 2004), thus positioning the teachers, as well as the children, as individuals who learn, grow and develop.

Moreover, the pedagogical aim of transformation provides learning tasks that are current and complex real-life problems (see also Engeström et al., 2002). These kinds of learning tasks expand the form of accountability by changing the nature of student contributions and bring in new audiences with whom students share and discuss their observations, opinions and reflections. In these situations, students find that the knowledge and cultural resources that they learn can become functional – that is, cultural tools – in other activity systems beyond school (Engeström, 2008b). Indeed, in order to determine the usefulness of an idea, it is essential to test it in practice. When doing so, new audiences respond, thus providing students with feedback about the feasibility of their ideas from multiple perspectives. The authority of a subject matter is just one background, albeit useful, against which the value of an understanding or a contribution can be evaluated (Scott et al., 2006). In addition, numerous other types of authority stem from other activity systems apart from those linked to school.

In essence, a pedagogy that advances the expansive chronotope calls for 'under-designing for emergent behavior' (Fischer, 2011, p. 52); that is, purposely leaving room for creativity, renegotiations and surprises. Addressing real-life problems and issues requires the teacher and students to work with open, flexible and tentative plans and goals that might not be clear from the outset and need reconfiguring along the way. Indeed, the *Bicycles on the Move!* project altered its plans in response to the tight schedules of city officials. This involved the students, along with one of the teachers, formulating a written plea to city planning officials concerning pedestrian and bicycle traffic solutions around a new subway line.

Expansive chronotopes also involve connecting learning across settings, communities and time. For instance, in order to connect learning and teaching to expert communities outside school, teachers and schools need to build partnerships and networks. Building networks and partnerships also requires new competences, such as multiprofessional collaboration (Kumpulainen et al., 2010), on the part of teachers. These issues need to be addressed as early as in teacher training. But, who should take responsibility and leadership for coordinating and managing these networks? In most cases, the teacher or the school is perhaps best aware of the learning needs of students. However, teachers are usually overburdened by their existing workloads, and the partners could therefore play a part in management and coordination of the partnerships and networks. Support and leadership for building networks and partnerships can be provided by projects or institutions – such as cultural or science centres. The teachers involved in *Bicycles on the Move!* actually reported that support from the larger government-funded project *On the Move!* was crucial for them when launching their own project.

However, students themselves should also have a say about the organisation of their own learning. It is not enough just to connect learning and teaching to expert communities. In addition, for learning to be meaningful to the learners, a connection should be made to their concerns and perspectives, and to the funds of knowledge embedded in their lifeworlds. In this respect, the school occupies a pivotal position in society as an institution through which children's perspectives and opinions on matters concerning them and their lives can be brought into the public debate. Here, children are not simply consulted or awarded superficial positions within the decision-making process, but rather are provided with a continued possibility to influence their own lives and practices. Yet, in the case of the *Bicycles on the Move!* project, the overall goal of improving local cycling conditions was given in advance by the teachers, and the students could exercise their agency by choosing to participate in the realisation of this goal. To overcome this limitation, teachers and students could launch similar projects stemming from and encompassing more of the students' own concerns and initiatives. This requires teachers to reconcile the demands of the curriculum and the contingencies of students' concerns (Thomson & Hall, 2008).

SUMMARY

To conclude, we do not argue that schooling should always strive to transform its local environment or society at large. Instead, an expansive chronotope, such as the one examined in this chapter, has a definite scope to be employed for the specific pedagogical purposes of promoting students' transformative, relational and conceptual agency. Yet, promotion of agency does not exhaust the role of schooling. In fact, as Jerome Bruner (1996) has put it, institutionalised schooling has a dual role in our societies, both preserving and passing on existing cultural heritage, as well as promoting cultural renewal and change (see also Rainio, 2010). Accordingly, the complexity of contemporary schooling calls for other kinds of chronotopes in order to serve the multiplicity of learning needs of twenty-first-century learners and associated pedagogical purposes. In all, there is room for further exploration of the novel and meaningful chronotopes of today's schooling. Further research could also set out to examine the following research questions: Over time, how do students take up the opportunities for agency provided by an expansive chronotope? To what extent is an expansive chronotope transferable to contexts of teaching and learning, other than those examined in this chapter?

ACKNOWLEDGEMENTS

We would like to thank the Learning Bridges Research Network and Giuseppe Ritella, as well as Anna Mikkola for her support in data collection and her analysis of the *On the Move!* project.

REFERENCES

Bakhtin, M. M. (1981). *The dialogic imagination: Four essays by M. M. Bakhtin* (M. Holquist, Ed., C. Emerson, & M. Holquist, Trans.). Austin, TX: University of Texas Press.

Bakhtin, M. M. (1986). *Speech genres and other late essays* (Vern W. McGee, Trans.). Austin, TX: University of Texas Press.

Bloome, D., Beierle, M., Grigorenko, M., & Goldman, S. (2009). Learning over time: Uses of intercontextuality, collective memories, and classroom chronotopes in the construction of learning opportunities in a ninth-grade language arts classroom. *Language and Education, 23*(4), 313–34.

Brown, R., & Renshaw, P. (2000). Collective argumentation: A sociocultural approach to reframing classroom teaching and learning. In H. Cowie & G. van der Aalsvoort (Eds.), *Social interaction in learning and instruction: The meaning of discourse for the construction of knowledge* (pp. 52–66). Amsterdam: Pergamon Press.

Brown, R., & Renshaw, P. (2006). Positioning students as actors and authors: A chronotopic analysis of collaborative learning activities. *Mind, Culture and Activity*, 13(3), 247–59.

Bruner, J. (1996). *The culture of education*. Cambridge, MA: Harvard University Press.

Daniels, H. (2008). Pedagogy. In H. Daniels, M. Cole, & J. V. Wertsch (Eds.), *The Cambridge companion to Vygotsky* (pp. 307–32). Cambridge: Cambridge University Press.

Edwards, A., & D'Arcy, C. (2004). Relational agency and disposition in sociocultural accounts of learning to teach. *Educational Review*, 56, 147–55.

Edwards, A., & Mackenzie, L. (2005). Steps towards participation: The social support of learning trajectories. *International Journal of Lifelong Education*, 24(4), 287–302.

Emirbayer, M., & Mische, A. (1998). What is agency? *The American Journal of Sociology*, 103(4), 962–1023.

Engeström, Y. (1987). *Learning by expanding: An activity-theoretical approach to developmental research*. Helsinki: Orienta-Konsultit.

Engeström, Y. (2008a). Putting Vygotsky to work. The change laboratory as an application of double stimulation. In H. Daniels, M. Cole, & J. V. Wertsch (Eds.), *The Cambridge companion to Vygotsky* (pp. 363–82). Cambridge: Cambridge University Press.

Engeström, Y. (2008b). *From teams to knots: Activity-theoretical studies of collaboration and learning at work*. Cambridge: Cambridge University Press.

Engeström, Y., Engeström, R., & Suntio, A. (2002). Can a school community learn to master its own future? An activity theoretical study of expansive learning among middle school teachers. In G. Wells & G. Claxton (Eds.), *Learning for life in the 21st century. Sociocultural perspectives on the future of education* (pp. 211–24). Cambridge, MA: Blackwell.

Engeström, Y., Puonti, A., & Seppänen, L. (2003). Spatial and temporal expansion of the object as a challenge for reorganizing work. In D. Nicolini, S. Gherardi, & D. Yanow (Eds.), *Knowing in organizations: A practice-based approach* (pp. 151–86). London: Sharpe.

Engle, R. (2006). Framing interactions to foster generative learning: A situative explanation of transfer in a community of learners classroom. *The Journal of the Learning Sciences*, 15(5), 451–98.

Engle, R., & Conant, F. (2002). Guiding principles for fostering productive disciplinary engagement: Explaining an emergent argument in a community of learners classroom. *Cognition and Instruction*, 20(4), 339–483.

Engle, R., Nguyen, P., & Mendelson, A. (2011). The influence of framing on transfer: Initial evidence from a tutoring experiment. *Instructional Science*, 39, 603–28.

Fischer, G. (2011). Understanding, fostering, and supporting cultures of participation. *ACM Interactions*, XVIII(3), 42–53. Retrieved from http://l3d.cs.colorado.edu/~gerhard/papers/2011/interactions-coverstory.pdf

González, N., Moll, L. C., & Amanti, C. (2005). *Funds of knowledge: Theorizing practices in households, communities, and classroom*. Mahwah, NJ: L. Erlbaum Associates.

Greeno, J. (2006). Authoritative, accountable positioning and connected, general knowing: Progressive themes in understanding transfer. *Journal of the Learning Sciences, 15*(4), 537–47.

Gresalfi, M., Martin, T., Hand, V., & Greeno, J. (2009). Constructing competence: An analysis of student participation in the activity systems of mathematics classrooms. *Educational Studies in Mathematics, 70,* 49–70.

Hakkarainen, K., Ritella, G., & Seitamaa-Hakkarainen, P. (2011, July). *Epistemic mediation, chronotope, and expansive knowledge practices.* Poster presentation at the 9th International Conference on Computer-Supported Collaborative Learning, Hong Kong.

Holland, D., Lachicotte, W., Jr., Skinner, D., & Cain, C. (1998). *Identity and agency in cultural worlds.* Cambridge, MA: Harvard University Press.

Hubbard, L., Mehan, H., & Stein, M. K. (2006). *Reform as learning: School reform, organizational culture, and community politics in San Diego.* New York: Routledge.

Kumpulainen, K., Krokfors, L., Lipponen, L., Tissari, V., Hilppö, J., & Rajala, A. (2010). *Learning bridges: Toward participatory learning environments.* Helsinki: CICERO Learning, University of Helsinki.

Kumpulainen, K., & Lipponen, L. (in press). The dialogic construction of agency in classroom communities. In B. Ligorio & M. César (Eds.), *The interplays between dialogical learning and dialogical self.* Greenwich CT: Information Age Publishing.

Kumpulainen, K., & Lipponen, L. (2010). Productive interaction as agentic participation in dialogic inquiry. In C. Howe & K. Littleton (Eds.), *Educational dialogues* (pp. 48–63). London: Taylor & Francis.

Kumpulainen, K., Vasama, S., & Kangassalo, M. (2003). The intertextuality of children's explanations in a technology-enriched early years science classroom. *International Journal of Educational Research, 39,* 793–805.

Leander, K. (2002). Polycontextual construction zones: Mapping the expansion of schooled space and identity. *Mind, Culture, and Activity, 9*(3), 211–37.

Lemke, J. (2004, April). *Learning across multiple places and their chronotope.* Paper presented at AERA 2004 Symposium, San Diego. Retrieved October 31, 2011, from http://www-personal.umich.edu/~jaylemke/papers/aera_2004.htm

Lipponen, L., & Kumpulainen, K. (2011). Acting as accountable authors: Creating interactional spaces for agency work in teacher education. *Teaching and Teacher Education, 27*(5), 812–19.

Mehan, H. (1979). *Learning lessons: Social organization in the classroom.* Cambridge, MA: Harvard University Press.

National Institute for Health and Welfare. (2011). *School health promotion study.* Helsinki: Author. Retrieved October 31, 2011, from http://info.stakes.fi/koulutervey skysely/EN/index.htm

OECD. (2010). *PISA 2009 results: What students know and can do – student performance in reading, mathematics and science* (Vol. I). Paris: Author. Retrieved December 22, 2011, from http://dx.doi.org/10.1787/9789264091450-en

Rainio, A. (2008). From resistance to involvement: Examining agency and control in a playworld activity. *Mind, Culture, and Activity 15*(2), 115–40.

Rainio, A. (2010). *Lionhearts of the playworld: An ethnographic case study of the development of agency in play pedagogy.* Helsinki: University of Helsinki, Institute of Behavioural Sciences.

Schulz, W., Ainley, J., Fraillon, J., Kerr, D., & Losito, B. (2010). *ICCS 2009 international report: Civic knowledge, attitudes, and engagement among lower-secondary school students in 38 countries*. Amsterdam: IEA.

Scott, P., Mortimer, E., & Aguiar, O. (2006). The tension between authoritative and dialogic discourse: A fundamental characteristic of meaning making interactions in high school science lessons. *Science Education, 90*(4), 605–31.

Stetsenko, A. (2008). From relational ontology to transformative activist stance on development and learning: Expanding Vygotsky's (CHAT) project. *Cultural Studies of Science Education, 3*(2), 471–91.

Thomson, P., & Hall, C. (2008). Opportunities missed and/or thwarted? 'Funds of knowledge' meet the English national curriculum. *Curriculum Journal, 19*(2), 87–103.

Tyack, D., & Cuban, L. (1997). *Tinkering toward Utopia: A century of public school reform*. Cambridge, MA: Harvard University Press.

Vadeboncoeur, J. (2005). The difference that time and space make: An analysis of institutional and narrative landscapes. In L. Stevens & J. Vadeboncoeur (Eds.), *Re/constructing 'the adolescent': Sign, symbol, and body* (pp. 123–52). New York: Peter Lang.

Chapter 8

Studying the Discursive Construction of Learning Lives for Individuals and the Collective

Judith Green, Audra Skukauskaite and Maria Lucia Castanheira

In exploring ways of conceptualising 'learning lives', Erstad, Gilje, Sefton-Green and Vasbø (2009) argue that to understand learning lives as they are developing requires examining 'how the individual learner relates to other people and objects, drawing on deeper trajectories or narratives of the self as it exists within and outside the immediate learning contexts' (p. 100). In this chapter, we bring together a range of theoretical arguments from anthropology, sociology and discourse studies to develop a logic of enquiry (Kaplan, 1964/1998) for examining how, in and through collective-individual interactions, learning lives are socially constructed. Our goal is to make visible how a discourse-based ethnographic logic of enquiry provides a way of conceptualising and studying the interactional work of individuals and the collective (social group) in discursively constructing local, situated learning lives within and across times, events and social spaces.

CONCEPTUALISING A LOGIC OF ENQUIRY THROUGH COMPLEMENTARY PERSPECTIVES

The logic of enquiry that we present brings together a complementary set of epistemological perspectives focusing on the social accomplishment and construction of life within social groups. Three bodies of conceptual arguments will be brought together to form a multifaceted logic of enquiry: arguments about ethnography as a philosophy of enquiry from anthropology, perspectives on social accomplishment of life from sociology and arguments on the discursive construction of everyday life from socio-linguistics and anthropology. As we will demonstrate, each of these perspectives provides a particular angle of vision on the complex work of individual-collective accomplishments of identities, literate practices and everyday life in a social group. Each angle, therefore, will foreground a particular dimension of the processes involved in constructing learning lives across times, events and groups of actors. Although we focus on the logic as applied to education, we argue that this logic of enquiry transcends educational contexts.

ETHNOGRAPHY AS EPISTEMOLOGY: PERSPECTIVES FROM ANTHROPOLOGY

We begin the discussion of the logic of enquiry with recent dialogues at the intersection of education and anthropology about ethnography as a philosophy of enquiry (Anderson-Levitt, 2006) and as epistemology, not method (Agar, 2006b). The view of ethnography as epistemology frames an interdependent relationship between theories and methods, in which theory cannot be separated from method because theory implicates methods and methods constitute the theory/theories about the phenomenon(a) under study. This ethnographic epistemology, Agar (2006b) argues, constitutes an iterative, recursive and abductive process of enquiry.

The goals of this ethnographic epistemology focus on examining and developing warranted claims about what counts as *emic*, or insider, knowledge guiding participants' actions, activity and local knowledge. Such knowledge, Agar (2006a) argues, requires developing understandings of the *languaculture* of a group, given that language and culture are interdependent, since language is imbued with culture and culture is realised through language. From this perspective, the ethnographer, like any newcomer entering an ongoing community or social group, brings his or her own *languaculture* to the task of perceiving, interpreting and understanding what is happening; this languaculture Agar calls *languaculture 1*.

When the ethnographer cannot understand what is happening, a *frame clash* occurs that makes visible the cultural knowledge and meanings of the group and individuals-within-the group that differ from those of the ethnographer. At such points, what Agar (2006a) calls *rich points*, a potential opportunity occurs for learning what insiders understand and know, or how they interpret the interaction. He argues that the insiders' languaculture is *languaculture 2* for the ethnographer (and newcomers alike).

Given the ethnographer's goal of constructing warranted claims about insider meanings, actions, knowledge, processes and practices, the ethnographer needs to wonder about how the observed phenomena that led to the frame clash were developed by members and how such knowledge was made available to new members. These questions require the ethnographer to *explore the roots and routes* leading to what may appear to an insider as ordinary actions, meanings or interpretations, but which, for an ethnographer, lead to a frame clash between what he or she expected and what was experienced. This analytic process requires *backward mapping* to the *roots of* particular processes, practices and sources of knowledge, among other cultural phenomena, or *forward mapping* in time to uncover *routes to* cultural knowledge necessary to understand the phenomena as members do (Green, Skukauskaite & Baker, 2012).

In this way, the ethnographer follows the data and moves backwards, forwards, and at times sideways, across times, events and spaces, to uncover the interrelated web of knowledge necessary to resolve the frame clash. Through these iterative and recursive processes of analysis, guided by abductive reasoning, the ethnographer seeks to develop warranted claims about the local knowledge necessary to participate in everyday activity of the group.

PERSPECTIVES ON SOCIAL ACCOMPLISHMENTS OF EVERYDAY LIFE

In this section, we shift the angle of vision from ethnography as a philosophy of enquiry to an interactional perspective grounded primarily in ethnomethodology. Our goal is to add to the logic of enquiry an orienting perspective on ways of conceptualising the relationships among and accomplishments of actors within a social system, as well as of the social system itself as an ongoing social construction. These conceptual arguments from ethnomethodology provide a theoretical language and associated principles of operation for examining how particular moments in classrooms are socially accomplished in and through the interactions among participants.

We begin developing this dimension of our logic of enquiry by drawing on the work of James Heap, a sociologist in education. Heap (1991) provides a set of conceptual arguments from ethnomethodology about the socially accomplished nature of everyday life. He argues that, from an ethnomethodological orientation, we must accept that the individual is defined as an actor in a social system; the situation must be defined as formulated by the actors; an actor defines his or her situation through interactions with others; an actor acts consciously; an actor has preferences; each actor aligns his or her actions to the actions of others by ascertaining what they are doing or intend to do – in other words, by 'getting at' the meaning of their acts; social structures are governed by rules (norms, values), which may or may not be complete; and social structures are observable through coordinated actions among actors.

In studying the work of participants in learning to be literate in the social events around the reading and writing of texts, Heap (1980, 1989) posed what has become an overarching question in work in discourse-based ethnography: What counts as a socially relevant practice for participants, and when do such practices count – for example, what counts as reading, and when does a particular reading count? To explore this question, Heap (1980) examined a reading lesson as it was developing. By closely examining the moment-by-moment interactions and social accomplishments of a teacher reading a text with a small group of students, Heap (1980) identified a problematic situation in which a student's prior knowledge did not count to the teacher. In the interactions, the teacher asked the question, 'Who helped the queen?' Mineen raised her hand, was called on, and answered, 'Rumplestiltskin'. The teacher responded: 'The little man. We don't know his name yet, since we haven't come to it in the story'. In responding in this manner, Heap argued, the teacher was signaling what counted to her as the answer to the question and what, and whose, knowledge counted.

In his ethnographic study from which this 'lesson' was taken, Heap had interviewed the students about their experiences with reading and found that the students had all seen the film *Rumpelstiltskin* the previous year, in first grade. The student's interpretation of the teacher's question can be viewed as framed by a social history that was not available to the teacher or visible to the ethnographer in the moment of observation. Heap's research further shows that, through the teacher's response, students were afforded information about what counted to the teacher as reading in this moment and what knowledge could be (or could not be) brought to bear to answer the question – only textual inscriptions from the book could be used to construct text interpretations and to provide evidence for answers to teacher questions.

From this perspective, to understand what counts as reading or literate practices, and identity or positions, the ethnographer examines what people in interaction are discursively constructing. From this perspective, participants in the dialogue are constructing 'a reading' of text or an event, and each time they engage with the text they are constructing a new reading. As part of these productions of readings, they are also potentially (re)constructing positions and identities. Thus, readings can be understood as social accomplishments (McHoul, 1991), just as identities and positions are social accomplishments. The arguments about *what counts as. . .*, therefore, frame a principle of operation for ethnography from an ethnomethodological perspective. The ethnographer, drawing on ethnomethodological arguments, applies this question to explorations of social, linguistic and cultural phenomena in order to identify meaningful actions and practices within a particular social group. *What counts as. . .* questions also provide a systematic basis for examining interactions to understand what participants are doing together, how and in what ways, under what conditions, with what outcomes or consequences for what participants can do and learn. This orientation, therefore, leads to questions about *what counts as learning lives* for an individual across social groups, as well as for the group itself.

One final aspect of ethnomethodologically oriented ethnographic work is needed to complete Heap's original conceptualization of what is required to understand the socially accomplished nature of everyday life. Heap argued that structures are governed by norms that may or may not be complete, and that social structures are observable through coordinated actions among actors. Work by Mehan (1979) provides a rationale for why examining such developing norms is necessary. Mehan argues that to understand social institutions such as schooling, the ethnographer needs to uncover how participants engage in a process he calls *structuring school structures*. In conceptualising structuring as a social accomplishment, not as a given, Mehan frames a need to study how norms are constructed in and through the moment-by-moment work of actors. He further argues that, through such processes, students are *learning lessons* (Mehan, 1979) about what counts as expected social actions (norms for partic-ipating), who counts as having access to what knowledge and that such lessons are constituted in and through discourse. Mehan's arguments implicate the need to explore how the collective is constructed and how, through that construction, individuals are afforded (or not) particular opportunities for learning.

STRUCTURING OPPORTUNITIES: AN EXAMPLE
FROM A FIFTH-GRADE CLASSROOM

We conclude this section by presenting an analysis of how, in the first moments of a school year (a social structure), an assigned group of students and their teacher, together with others (teaching assistant, student teacher, parents and researcher), begin a process of structuring what counts as ways of knowing, being and doing among participants in their class. As part of the presentation and analysis of this process, we examine how identities and literate practices were produced in and through the developing events of classroom life, and how these social accomplishments became part of the developing languaculture and local knowledge of the group. Although not strictly an ethnomethodological study, these analyses are grounded in the arguments in this section, creating an example of how ethnomethodological constructs contributed to the developing logic of enquiry.

Table 8.1 provides a record of the actions taken by members of the class. The map (Green & Meyer, 1991; Castanheira et al., 2001) moves between teacher actions and those of students (and others) to make visible how members were structuring the events of the first hour of class. The table also presents an

TABLE 8.1 *Mapping two events of the first day of class: Onset of community*

Time	Speak	Actions	Language	Interaction Space	Sub-event	Event	Opportunities for Exploring Self, Others and Physical Environment as Texts
8:10	St/P	**arriving** in the classroom		T–I			– seeing and 'reading' what other participants are doing – reestablishing contact with friends
	St/P	**meeting** teacher		I–TG			
	T	**greeting** St/P	S/E				– meeting new people
	St/P	**responding** to T	S/E				– listening to English or Spanish being spoken
	T	**orienting** students to **finding** name card, **choosing** place to sit	S/E				– speaking English or Spanish
	St	**choosing** where to sit		I–I			
	St	**decorating** name square	S/E				– meeting new people – getting acquainted with others – choosing language to interact with others
8:45	St	**talking** to classmates sitting at table group	S/E				
	T/TA/St	**talking** to Sts at table groups	S/E				
	St	**talking** to T/Teaching Assistant and St. Teacher	S/E				
					ENTERING THE TOWER	ONSET OF COMMUNITY	
8:55	T	**introducing** chime as a sign	S/E	WC			– resituating self within large group
	T	**welcoming** participants	S/E	St–WC			– getting support from adults and classmates
	T		S/E				– helping St learn her job partner

TABLE 8.1 (cont.)

Time	Speak	Actions	Language	Interaction Space	Sub-event	Event	Opportunities for Exploring Self, Others and Physical Environment as Texts
		celebrating the languages of the Tower Community: Spanish and English					
9:40	T	*explaining* way of using Spanish and English in the classroom	S/E				– becoming ethnographer
	T	*introducing* adult members to students	S/E				– knowing local community ways of leaving
	T	*introducing* ethnography as community practice	S/E				– making decisions about routine aspects within the norms being established for the group
	T	*talking* about basic routines: drinking water, signing up for lunch, bathroom, recess, etc.	S/E				– becoming a Tower community member
	T	*exploring* students' knowledge about Tower community	S/E				– exploring own knowledge and experience in constructing Tower community in 96/97
	T	*introducing* Tower as community with traditions					– defining uses and exploring multiple spaces
	T	*presenting* multiple physical spaces of Tower classroom					– hearing S/E and speaking language of choice

WELCOMING TO THE TOWER COMMUNITY

Key: **I S**: Interactional Space; **T–I**: Teacher–Individual Student; **I–TG**: Individual–Table Group; **I–I**: Individual–Individual; **St–WC**: Student–Whole Class; **TA**: Teaching Assistant; **ST**: Student teacher; and Language– **S**: Spanish; **E**: English analysis of how the structuring involved different levels of timescale, and how, in and through this developing structuring process, students were afforded opportunities to produce and engage with different texts, to inscribe and position self. The analysis also makes visible how students were (re)positioned by the teacher (and others) in particular communications within and across times and events.

In presenting the developing *flow of conduct* (Giddens, 1979, p. 55) as a map, we constructed a text that can be used to examine how norms and expectations for being a member of this developing social group were proposed and recognised by particular participants, how students oriented to the proposed actions and how, through this process of proposing, orienting to and taking actions in response to what was proposed, participants created local and situated views of what counts as being a student in this social group in different events.

Table 8.1 is a graphic (re)presentation of the dynamic and developing process of the first forty-five minutes of the first day of school (1996) in a fifth-grade linguistically diverse class. This map includes a period prior to the official start time of school (8:30), a period that began with the entry of the first student and his parent, as indicated in column 3 (Actions). By including this period, we illustrate Mehan's (1979) argument that participants construct schooling structures, given that the structuring process did not begin with the bell as a signal of the official start of school but with the entry of the students. This analysis also makes visible the necessity of examining the developing work of participants in social settings in structuring their world(s).

In following the chain of actions (column 3), (re)presented as present continuous verbs, we were able to identify the flow of conduct within the developing community. That is, once a student was greeted by the teacher, he or she was invited to locate his or her name card, select a place to sit at a table group and personalise his or her name card to represent him- or herself to others. In this way, as indicated in the last column (Opportunities for Exploring Self, Others and Physical Environment as Texts), these small moments afforded individuals opportunities to explore self in relationship to others, to situate self in the developing social group and to engage in a process of exploring self–other relationships as potential texts for constructing and accomplishing life within this group.

Analysis of the developing actions and objects (column 3) also showed that, as students entered the classroom alone or with a parent, they were welcomed at the door by the teacher in their heritage language (Spanish or English). In greeting students this way, the teacher signaled to students and their parents that she valued both languages. These actions were also available to students as overhearing audiences (Larson, 1996), thus providing those present with a continuous source of information about the use of language in the class. These small moments can also be viewed as part of the process of developing the norms for language use and for initiating a process of developing a langua-culture for the class.

Analysis of the second event in column 1 (Welcoming to the tower commun-ity), provides further evidence of how moments of structuring classroom spaces and activity were being (re)formulated. In shifting the floor (Goffman, 1981) from individual and small-group interactions in self-selected spaces, the teacher initiated a process of reorienting the group, creating a common floor for collective work. As indicated in columns 2, 3 and 4, while the use of two languages continued to be visible to participants, the reformulating of the space changed speakers and the ways in which speakers could be recognised, thus initiating a norm for whole-class activity.

In the pattern of actions and choices of language use and speaker in this new space, students were afforded opportunities to learn about what they would do in the future, to hear a language about what they will be doing together (becoming ethnographers, Tower community members) and to begin exploring the space of the classroom. In engaging students in resitu-ating self, the teacher initiated a process of (re)formulating individual–collective relationships, a process that our research across the school year showed was a recurring pattern. That is, in each new activity or area of study, the teacher engaged students in (re)formulating social, cultural and linguistic practices relevant to the tasks in which they would engage.

This example of analysis makes visible how in and across multifaceted social spaces individuals, as well as groups, are structuring their everyday worlds through the discursive work among participants. Moreover, the con-ceptual arguments in this section foreshadow the need to explore further the role of discourse in constructing possibilities for (re)formulating the material resources that individuals draw on (or not) in developing local, situated learning lives for themselves, as well as for the collective.

PERSPECTIVES ON DISCURSIVE CONSTRUCTIONS OF SOCIAL LIFE

In this section, we shift the angle of view from structuring the environment to a focus on the nature of language and social life. Drawing on theories at the intersection of sociolinguistics, critical discourse analysis and ethnography, we present a series of conceptual arguments that guide the analysis of how cultural, linguistic and social processes, meanings, identities and literate practices are constructed by members of a social group in and through language in use. These arguments constitute an *orienting theory* for exploring what members say to each other, in what ways, under what conditions, when and where, in relationship to what objects (artefacts) and with what outcomes or consequences for individuals, as well as for the collective. The orienting theory thus provides a basis for examining the relationship of language and social life as discursive constructions from an *emic* (insider) point of view.

Bloome and Egan-Robertson (1993), drawing on Bakhtin (1979/1986) and Fairclough (1992), provide a conceptual argument about the ways in which language is a dynamic and complex process of meaning construction central to our developing logic of enquiry:

The meaning of an utterance or other language act derives not from the content of its words, but rather from its interplay with what went before and what will come later. When language is viewed as part of an ongoing dialogue, as part of how people act and react to each other, then it is seen not as meaning per se but as meaningful, strategic action that is materially realized. That is, in order to engage in a dialogue, regardless of whether that dialogue is a face-to-face conversation or something else (e.g. an exchange of letters, this article), people must do so in ways such that others can understand their actions and intentions in the event. (p. 309)

In this argument, Bloome and Egan-Robertson (1993) capture succinctly the dialogic nature of discourse and make visible what speakers (writers) must consider in selecting how to interact and orient to others. At the centre of this dialogic interaction is a process of both joint construction of identity potentials and of inscription of others (hearers).

To make visible the implications of these arguments on the relationship of language-in-use and social life, we focus on four additional conceptual arguments: utterances as texts, social processes and discourse practices; intertextuality as socially constructed everyday practice of people in interactions; responses to complex communication as visible sooner or later in the actions of speakers/hearers/writers; and contrastive relevance as a principle of operation for examining what is socially significant in a particular social group. These theories provide ways of conceptualising what counts as language/discourse-in-use; how language used by participants makes visible the social, cultural and linguistic presuppositions that participants bring to a developing event (Gumperz, 1986); how, in and through the moment-by-moment and over time discourse-in-use, common knowledge is constructed (Edwards & Mercer, 1987); how the study of discourse-in-use makes visible situated understandings of the ways of knowing, being and doing everyday life within a social group;

and how the study of language requires exploration of individual–collective interactions central to the developing knowledge, identities and literate practices of both the individual and the collective.

INTERTEXTUALITY AS A SOCIAL CONSTRUCTION

Building on the analyses and concepts just described, we present arguments that help frame an understanding of language/utterances (oral and written) as developing texts. Underlying these arguments is a view of texts as complex social phenomena that are being developed within a particular social group. Not only are texts spoken, written or graphic constructions, but people (or other dimensions of social worlds) become texts for each other (Erickson & Shultz, 1981). Thus, reading and interpreting what people orient to, hold each other accountable for and build on (or not) requires ethnographers, as well as participants, to ground their claims about emic (insider) knowledge in what is being proposed and/or accomplished by self and others. Viewed in this way, people, through their moment-by-moment and overtime communication and activity, are engaged in a process of textualising the local worlds of the classroom both collectively and individually (Bloome & Egan-Robertson, 1993).

These conceptualisations of text central to the developing logic of enquiry build on arguments by Fairclough (1992) that a bit of talk or writing is simultaneously a text, a social process and a discourse practice, and that, in texts, are traces of prior texts, practices and processes. If we apply Fairclough's argument to what is visible in the chains of actions represented in Table 8.1, we can now interpret the developing text as affording students opportunities to develop social, linguistic and textual processes and practices that constitute a developing languaculture. The boundaries of texts can be identified at multiple levels of analytic scale (utterance, events and intertextual cycles of activity [Bloome et al., 2005]). Examining developing classroom interactions as a collective text provides a basis for identifying ways in which members construct their learning lives and how their individual and collective past informs the present and possible future actions. From this perspective, meanings and activities are foreshadowed in the work of individuals-within-the-collective and the collective as a whole.

Bakhtin (1979/1986) captures the significance of analysing intertextual connections among past, present and future developing events and learning lives by emphasising the complex and 'actively responsive' nature of human communication within and across times. He argues that

Sooner or later what is heard and actively understood will find its response in the subsequent speech or behavior of the listener. In most cases, genres of complex cultural communication are intended precisely for this kind of actively responsive understanding with delayed action. Everything that we have said here also pertains to written and read speech, with the appropriate adjustments and additions. (p. 69)

In this argument, Bakhtin points to the need for over-time analysis to examine what actors in communicative contexts understand. From this perspective, learning lives, identities and literate practices may not be visible in a particular event. Therefore, examining the interactions among speakers (writers) and hearers (readers) as processes of cultural communication requires tracing ways in which actors actively respond to and construct different speech genres. Bakhtin's argument that all cultural communication involves delayed action supports a *principle of over-time analysis* of the developing knowledge, meanings, social and literate processes, practices and identities, among other social phenomena.

CONTRASTIVE RELEVANCE

We conclude the discussion of the discursive construction of social life by drawing on the work of Hymes (1977) to present contrastive relevance as an underlying principle for discourse-based ethnographic logic of enquiry. Hymes (1977) argues that, in linguistic ethnography, a shift in focus from the study of social life as a linguistic process to the study of language as a way of organising social life influences what questions can be asked and how social life will be represented. He states that the linguistic aspect of ethnography in the *study of social life* requires the researcher to ask what communicative means, verbal and other, were used by participants to conduct and interpret a particular 'bit of social life'; what is their mode of organization from the standpoint of verbal repertoires; what counts as appropriate and inappropriate, better and worse, uses of these means; and how are skills entailed by the means acquired, and to whom they are accessible. Hymes further argues that if one starts with *language*, the questions change, providing a basis for exploring who employs particular verbal means, to what ends, when and where, under what conditions, in what ways; and what their organization is from the standpoint of the patterns of social life. His distinction between a focus on social life and language makes visible how the choice of area of study requires a particular conceptualisation of the relationships among language, culture and activity and how this choice guides the ways in which social life is perceived and interpreted as discursively constructed.

To construct warranted claims about the role of language in the construction of everyday life, Hymes proposes the *principle of contrastive relevance*, which he defines as 'the demonstration of functional relevance through contrast, showing that a particular change or choice counts as a difference within the frame of reference' (p. 92). In arguing that contrastive relevance is central to the study of language development and social life, Hymes frames a systematic approach to identifying what is meaningful within a particular social group. The process of analysis through contrastive relevance, he argues, needs to work 'back and forth between form and meaning in practice to discover the individual devices and the codes of which they are part' (pp. 92–3). From this perspective, the principle of contrastive relevance provides a basis for examining meaning–form relationships in language and for identifying how particular forms and meanings have consequences for members (as well as for the ethnographer). Building on Hymes (1977), we argue that contrastive relevance is a principle that makes visible the need for *different levels of analytic scale* (human and timescale).

An Illustrative Example of Contrastive Relevance

To make visible how contrastive relevance provides a means of examining the opportunities for learning constructed by members of a social group at different levels of analytic scale (human and timescales), we trace the ways in which a bilingual fifth-grade teacher engaged students in becoming mathematicians in her class (Brilliant-Mills, 1994; Castanheira, 2004; Castanheira et al., 2007). Figure 8.1 presents an analysis of how becoming a mathematician involved collective–individual interactions in multiple ways and physical configurations. The chain of actions within each space was obtained by examining what members proposed to each other, how a text was constructed in each group and how individuals were afforded opportunities to construct personal texts drawing on the spoken, written, visual and activity resources developing across times, activities and differing groups of actors.

As represented in Figure 8.1, the teacher engaged the whole class in a series of actions that led to individual estimates of the weight and cost of the watermelon assigned to each table group. Once this was complete, the individual was then asked to contrast his or her estimate with those of other table group members to arrive at a common group estimate of weight and cost. Next, two members of the group, one who spoke Spanish and one who spoke English, were asked to report to the whole class the group's negotiated estimate. This process afforded students with a new opportunity to explore how their processes in constructing the estimates contrasted with those of other groups.

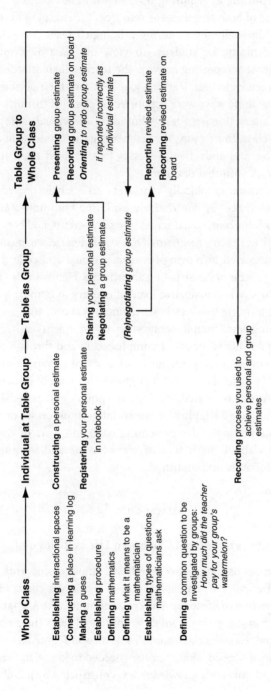

FIGURE 8.1 Patterns of structuring participation

By framing reporting as requiring both English and Spanish, the teacher signaled the value of both languages as resources for engaging in mathematical enquiry. Additionally, by requiring a bilingual team presentation, she created an opportunity for students to view the class as a multilingual community. After this reporting activity, the teacher then afforded students opportunities to return to their learning logs to record their personal ways of thinking and how these ways were supported or changed through participation in different interactional spaces – whole class, individual, table group and reporting to the class. In this way, the teacher engaged students in a series of iterative, recursive and abductive processes that enabled them to contrast their personal work with that of others.

Figure 8.1, therefore, graphically represents an analytic procedure based on contrastive relevance. By contrastively exploring both how a *language of mathematics was being constructed* across times and events, and how particular forms of *social life were being constructed through language*, we uncovered how students were supported in moving between personal and collective understandings of the process of constructing an estimate. Figure 8.1 also represents the iterative, recursive and abductive logic of enquiry in ethnography, which parallels ways of learning in educational settings (Walford, 2008).

The intersecting and complementary set of arguments in this section, about how everyday life is socially accomplished in and through purposeful actions and discourse among members of a social group, constitutes an *orienting theory* (a logic of enquiry) that guides the work of discourse-based ethnographers. As demonstrated, this logic of enquiry guides decisions about questions that can be asked; phenomena of interest; processes of collecting, constructing, interpreting and representing data; and ways of constructing warranted claims about the nature of everyday life and learning lives as socially and discursively accomplished.

SUMMARY

Narratives of Self and Classroom Life as Rich Points

We conclude the discussion of discourse-based ethnographic work by applying this logic of enquiry to an exploration of narratives about individual–collective construction of life in the Tower Community (the fifth-grade class). Through analysis of two essays from different school years (1992 and 1995) in the same bilingual teacher's classroom (Table 8.1 and Figure 8.1), we explore how two students inscribed what members needed to know, understand and do in the class and how such knowledge was constructed by members across times and events. These essays were written for the audience of students who would enter the Tower Community in the next school year (Santa Barbara Classroom Discourse Group, 1992a, b; Green, Yeager & Castanheira, 2008).

One additional piece of information is needed to understand the significance and origins of these essays. The practice of writing these essays was originally initiated by a student (1991), who asked to write about her class as part of a writing workshop. The teacher agreed and, when the student read her essay to the class, other members of the class asked to write a similar essay. Across the years (1992–2000), the teacher took up this task and incorporated it into her final reflexive writing assignments at the end of the year (Castanheira et al., 2007).

The contrastive analysis of these essays is designed to make visible how, in their narratives about classroom community, students inscribed a common set of processes involved in constructing life-world(s) of their class, their positions and identities within their world and their agency in this developing world (Ivanič, 1994). The first essay was selected to demonstrate how students inscribe individual–collective relationships involved in becoming a member of the class. The second essay was selected because it expands this focus and also inscribes in more depth how collective knowledge was developed (Yeager, Floriani & Green, 1998).

The first essay was written by Israel, a student who entered the class halfway through the school year (Castanheira et al., 2007):

Our community has a lot to do over the year. Sometimes our community gets different during the year. What I mean is like the first day I walked in the door. I was new and nervous just me thinking who am I trying to make friends. I came in the door. Other students explained how to do the Writer's Workshop. I didn't understand the three logs. Other kids and the teacher explained. Now I'm just part of everyone else. (Israel 1992)

In his essay, Israel positions himself initially as a newcomer who needed to develop and gain access to the particular language of the class, as well as to ways of doing particular social action/activity (Writer's Workshop). He argues that such knowledge was a material resource that he needed to become 'part of everyone else'.

The second essay was selected from a class in 1995 (three years after Israel's). We selected Arturo's essay from published work from our ongoing program of research (Yeager & Green, 2008) to make visible how he viewed the situated and constructed nature of language–culture relationships within the developing collective (the Tower Community).

COMMUNITY

In our tower community, we have our own language as well as the languages we bring from outside (like Spanish and English) which helped us make our own language. So, for example, someone that is not from our classroom community would not understand what insider, outsider, think twice, notetaking/notemaking, literature log and learning log mean. If Ms. Yeager says we are going to 'make a sandwich', the people from another class or room would think that we were going to make a sandwich to eat. Of course we aren't, but that is part of our common language.

To be an insider, which means a person from the class, you also need to know our Bill of Rights and Responsibilities which was made by the members of the Tower community. And if Ms. Yeager said, 'Leave your H.R.L. on your desk,' people would not understand unless someone from the Tower community told him/her and even if we told him/her that H.R.L. stands for 'Home Reading Log', they still would not understand what it is and what you write in it. If we told a new student, 'It's time for SSL and ESL', he would not understand.

These words are all part of the common Tower community language and if someone new were to come in, we would have to explain how we got them and what they mean. We also would tell them that we got this language by reports, information, investigations, and what we do and learn in our Tower community. (Arturo 1995)

In this essay, Arturo inscribes processes through which the community was constructed. He frames the (re)formulation of language as a collective resource constructed by members, not simply the resource that individual participants brought to the classroom. In contrasting three types of language, he creates a theoretical argument about life in the classroom as constituted in and through what people do and say to each other, and how such sayings become a material resource for members (Gee & Green, 1998). Like Israel, Arturo states that outsiders would not know what members know, thus creating insiders/outsiders as different positions that lead to differential knowledge. He further claims that to understand this language you would need to know that 'we got this language by reports, information, investigations *and* [emphasis added] what we do and learn in our Tower community'. In setting these conditions for the outsider, Arturo makes visible the interdependence between language and activity, and social and cultural processes.

By including cross-year examples of the narratives by students about community life, we were able to locate insider information about self–other relationships, community as a developing learning space, insider–outsider relationships and language–culture relationships. The essays also make visible that students take a reflexive stance to being in the world; that is, they make visible how they view themselves in relationship to current, past and future groups. Their essays show that students read the social, cultural and linguistic processes that are material resources in the world, and they understand how what they are doing and learning are interdependent. These essays, therefore, make visible how students read the world (Freire & Macedo, 1987), are aware of who is and is not part of the community and how the common knowledge of a group is an ongoing process of developing activity, language, identities, literate practices and individual and collective learning lives. Students' inscriptions of the social and discursive construction of life in classrooms demonstrate how a discourse-based ethnographic logic of enquiry constitutes a conceptual language (theories) for both the university-based ethnographer and students (and others) about the interdependence of individual and collective learning lives.

REFERENCES

Agar, M. (2006a). Culture: Can you take it anywhere? *International Journal of Qualitative Methods*, 5(2), 1–12. Retrieved from http://www.ualberta.ca/~iiqm/backissues/5_2/PDF/agar.pdf

Agar, M. (2006b). An ethnography by any other name ... *Forum Qualitative Sozialforschung / Forum: Qualitative Social Research*, 7(4). Retrieved from http://www.qualitative-research.net/fqs

Anderson-Levitt, K. M. (2006). Ethnography. In J. L. Green, G. Camilli, & P. B. Elmore (Eds.), *Handbook of complementary methods in education research* (pp. 279–96). Mahwah, NJ: Lawrence Erlbaum & Associates for AERA.

Bakhtin, M. M. (1979/1986). *Speech genres and other late essays* (V. W. McGee, Trans.). Austin: University of Texas Press.

Bloome, D., Carter, S. P., Christian, B. M., Otto, S., & Shuart-Faris, N. (2005). *Discourse analysis and the study of classroom language and literacy events: A microethnographic perspective*. Mahwah, NJ: Lawrence Erlbaum Associates.

Bloome, D., & Egan-Robertson, A. (1993). The social construction of intertextuality in classroom reading and writing lessons. *Reading Research Quarterly*, 28(4), 305–33.

Brilliant-Mills, H. (1994). Becoming a mathematician: Building a situated definition of mathematics. *Linguistics and Education*, 5, 301–34.

Castanheira, M. L. (2004). *Aprendizagem contextualizada: Discurso e inclusão na sala de aula*. Belo Horizonte, Brazil: Ceale; Autêntica.

Castanheira, M. L., Crawford, T., Dixon, C. N., & Green, J. L. (2001). Interactional ethnography: An approach to studying the social construction of literate practices. *Linguistics and Education*, 11(4), 353–400. doi: 10.1016/s0898–5898(00)00032–2

Castanheira, M. L., Green, J. L., Dixon, C. N., & Yeager, B. (2007). (Re)formulating identities in the face of fluid modernity: An interactional ethnographic approach. *International Journal of Education Research*, 46(3–4), 172–89.

Edwards, D., & Mercer, N. (1987). *Common knowledge: The development of understanding in the classroom.* New York: Falmer Press.

Erickson, F., & Shultz, J. (1981). When is context? Some issues and methods in the analysis of social competence. In J. L. Green & C. Wallat (Eds.), *Ethnography and language in educational settings* (Vol. V, pp. 147–50). Norwood, NJ: Ablex Publishing Corporation.

Erstad, O., Gilje, Ø., Sefton-Green, J., & Vasbø, K. (2009). Exploring 'learning lives': Community, identity, literacy and meaning. *Literacy, 43*(2), 100–6.

Fairclough, N. (1992). *Disourse and social change.* Cambridge: Polity.

Freire, P., & Macedo, D. (1987). *Literacy: Reading the word and the world.* South Hadley, MA: Bergin and Garvey.

Gee, J. P., & Green, J. L. (1998). Discourse analysis, learning, and social practice: A methodological study. *Review of Research in Education, 23*, 119–69.

Giddens, A. (1979). *Central problems in social theory: Action, structure and contradiction in social analysis.* Berkeley: University of California Press.

Goffman, E. (1981). *Forms of talk.* Philadelphia: University of Pennsylvania.

Green, J. L., & Meyer, L. A. (1991). The embeddedness of reading in classroom life: Reading as a situated process. In C. Baker & A. Luke (Eds.), *Toward a critical sociology of reading pedagogy* (pp. 142–60). Amsterdam: John Benjamins.

Green, J. L., Skukauskaite, A., & Baker, W. D. (2012). Ethnography as epistemology: An introduction to educational ethnography. In J. Arthur, M. J. Waring, R. Coe, & L. V. Hedges (Eds.), *Research methodologies and methods in education* (pp. 309–21). London: Sage.

Green, J. L., Yeager, B., & Castanheira, M. L. (2008). Talking texts into being: On the social construction of everyday life and academic knowledge in the classroom. In N. Mercer, & S. Hodgkinson (Eds.), *Exploring talk in school: Inspired by the work of Douglas Barnes.* London, UK: Sage Publications Ltd.

Gumperz, J. J. (1986). Interactive sociolinguistics on the study of schooling. In J. Cook-Gumperz (Ed.), *The social construction of literacy* (pp. 45–68). New York: Cambridge University Press.

Heap, J. L. (1980). What counts as reading? Limits to certainty in assessment. *Curriculum Inquiry, 10*(3), 265–92.

Heap, J. L. (1989). Writing as social action. *Theory into Practice, 28*(2), 148–53.

Heap, J. L. (1991). A situated perspective of what counts as reading. In C. D. Baker, & A. Luke (Eds.), *Towards a critical sociology of reading pedagogy* (pp. 103–39). Philadelphia: John Benjamin.

Hymes, D. (1977). Critique. *Anthropology & Education Quarterly, 8*(2), 91–3.

Ivanič, R. (1994). I is for interpersonal: Discoursal construction of writer identities and the teaching of writing. *Linguistics and Education, 6*(1), 3–15.

Kaplan, A. (1964/1998). *The conduct of inquiry.* San Francisco, CA: Chandler Publishing Company.

Larson, J. (1996). The participation framework as a mediating tool in kindergarten journal writing activity. *Issues in Applied Linguistics, 7*(1), 135–51.

McHoul, A. (1991). Readings. In C. D. Baker, & A. Luke (Eds.), *Towards a critical sociology of reading pedagogy* (pp. 191–210). Philadelphia: John Benjamin.

Mehan, H. (1979). *Learning lessons.* Cambridge, MA: Harvard University Press.

Santa Barbara Classroom Discourse Group. (1992a). Constructing literacy in classrooms: Literate action as social accomplishment. In H. H. Marshall (Ed.), *Redefining student learning: Roots of educational change* (pp. 119–50). Norwood, NJ: Ablex.

Santa Barbara Classroom Discourse Group. (1992b). Do you see what we see? The referential and intertextual nature of classroom life. *Journal of Classroom Interaction, 27*(2), 29–36.

Walford, G. (2008). The nature of educational ethnography. In G. Walford (Ed.), *How to do educational ethnography* (pp. 1–15). London: Tufnell Press.

Yeager, B., Floriani, A., & Green, J. L. (1998). Learning to see learning in the classroom: Developing an ethnographic perspective. In D. Bloome & A. Egan -Robertson (Eds.), *Students as inquirers of language and culture in their classrooms* (pp. 115–39). Cresskill, NJ: Hampton Press.

Yeager, B., & Green, J. L. (2008). 'We have our own language as well as the languages we bring': Constructing opportunities for learning through a language of the class-room. In J. Scott, D. Straker, & L. Katz (Eds.), *Affirming students' right to their own language: Bridging language policies and pedagogical practices* (pp. 153–75). New York: Routledge with National Council of Teachers of English.

Chapter 9

Social Entrepreneurship: Learning Environments with Exchange Value

Shirley Brice Heath

In Boston, Massachusetts, teenagers move quickly up and down the three floors of Artists for Humanity (AFH), a youth-centred arts enterprise in which teenagers (14–18) learn to design and create art works. Founded in 1991 by six middle-school boys and a resident artist of their school, AFH evolved into a grassroots community organisation that operates as a blended-value for-profit/nonprofit entity, providing after-school art and design instruction and developing products on commission from individuals, corporations, and city government offices. (Heath & Smyth, 1999; www.afhboston.com)

In Lund, Sweden, *mejeriet* [The Dairy], a youth performance venue that spawns and fosters entrepreneurial pursuits by young people of the region, is supported in part by an annual budget from the city. Mejeriet's state of the art concert hall, one of the most sought-after public-performance venues in Sweden, is rented out for appearances by entertainers from around the world. On-going support of the facility also comes from membership fees for various areas of programming (e.g. film, jazz and classical music, folk and popular music). Daily film events plus weekly concerts and recitals draw local fans. In the after-school hours, students work with their local music instructors in the facility's numerous rehearsal and practice spaces. (Heath, 2002; www.mejeriet.org)

These two cases provide a glimpse of the range of social enterprise developments with art, science and management that young people living in modern economies initiate and sustain. In these environments, young people 'learn by doing'. As they become immersed in roles critical to maintaining daily operations of their social enterprises, the young work under the guidance of professionals from different arenas of the art, science and business worlds. Young people observe and learn to take part in the business side of their organisations: marketing, management and security, health and safety and record-keeping related to income and expenditures. The young see themselves as vital contributors to the well-being of the entity to which they voluntarily come in order to learn and work. The social entrepreneurial work of young people in these enterprises surrounds them with *playwork* that gives them public visibility as good citizens of their local region.

As they gain expertise in the range of roles they play to keep their operations viable, young people see the real benefits of working towards excellence in public speaking, reading and writing, and in understanding different types of symbol systems (e.g. those of mathematics, chemistry, copyediting, web development, and health and safety). As they gain direct experience with the ubiquitous use of symbol systems in the daily life of organisations, young people absorb the reality that competence with these systems will be vital to their future education and employment.

The first two sections of this chapter define social entrepreneurship (SE) and position its contributions within democracies. The third section examines the two cases of collaborative invention of youth-centred social enterprises that opened this chapter. Specific modes and principles of operation define community initiatives led by savvy adults who value the roles and competencies of young people. Adult leaders – who are often founders – insist that these entities meet social goals while simultaneously contributing financially to the organisation's budget. These entities do so by enacting and enforcing operational principles that also characterise effective and humane businesses, governmental offices and health facilities. In addition to examining two cases of collaborative invention, this section also recounts the initiation by an individual youth of an international SE, a phenomenon that began in the late 1990s to appeal to students in US colleges and universities.

A subsequent section considers methods of data collection and analysis needed for research in youth-centred social enterprises. The chapter closes by considering features of learning environments of community organisations in terms of their complementarity with institutions such as schools and families. Raised here is the need for a synergy of efforts within modern economies to respond to the reality that leadership in the coming decades will require more skills and knowledge than today's elders are able to offer the young.

SOCIAL ENTERPRISE AS ENTREPRENEURSHIP

Devised in the 1980s to respond to the social motives of enterprising individuals around the world, SE evolved quickly into a legitimate area of study and claim for identity by community organisations.[1] Community organisations

---

[1] For a sampling of the geographical and functional range of these enterprises, see Youth Ventures at www.ashoka.org and Bornstein (2004); Dees, Emerson & Economy (2002); Elkington & Hartigan (2008).

that either begin or evolve as social entrepreneurial ventures bring to bear the energy, imagination and desire of their voluntary members in situations in which governmental institutions and for-profit enterprises have insufficient social value and fail to meet the needs of particular populations (e.g. disenfranchised or under-resourced groups, such as migrant workers, street dwellers and young people).

Consistently geared towards such populations, as well as to situational crises related to environmental issues, social enterprise organisations carry risks. The majority of start-ups do not survive when they face the realities of zoning and tax codes and recruitment and retention of newcomers in rapidly changing local economies. Trial and error in tactics and strategies characterise these organisations. Leaders must adhere to a simple, limited and clear mission that targets markets and participants carefully. Choice of paid employees is critical because they must do their own work and also find volunteer professionals who will guide – not direct or do for – youth. Rules, roles and risks matter. Social enterprises are tough places in which to work and learn, for they invariably exist in the midst of personal crises and on the edge of financial collapse. Paid adult employees, as well as volunteers, have to hold youth and other member constituents accountable, never letting pity or sympathy mitigate demands for responsibility and loyalty to a balance of personal and organisational needs and goals.

SUSTAINING DEMOCRACIES

Essential to the success of these organisations are roles with meaning and clear designations for advancement. To the young, especially those from disenfranchised groups, having a clearly defined role supported by clear rules gives meaning to voluntary participation. Community organisations dedicated to social enterprise truly *need* the work of young participants. Thus, the enterprises ensure that advancement of expertise with particular skill sets becomes an expected and accepted part of operations. For those who remain with a specific organisation over several years, responsibility and visibility within leadership roles increase, often giving access to entirely new areas of expertise and visibility. The centrality of this advancement principle within social enterprises differs significantly from modes of operation that characterise institutions such as schools and civic bureaucracies.

For example, educators and policy makers in economically advanced nations identify young people in secondary schools primarily by their role as students. National policies directed towards this segment of the population generally reference the group as 'our national youth' and 'the future of our country'. Good intentions and considerable public financing support formal education and special programs designed to teach students to read, interpret, produce and use extended printed texts specific to academic settings. The functions and purposes of these texts generally lie wholly within the operational norms of academic settings and not in the flow of realities of being family members and economically productive citizens of a capitalist democracy.

The production of a literate citizenry is seen as critical to the continuity of democracy in modern economies around the world. Nations expect citizens to be able to read extended written texts in order to stay informed about events occurring and choices available in democracies. Catching short snatches of information and opinion from television, blogs and tweets may meet immediate needs, but these sources lack extended, deliberative, information-rich well-formed arguments.[2] Democratic governments rely on the reasoning of literate citizens who read and consider routes to the achievement of ends beyond the self-interests of powerful individuals or groups. Ideally, a key reward of being literate comes in the privileges and rights granted to citizens of democracies. In modern economies, reading and writing skills also enhance the facility with which individuals manipulate other symbol systems of daily transactions in political, economic, social, religious and aesthetic spheres. Individuals fluent in receptive and productive competencies of multiple symbol systems can operate in ever-widening roles and levels of power – local, national and international.

Modern economies expect the young to learn to be good citizens in large part by preparing to take part in a vibrant workforce. Strong linkages prevail in the public mind between acquisition of literate skills and values and achievement of the knowledge essential to employment within manufacturing, commerce and the professions of education, engineering, law and medicine. Foundational within values that surround formal schooling is the expectation that what is learnt in school will have relevance and transfer value in a modern economy. Yet, school systems of modern economies generally fail to make the vital link between school learning and skills and information needed to operate effectively as a voter, worker and healthy citizen and family member.

In contrast, within social enterprises, the exchange value of learning to read and write becomes evident to the young, as does the need to know how to manage finances and to take part in financial transactions involving assets

---

[2] See Gutmann & Thompson (1966) and Mutz (2006) on the role of deliberative discourse and informed citizens in the future of democracies.

and liabilities, credit and debt. In fact, these organisations excel in embedding such skills in the everyday behaviours of the young.

However, social enterprises fall short of ensuring that their members acquire fluency and ease with knowledge of the humanities, as well as depth of skill development in specific subject areas, such as calculus and laboratory sciences. Schools, therefore, remain vital in their role of providing personnel trained in these subject areas and dedicated to ensuring that the young know how to seek, assess and use information accessible through multiple types of sources. Schooling, along with participation in community-based organisations, habituates the young to processes of remaining well-informed, broadly knowledgeable citizens.

The informational content usually gained through participation within youth-centred social enterprises relates directly to the primary activity realm (e.g. organic gardening and other science-based enterprises, as well as specific art forms, such as dance, music and video production). Through roles within the organisation, individuals become familiar with broad areas of information related to public relations, marketing, audience development and financial planning. Essential to keeping SE tuned to social needs and market values and competition is the experience that leads to understanding of what it takes to maintain a business and to make decisions to ensure a future for the enterprise. In many instances, young people also have to learn skills related to one or more of the following: intellectual property, privacy and security, invention and patents, tax-related record-keeping and reporting, health and safety regulations, protocol in relationships with public figures and booking venues and managing publicity. In almost every instance of a community organisation involving social enterprise, international as well as national factors shape the presuppositions and courses of action related to public representations of the group and the actions of its members.

Communication using media of many different types takes place within these organisations on a regular basis. This power to connect and to be 'in' on what happens elsewhere conveys to young people a sense that individuals, neighbourhoods and small communities can and must be agents of change, now and into the future.

SOCIAL ENTERPRISES AT WORK

Opening this chapter is the case of AFH, based in Boston, Massachusetts. In 1991, Susan Rodgerson, an art teacher, had a short-term residency in an urban middle school (serving students aged 12–15). There, she invited students to join her in the school library to create a mural. Eager to escape from classes they did not enjoy, several boys joined her. When the residency ended, Rodgerson moved on to another school, and the boys returned to the routine of school. However, when the summer vacation came for these thirteen-year-olds, in a year when Boston's poorest neighbourhoods were racked by gang violence, drug trafficking and random shootings, six of the boys determined that they needed to be anywhere but their own neighbourhoods. One of them recalled Rodgerson's having mentioned that she worked at home in something called a 'studio'. An idea developed. Another boy remembered the address of Rodgerson's home, and they showed up at her door asking to see the 'studio' – the garage next to her rented house. Jointly, they announced: 'This will do fine'. Puzzled, Rodgerson asked: 'Do what?' The boys created on the spot a plan for escaping their neighbourhoods that summer. They would work in Rodgerson's studio, doing the artwork they had come to enjoy during her residency at their school.[3]

From the series of happy accidents in this story emerged AFH, a grassroots community organisation that introduces young people to social entrepreneurial work that combines art, science and design. In 2001, after a decade of moving from one low-cost rental space to another, the organisation created designs for its own building. One of the original middle-schoolers, now an architect, helped with the design for the all-green 23,500-square-foot 'epicentre' that opened in 2004. Dedicated to bridging 'economic, racial, and social divisions by providing underserved youth with the keys to self-sufficiency through paid employment in the arts,' AFH operates as combined living room, studio, laboratory, rehearsal zone for career entry and academic and career counseling centre.

In 2011, twenty years after its founding, three of the original middle-school boys held management positions in the organisation. In that year, the products and services of AFH provided over a million dollars of income for the for-profit/nonprofit organisation. This income, along with grant money and charitable donations, plus some support from the city of Boston, enables AFH to operate year-round. During the academic terms, on three afternoons a week, AFH opens its studios to young people (aged 14–18). During the summers, young people come every weekday. They study photography, silk-screening, painting, drawing, welding, video production, animation and design. Rules of participation require that newcomers orient themselves by working for six weeks through all the studios. If they have adhered to the organisation's norms regarding punctuality, regular attendance and commitment, they are invited to stay and are paid a minimum wage. Each individual

---

[3] For the history of this organisation, see Heath & Smyth (1999) and www.afhboston.org.

must then decide on one or two studios for focused study and gradually take on increasing levels of responsibility in the many public activities of the organisation.

In the studios of AFH, students experiment with technologies, curation, program development, financial accounting and oral and written presentation of art work, design plans and service contracts. The young do so under the guidance of professional artists as mentors whose 'day job' is often elsewhere in their own studios, galleries or offices. Central to the operations of AFH are expectations of responsible work within the context of individual creation, group projects and the organisation as a whole. For example, commissioned in 2011 to design bicycle racks for placement throughout the city of Boston, AFH members from novices to experienced members contributed ideas, critiqued designs and helped sustain within the building an atmosphere of commitment to deadline and to quality of product and presentation. Commissions and individual sales (shared 50–50 with AFH) enable young artists to earn their own money, as well as to give back to the organisation that has nourished their talents and ambitions. Many of the students who complete secondary school as they work within AFH find further education opportunities, apprentice with crafts workers in the region and initiate their own small businesses.

Students who remain within the AFH program for at least a year develop a strong sense of the need to innovate and to break out of the mold of what the enterprise has done in years past. Sometimes these initiatives meet with failure, obvious to the individual artist as well as to curating peers. At other times, innovations, after significant trial-and-error efforts, succeed. Such was the case when several young artists set out to devise creative ways to use discarded glossy color advertising inserts from weekend newspapers. They created a new line of furniture using the inserts and earned recognition from national furniture chains and major architectural and home design magazines for their products. For students at AFH, such creative projects are often their initial experience in intention-based learning. Individuals propose projects on their own or for small groups and sometimes for entire studios. When they do so, they take responsibility for 'pitching' the idea to others and guiding and following as others join in on the project. This process encourages metacognitive understanding of how learning works within different kinds of learning environments. Self-regulation, even for young men and women with a history of unsatisfactory behavioural management in classrooms, becomes the expected social norm within studios where students have a joint commitment to the best use by all of the valuable resource of studio time and guidance from professional artists.

The second case opening this chapter tells the story of *mejeriet* (The Dairy) in Lund, Sweden. Initiated in 1990, this music centre has consistently been supported by a substantial annual budget from the city of Lund, which requires the young directors to report semi-annually on operations, including attendance figures, maintenance costs and assets and liabilities. The Dairy houses a concert hall outfitted with the latest in sound and lighting equipment, more than a dozen soundproof rehearsal rooms open for use by local music teachers, a small theatre and a café with performing space. The for-profit cultural organisations within The Dairy cater to special interest groups in different types of music and film. Each of these sends representatives to the governing board, usually headed by a young person.

The Dairy is open daily, and its café (with large television screens for viewing special sports events or concerts taking place elsewhere in Sweden) draws young and old from morning until the evening. At daily events, as well as annual events such as the Hip Hop Festival, young people hold responsibility for operation of the sound equipment, ticketing, security and crowd control. The Dairy buzzes daily with activity, as young people go from music lessons in rehearsal rooms to the café, to the sound booth and practice rooms, to the bulletin board of upcoming events.

The Dairy prides itself on building cross-age cross-interest communities. In addition, throughout Sweden, Lund is acknowledged as a city that respects its young people and provides a widely renowned learning environment that encourages professional development of musical talents and lifelong interest in music and film. When unemployment of young people increased in the first decade of the twenty-first century and university enrollment did not gain in appeal, Lund's *mejeriet* offered young men and women valuable apprenticeship opportunities in a concert facility with world-class recording and production equipment and a first-rate reputation as a performance venue.

These two cases come from a vast collection of social enterprises that spring from collaborative efforts that cater to the special interests of groups of young people. An additional type of social enterprise springs from individuals who dedicate themselves at a young age to specific problems in a particular geographic location. Such initiatives typically concern needy population cohorts and require considerable scientific knowledge, most often in the fields of health and environment. In these instances, the radical specificity of the project demands intellectual (and financial) capital beyond the resources of a single young person. Thus, such individuals tend to incubate their ideas over some years until they can recruit experts willing to bring networks of knowledge and power to mix with an individual's creativity and energy.

At the age of twelve, in an elementary school geography class, EQ drew Ecuador as his assignment. Ecuador, its history, language, architecture and Amazonian ecology led the youngster to immerse himself in learning more. On a trip to Eastern Ecuador with his father, EQ saw students walk through oil-contaminated soils in the Amazonian forests. Upon his return to the United States, he organised a large-scale collection of used footwear and persuaded three international corporations to transport the shipments free of charge. Local Ecuadorian law at the time prohibited the importation of used shoes. EQ battled the government in a campaign to expose the consequences of oil industry drilling practices in the Amazon Basin. His efforts earned him poster child status (at age sixteen) as 'the good gringo'. EQ then leveraged his position to develop full-scale school exchanges, bringing thousands of US secondary students to the Amazon and fomenting their interest in Latin America and environmental sciences. Such direct experience raised student consciousness around issues related to the role of the Amazonian rain forest (whose plants contribute to 70 per cent of modern medicines) in contemporary life. Subsequently, EQ was hired by an international environmental law attorney as a legal assistant in what proved to be one of the largest environmental litigations in US history.

EQ attended an elite private college and chose to major in both Latin American studies and development studies. After two years at the university, he left academic study to shuttle between New York and Ecuador. He succeeded in incorporating his first social entrepreneurial venture – the world's first fair-trade and 'greenly extracted' oil company. Applying fair-trade principles pioneered by Fair Trade USA, his fair-trade oil corporation would operate primarily out of Ecuador. Using his position as 'the good gringo' and extensive local contacts built up over years of pro-bono work, EQ persuaded the Ecuadorian government and formerly intractable local municipalities to enter into agreement with the goals and operational plans of the corporation. On the verge of economic extinction and violent social unrest fed by growing awareness of the environmental destruction of their traditional lands, these communities chose to place considerable hope in EQ's continuing dedication to their quality of life and the healthy future of their children. The corporation plans to develop an environmental scorecard by which to measure the invasiveness of the extraction process. A base line will then be established, and a compliance accountability and improvement plan specified for continuing certification.[4] In the future, the corporation expects

---

[4] See www.equitableorigin.com for details on the operation of the company. The board includes not only energy experts from for-profit companies, but also other youthful social entrepreneurs and representatives from Ecuadorian interests.

to participate in incremental profits generated by the sale of 'green' oil. EQ persuaded key players in the Ecuadorian industry to move beyond the 'reparations pattern' in use in countries such as Nigeria.[5] He judged profit-sharing, medical clinics and training programs as insufficient for communities already tarred with the oil industry's brush. He insisted on and won the industry's pledge to take on 'negative injunctions' whereby the most toxic practices (unrestricted road construction, forest destruction, oil seepage prophylaxis and oil flaring) would be prohibited. These destructive practices would not go forward with the 'out' that reparations and compensation could erase their effects in the minds of local communities. The resulting extraction costs are estimated to be 10–12 per cent higher than comparable costs. EQ plans for two sources of incremental profitability to the social venture – the savings of expense, as well as incremental premium revenues to be collected because 'green' oil is expected to sell for more than comparable 'black oil'. The 'green' premium is expected to be particularly valuable for consumer product companies eager to distinguish their products in a credible way as environmentally friendly. The green premium is to be shared between the government owners and the SE venture, with both parties 'recycling' a portion of their share to community needs and environmental conservation. Thus does the social entrepreneur start to convert the vicious cycle of exploitation and environmental degradation into the virtuous circle of participation and limited profitability.

EQ and other social entrepreneurs with similar passions for 'making the world a better place' (as distinct from cases such as AFH, which show dedication to improving the quality of life for specific local communities) have significant social capital defined as the ability to persuade, but not coerce, people to act in concert. EQ's case, along with those of *mejeriet* and AFH, illustrates how social enterprise development envelopes the young in systems of knowledge and skills that go far beyond academic reliance on print literacy and subject area assessment. Once initiated, these enterprises pull young people into areas of knowledge they could not have previously imagined. Whether design of furniture from the toxic inserts in weekend newspapers or development of 'green oil' fields, the young enter into relentlessly expanding situations that give value in exchange for their ideas, commitment and skills (in multiple symbol systems, persuasive

---

[5] This move may prove to be a deterrent to the business interruptions that have plagued, for example, the Nigerian oil industry, where social programs are administered as a form of reparations, and community involvement consists of standing in line for free clinics necessitated often by environmental poisoning (Idemudia, 2007).

powers and adherence to health and safety requirements, as well as in international market regulations).

How can scholars conduct research within operations such as AFH, *mejeriet*, and EQ's international enterprise? SEs are organisations of rapid change, extensive networking and shifting key players, especially volunteers or experts temporarily called in to assist with special projects. Much that happens within these organisations involves privileged information, with legal and financial repercussions if leaked.

Research in SEs relies on respecting young people who undertake either collectively or individually high-risk ventures towards which adults may (understandably) be skeptical and even resistant. Adult researchers, armed with recording equipment, questions and theories, alter the natural flow of interactions among the young, many of whom prefer to work out their ideas within their own groups of interlocutors and without the risk of adult interference or 'help'. Research within SEs means longitudinal study critical to revealing how their rapidly developing ideas play out in the long run.

Linguistic anthropologists who use methods associated with participant observation tend to be those scholars who can, to some extent, immerse themselves in the everyday life of SEs. They rely on field notes and recordings (video and audio), as well as occasional use of interview-like questions, test-like situations and the introduction of tasks not generally part of the everyday life of the setting. In the latter means of collecting data, linguistic anthropologists also join with individual young people to collect data and take part in devising questions, test-like experiences and novel tasks.[6]

Partnership with young people during data analysis helps ensure validity and also provides additional data. Young people regard themselves as highly interesting subjects. When they see the minutiae of their lives laid out in transcripts, quantified charts and graphs, they respond with valuable meta-commentaries, as well as suggestions for ways to collect data more effectively in the future. Analysis of data from linguistic anthropologists relies on varieties of processes for examining discourse features such as vocabulary, syntax, genre, patterns of turn-taking and interruption and referencing of co-participants, as well as distant verifiable sources (Heath & Street, 2008). Video recordings enable examination of gestures accompanying speech, as well as uses of written

---

[6] For further information on such methods, see Heath & Street (2008) and Heath (2012).

materials and sources created in other symbol systems (e.g. musical notation, schematic drawings, graphs and charts, photographs, video). Linguistic anthropologists give particular attention in both note taking and analysis of video records to visuomotor behaviours that involve creation of artefacts and representations of current work through means beyond verbal records (e.g. architectural models, photography, sculpture). Analysis of these records also enables researchers to correlate specific language behaviours with ways that young people use their hands to enact, illustrate, model or emphasise aspects of the ongoing work of their social enterprise.

EXCHANGE LEARNING

Every case, story or ethnography centred on learning leads us to question how specific instances, such as those given here, may help us improve current theories of learning across the lifespan. What can we learn from these particular cases that may be extractable for comparison with any other set?

The introduction to this volume draws attention to the need to specify how features of particular learning environments influence habits of lifelong learning. The cases given here suggest that in the 'liquidity' of life in modern economies saturated with technologies, risk-taking is an essential aspect of learning. The young, in particular, have to experience opportunities to stretch their talents and build knowledge and skills that will not be confined to their usual identities and roles as *child* or *student*. By their prepuberty years, young people begin to recognise that technical expertise and worldly knowledge provide their entry ticket for inclusiveness in peer groups that relish high-risk and 'out-there' ventures in which contexts have no boundaries. Whether as designers of the only all-green building of a major metropolitan area or the first nationally acclaimed concert venue doubling as learning environment for young musicians and music entrepreneurs, the young in modern economies see no reason to rely on limits (of age, imagination or possibility). Collaboration around common interests offers sufficient motivation, intellectual energy and incentive for finding needed guidance from external experts. Individual social entrepreneurs follow paths of learning similar to those of collaborative groups; they differ primarily in their adoption of business models that emphasise stockholders and stakeholders, as well as leadership through chief executive officers (CEOs).[7]

---

[7] Dutton (2011) provides case studies of adolescents who broke boundaries of learning in the sciences in response to their sense of local needs and unresolved problems related to environmental degradation, health sciences and national security.

All cases of SE initiated and maintained by young people bring us face-to-face with the reality that certain groups and individuals among the young choose and create exceptional learning environments. Within these contexts, the young voluntarily learn complex information and highly technical and interrelated skills that incorporate numerous academic skills as well (e.g. literacy, numeracy, science and geography). SEs provide one such context that integrates visual, performative and verbal demands by placing responsibility on youth taking real roles for true purposes that they create and uphold.

Unlike community-based organisations, schools are institutions that bear special legal responsibilities and positioning in relation to governmental expectations. Therefore, schools cannot provide voluntary, flexible and ever-adapting environments of learning. Compulsory attendance, predictability of operations and standard accounting for quality of output in relation to amount of financial input have to be core features of publicly funded formal instruction provided for all children up to a certain age.

In large part, the voluntary nature of participation that characterises SEs and other types of community-based organisations lays the groundwork for all else that happens in these learning environments for young people. When newcomers to these contexts recognise that what and how they learn determines the future of the entire entity, incentive for speed and excellence multiplies. Social control by cross-age peers with different years of experience in the organisation works interdependently with both individual behaviour regulation and group curation of products and services. Regular interactions with members of the public as clients and audience members remind young people that expectations of quality surround them. Learning in such situations, week after week and year after year, lies well outside any definitions that may attempt to specify limits on where imagination, energy, determination and creativity can lead.

For the stories or cases noted in this chapter, two primary questions hold. The first asks how scholars have failed to address the inadequacy of accounts and theories of voluntary (or 'informal') learning. This kind of learning is ubiquitous, taking place primarily outside institutional settings and within situations in which individuals voluntarily choose to learn to go beyond what is expected or even accepted in the broader society. Collaborative groups and individuals use what they have learnt in other settings, such as school, travel and harsh living circumstances, to go beyond normal or normed lessons of reading, writing and mathematics, as well as other subject matter courses. As they do so, they learn from the doing of the projects as well as from models and principles they seek out or invent to meet the particular needs they identify. Voluntary learning in SEs brings in technical expertise, specific bodies of both scientific and artistic knowledge and the production of goods and services for locals, as well as for clients or customers whom the young entrepreneurs may never meet face to face.

A second question reaches into interdisciplinary studies of *playwork* – contexts in which individuals see their work as like play, in that it involves intense engagement, high risk and emotional feedback, as well as the promises and perils inherent in games of chance and competition.[8] Theories amplified through the few studies we have of such contexts emphasise the meta-linguistic and meta-cognitive effects of learning that depends on envision-ment and embodiment. Imagining a future not previously designed or experienced intensifies visual perception of details. Embodying roles, such as that of publicist, artist or musician, becomes possible when learning takes place regularly in the company of professionals or experts who guide, facil-itate and model, rather than teach. Apprenticeship stretches learning and involves risks that the stimulate visual, motor and verbal centres of the brain, thereby reinforcing long-term memory and formation of 'future memories'.[9]

The exchange values that come through SE membership contradict long-standing premises of formal approaches to learning that emphasise the need for teacher-directed scope and sequence, expectation of monolinear devel-opmental stages and reliance on the primacy of verbal exposition over visual representation.[10] In formal educational systems of many nations, these prem-ises guide practices of instruction and assessment, especially those devoted to reading, mathematics and the sciences. Teachers receive their training so that the institution of schooling will feel confident in predicting that learners of the same age will acquire the same skills and knowledge at approximately the same rate. Room for creativity in the process of teaching and acknowledging learning of the young must therefore be minimal. In contradiction with these theories and practices are stories such as those recounted here of creative and advanced learning by individuals outside the customary purview and scope of formal schooling and within opportunities for emotional engagement and innovative moves for social and economic change.

---

[8]   Sutton-Smith (1997) provides an interdisciplinary overview of how activities and expectations of play forms and experiences are essential to human learning. He maintains that 'play variability is analogous to adaptive variability; that play potential is analogous to neural potential; that play's psychological characteristics of unrealistic optimism, egocentricity, and reactivity are analogous to the normal behaviour of the very young; and finally that play's engineered predicaments model the struggle for survival' (p. 229).

[9]   For discussions of the cognitive neuroscience behind enactment, envisionment and embodi-ment in learning, see Heath (2011).

[10] For further discussion of these points, see Banks (2007); Bransford et al. (2005); Miles et al. (2002); Perret-Clermont et al. (2004); Turner (2006).

In developed and developing countries throughout the world, governments, nongovernmental and nonprofit organisations, health officials and education leaders recognise that creating a knowledge-based, civic-minded, global workforce is complex and challenging. Many look to school systems, already burdened by bureaucracy, to adapt existing learning environments to meet the shifting knowledge and skill demands of a global economy. An equivalent emphasis goes to expectations of family socialisation, in spite of the fact that the majority of families living in modern consumer-driven economies lack the expertise, knowledge, time and willingness to undertake advancement of their children's creativity in projects of science and the arts.

Organisations of social enterprise employ professionals and recruit volunteers in these fields who guide, model and critique the creative ideas and projects of young people. Many of these organisations are ready partners with schools and businesses willing to allow young people to use and extend information and skills gained in school and to build interests and specialisations that will make them valuable to future employers. Moreover, social enterprises encourage (and in some cases insist) on involvement over several years in specific roles, so that learning moves from beginning through intermediate and, in some cases, to advanced levels of accomplishment and knowledge. Often, high levels of achievement in special areas of expertise require apprenticeships and internships that can become available through association with the professionals in higher education institutions and civic and commercial business.[11]

Schools have to institute ways to give credit to young learners who have SE experience. Educational systems must do so by breaking out of current spatial and temporal boundaries. Local governmental agencies need to provide tax incentives for businesses that partner with community organisations to enable the entrepreneurial energies of the young to flourish. For their part, community SE organisations need to become resourceful in their search for partners. Some few political leaders and public media outlets around the world recognise that the hours, days and sometimes years outside of formal education for the world's growing population of young people are an untapped resource for civic engagement, public responsibility, healthy lifestyles and productive workers.[12] United Nations committees, development agencies and local leaders are beginning to look to SEs as one resource that can sustain

---

[11]   See Dutton (2011) for examples of ways in which young entrepreneurs in secondary schools called on individual professors working in nearby universities to search out, in creative ways, resources and assistance both locally and through the internet.

[12]   For more on this point, see Bentley (1998) and Soep & Chávez (2010).

older children and adolescents in positive learning situations while providing critical socialisation contexts and future-looking roles.

Without ongoing attention to youth SE from leaders of international organisations and modern economies – especially the wealthy nations of the world – the potential of community SEs will remain invisible except for the occasional blip on television screens or short feature on the news page. The absence of a place in national and international thinking cannot, however, keep creation of the arts and sciences out of the hands and heads of the young. In spite of the lack of recognition and support for their learning through SE, small groups of young people working in combination with resourceful adults will continue to try to transform the cultural commons of their communities and the awareness of corporate and government leaders to their responsibilities for radical education restructuring.

REFERENCES

Banks, J. (2007). *Learning in and out of school in diverse environments*. Seattle, WA: LIFE Center and Center for Multicultural Education, University of Washington.

Bentley, T. (1998). *Learning beyond the classroom: Education for a changing world*. London: Routledge.

Bornstein, D. (2004). *How to change the world: Social entrepreneurs and the power of new ideas*. New York: Oxford University Press.

Bransford, J. D., Vye, N. J., Stevens, R., Kuhl, P., Schwartz, D., Bell, P., et al. (2005). Learning theories and education: Toward a decade of synergy. In P. Alexander & P Winne (Eds.), *Handbook of educational psychology* (2nd ed., pp. 209–44). Mahwah, NJ: Lawrence Erlbaum.

Dees, J. G., Emerson, J., & Economy, P. (2002). *Strategic tools for social entrepreneurs: Enhancing the performance of your enterprising nonprofit*. New York: John Wiley & Sons.

Dutton, J. (2011). *Science fair season: Twelve kids, a robot named Scorch. . . and what it takes to win*. New York: Hyperion.

Elkington, J., & Hartigan, P. (2008). *The power of unreasonable people: How social entrepreneurs create markets that change the world*. Cambridge, MA: Harvard Business Press.

Gutmann, A., & Thompson, D. (1996). *Democracy and disagreement*. Cambridge, MA: Harvard University Press.

Heath, S. B. (2002). Working with community. In G. Dees, J. Emerson, & P. Economy (Eds.), *Strategic tools for social entrepreneurs* (pp. 204–43). New York: John Wiley.

Heath, S. B. (2012). *Words at work and play: Three decades in family and community life*. Cambridge: Cambridge University Press.

Heath, S. B., & Smyth, L. (1999). *ArtShow: Youth and community development*. Washington, DC: Partners for Livable Communities.

Heath, S. B., & Street, B. (2008). *On ethnography: Approaches to language and literacy research*. New York: Teachers College Press.

Idemudia, U. (2007). *Corporate partnerships and community development in the Nigerian oil industry: Strengths and limitations.* Markets, Business and Regulation Programme Paper 2. Geneva: United Nations Research Institute for Social Development.

Miles, S., Pohl, A., Stauber, B., Walther, A., Banha, R. M. B., & Gomes, M. (2002). *Communities of youth: Cultural practice and informal learning.* Hants, UK: Ashgate Publishing.

Mutz, D. C. (2006). *Hearing the other side: Deliberative versus participatory democracy.* Cambridge: Cambridge University Press.

Perret-Clermont, A. -N., Pontecorvo, C., Resnick, L. B., Zittoun, T., & Burge, B. (2004). *Joining society: Social interaction and learning in adolescence and youth.* New York: Cambridge University Press.

Soep, E., & Chávez, V. (2010). *Drop that knowledge: Youth radio stories.* Berkeley: University of California Press.

Sutton-Smith, B. (1997). *The ambiguity of play.* Cambridge, MA: Harvard University Press.

Turner, M. (Ed.). (2006). *The artful mind: Cognitive science and the riddle of human creativity.* New York: Oxford University Press.

Chapter 10

The Construction of Parents as Learners About Preschool Children's Development

Helen Nixon

The concept of the lifelong learner – the idea that people should be active learners throughout the lifespan – has, since the 1990s, gained importance in public policy. Governments in relatively wealthy countries have made the argument that the economic future of nations is tied to the ongoing participation of citizens in learning opportunities that will assist them to participate fully in society and increase their chances of employment in changing workforce conditions. More recently, policy attention has focused on the other end of the lifespan, the first years of life. With the early years now recognised as crucial for later educational success, policy attention has also focused on the importance of *parenting* in the early years. In the United Kingdom and Australia, for example, the effects of state interventions to facilitate 'good parenting' and preschool children's 'readiness' for formal schooling have been felt in a range of settings, including community health services, the home and the preschool (Gillies, 2005; Millei & Lee, 2007; Nichols & Jurvansuu, 2008; Vincent, Ball & Braun, 2010).

In Australia, government policy has explicitly proposed a model of parenting as a learning process, and has urged people to cultivate their *identities as learners* in order to carry out their *responsibilities as parents*. In part, the policy objectives have been to support parents to ensure that all children get a healthy and successful start to life. As a federal government discussion paper puts it (Commonwealth of Australia, 2008):

The early years last a lifetime. ... There is now an impressive body of evidence, from a wide range of sources, demonstrating that early child development affects health, wellbeing and competence across the balance of the life course. (p. 29)

Children who come from rich and engaging early childhood educational environments have the foundations laid to become successful learners on their life-long journey. (p. 31)

A related policy objective has been to minimise the future costs to the public purse of health, education and social welfare. As analysts have noted, lifelong learning initiatives developed in the name of social inclusion have tended to encourage adults to develop dispositions as learners or 'learner identities' (Clegg & McNulty, 2002). At the same time, these initiatives have shifted the responsibility for developing those learning opportunities from the state to individuals and employers (Raggatt, Edwards & Small, 1996). In this process, the role of the market, 'partners' and 'stakeholders' has assumed greater importance:

The strategy of governments is to create the conditions in which people, families, communities, and organisations are most *likely* to learn for themselves, thus obviating the need for educational policy in the traditional sense. (Griffin, 1999, p. 440; cited in Griffin, 2000, p. 12)

In the United Kingdom, pressure on adults to locate and take up learning opportunities has been achieved by means of 'financial incentives. . . but also persuasion, veiled threat or even moral bullying' (Griffin, 2000, p. 12).

Similarly, early-years policy initiatives are currently shifting the burden of responsibility for preschool education and care from the state to individual parents and families. This neo-liberal policy climate has fostered many government – as well as commercially sponsored services and products designed to assist individuals to become the kind of 'good' parent that is normalised in policy discourse (Nichols, Nixon & Rowsell, 2009). In this chapter, I draw on a study that investigated this phenomenon.[1] The research had two main foci. First, it aimed to analyse the discourses that 'both constitute and reconstitute the family, parent and the child and their care and education' (Sunderland, 2000; Millei & Lee, 2007). This is not to suggest that the lived lives of actual parents are necessarily limited by these discursive constructions. Rather, their identities as parents are 'fragmented and fractured; never singular but multiply constructed across different, often intersecting and antagonistic, discourses, practices and positions' (Hall, 1996, p. 4). Second, the study enlisted a geosemiotic perspective (Scollon & Scollon, 2003). That is, it sought to examine how parents were discursively positioned by the semiotics of places they encounter and use as information sources in

[1]   *Parents' networks: The circulation of knowledge about children's literacy learning* was an Australian Research Council–funded Discovery Project (DP0772700) conducted by Chief Investigators Sue Nichols and Helen Nixon and Research Assistant Sophia Rainbird from the University of South Australia, Australia, and Partner Investigator Jennifer Rowsell from Rutgers University, United States.

everyday life, such as pharmacies, supermarkets, toy stores and churches (Nichols et al., 2009). While these places are rarely explored by educational researchers as sites for learning, it would seem that this kind of approach is necessary if we are to adequately study the multiple dimensions of people's lifewide as well as lifelong learning lives in contemporary conditions.

The geographic regions chosen for the study were selected on the basis of prior knowledge, proximity and census information. Regions were studied systematically for the places where parents of young children were hailed by semiotic means (e.g. in language and image in signs, notices or displays) and where resources that promised to assist them were produced, displayed and distributed or sold. Over a three-year period, multiple visits were made to these places, and methods of observation, note-taking, photography and interviews with seventeen volunteer information providers and forty-five parents were used to explore the incitements and affordances provided by these local environments for parents to engage in forms of information-sourcing about children's education and care (for more detail, see Nichols & Rainbird, 2012). The objective was to interrogate the complex ensemble of articulated discourses, practices and ideologies surrounding the figure of the 'proper' parent in these 'situated' materials that were produced and disseminated by the state, by commercial providers and by partnerships between the two.

I am not suggesting that the provision of advice by the state and other 'experts' designed to assist parents to raise healthy children is a new phenomenon. Indeed, the first years of life have been a significant focus of this kind of advice since the publication, in the 1920s, of behaviourist J.B. Watson's best-selling book on infant and child care (Seiter, 1995). And, while certain features of parenting advice literature persist – such as an assumed audience of middle-class mothers – histories of the social contexts of consumption show that the nature and potential implications of the advice on child rearing have changed with economic and social conditions (Seiter, 1993). An important difference in the contemporary context is that the burden of responsibility for learning how to carry out one's responsibilities as parents has shifted away from the welfare state. Rather, parents are now considered to have individual responsibilities to take on learner identities in order to carry out the increasingly complex social roles envisaged for them. That is, parents are discursively positioned as *pedagogical subjects* (Luke, 1994; Buckingham & Scanlon, 2001). As childhood has become increasingly commodified (Kenway & Bullen, 2001), parents are positioned this way not only by the state, but also by consumer culture (Seiter, 1993), with the distinctions between the public and commercial spheres of influence becoming increasingly hard to distinguish (Buckingham, 2011). With respect to parents of babies and infants, the commercial sector has recently expanded very rapidly. As Hughes (2005) puts it, 'international capital has discovered the under threes'. Further, in a knowledge economy (Lyotard, 1979/1984) or learning society (Organisation for Economic Co-operation and Development [OECD], 2000), babies have been redefined from largely the 'medical subjects' they were in the early twentieth century to individual 'early learners', whose potential, it is claimed, needs to be understood and realised by the efforts of adult carers. One result of this, in an increasingly competitive education and employment marketplace, is that contemporary parents face a good deal of pressure to ensure that they know how to give babies the best possible chance to be considered 'school ready' by the time they enter formal education, when, in the United Kingdom and Australia at least, this is formally assessed by the state.

In what follows, I illustrate my discussion of the figure of the parent as learner about young children's education and care, with reference to how this plays out in two places commonly encountered in local neighbourhoods: the state-sponsored health clinic and the retail consumption environment of the shopping mall. I also consider how the new media of online environments are increasingly made central to the processes of self-directed and experiential learning envisaged for parents. That is, I understand the life stage of 'early parenting' as comprising two instances in lifelong trajectories of 'learning'. First, it is a time in which babies and infants are increasingly understood to be, and to need to be seen as, *learners*. Second, it is a time when – because of pressures from the state, the media and advertisers – the *learner identity* of parents is an aspect of identity formation that looms large in what Giddens (1991) and others describe as 'parents' reflexive narration of self-identity' that continues throughout the life course (Martens, Southerton & Scott, 2004).

LEARNING TO BECOME A 'PROPER' PARENT
IN THE HEALTH CLINIC

From the very beginning of a child's life, parents are drawn in to an array of services and information networks that offer to advise them about how they can learn to stay healthy, nurture their relationships with partners, raise healthy children and become well-informed and responsible parents. Women in particular are a target audience for both state- and commercially funded organisations from the very first stages of pregnancy, when they are invited to attend antenatal classes, learn about 'pregnancy week by week' by reading books and pamphlets, consulting websites and subscribing to regular

SMS text messages and RSS feeds. This process of inscribing parents as pedagogical subjects – as people who explicitly need to source particular kinds of information in order to learn how to parent well – continues as their children grow older. However, my interest in this section of the chapter lies in how parents of preschool children are discursively constructed by the information resources and services offered and promoted in the community clinic or state-sponsored health service. How are parents inscribed as pedagogic subjects in these spaces? What are they told they need to learn and do in order to successfully carry out their duties as parents? And what is at stake in these processes, and for whom?

Because the state, via the public health system, is often the first to systematically target future parents, it plays a potentially significant role in shaping parents' views and practices in relation to children's education and care. Once a pregnancy is registered with a doctor or at a hospital, various state-sponsored health agencies, as well as partnerships they have with commercial organisations, are activated to target and reach mothers-to-be. In turn, women become recipients of parenting information and trial product samples, regardless of whether these have been sought. Typically, these resources are hand-delivered in hospitals and clinics, and many first reach parents via 'maternity samplers' known as *Bounty Bags* in Australia and the United Kingdom. Enclosed materials and products address the physical health of parents and babies, but they also draw attention to the fact that children are learners from birth who need support from their parents in order to successfully learn and develop (Nichols, Nixon & Rowsell, 2009). For example, in maternity samplers, the attention of parents is directed to the importance of exposing babies to literature, fairytales and song, and the need to begin as soon as possible to prepare children for 'school readiness'. Suggested ways to do this – embedded in information resources – include exposing infants to adult talk, adults regularly reading to children, and encouraging children's exploratory play and active learning. That is, right from the start of a child's life, parents – and especially mothers – are constructed as needing to develop themselves as learners. For the future welfare of their child, they need to learn how to enact a complex role that combines physical carer with academic teacher, and they are at once coerced and supported by the state to take up that role (Vincent et al., 2010).

In Australia, postnatal contact between public health systems and new mothers and babies is maintained by state-government Departments of Health that offer three main forms of service provision: a telephone helpline, a website and a community nurse who operates from local and regional health clinics. All parents we interviewed reported that they had used the telephone helpline in cases of emergency or uncertainty, and especially in the first months and years of a child's life. However, newer communications technologies play an increasingly important role. Not only is the department's website now the primary resource used by health workers when they converse with helpline callers, it is also recommended to parents during health clinic visits as an authoritative and up-to-date resource. This aligns with both state and commercial visions for 'networking' providers and consumers and making information always and everywhere available so that, in theory, anyone can be a learner and consumer at any time.

Other state-funded health services that support families include 'universal contact visits' to the homes of all newborn babies within the first four weeks of leaving hospital. Return visits are made if nurses assess that mothers or children might be 'at risk'. Nurses also conduct parenting programs at the clinic and health checks for babies at the 'key milestone' ages of 6 weeks, and 6, 18 and 24 months. Since comparatively recently, even in these face-to-face contact scenarios, new technologies have become closely aligned with learning opportunities that parents are encouraged to take up. As one nurse explained, she invariably points to the website as a key resource that should be consulted:

What I normally do ... if parents are struggling ... they're not quite sure how to start, and so forth, the first thing I will do is go on the internet, which is always open anyway ... I ask them what information they have already, what they know ... and I go onto the site and I show them all the wonderful parts and bits and pieces.

These practices illustrate how the networking of resources, organisations and agencies across digital media is increasingly being adopted by the state as a preferred method of making resources and services available to citizens who are, in turn, encouraged to assume responsibility for consulting and acting on them.

A web manager and dedicated content writers facilitate this process, and a significant increase in the number of hits to the state health department website was recorded in 2010 compared with the previous year. This suggests that parents are not only being urged to use digital media to access information, but they are also increasingly doing so in practice. However, interviews with parents suggested that the web is not always their preferred method for accessing information, nor is it even possible for some due to cost or lack of time, hardware or broadband access. Several parents referred to 'word of mouth' as the most common method of sourcing advice about how to parent young children, even if this was later supplemented by other methods. For example, parents reported that: 'It's much better, from my point of view to hear it', and 'You talk among your mates at playgroup . . . it's more talking, I suppose, than actually the internet'. Where the internet was consulted, the state-supported health website was used to source information about children's development milestones and common medical conditions. Commercially produced websites produced for supermarket chains and baby products, on the other hand, were consulted for 'educational' activities (largely school-type 'worksheets') that parents could download for children to engage in at home. Information about how to access these sites was largely sourced from advertising, talking to other mothers and attending playgroups. If not available at home, some parents took advantage of internet and print facilities at their workplace to source materials that they considered to be educationally valuable for their children.

Although the nurse makes the website central to face-to-face consultations, in the clinic waiting room, parents are faced with a vast array of print media in the form of posters and pamphlets (see Figure 10.1). These materials convey strongly moral messages about how responsible parents can and should learn to prevent, diagnose and remediate health and development problems in babies and infants. The most prominent display in a waiting room we studied consisted of *Parent Easy Guides* (PEGS) that addressed over eighty topics:

FIGURE 10.1 Advice for parents in health clinic waiting room

Parent Easy Guides (PEGS)... bring simple, easy-to-read information on many of the issues faced by parents from birth through adolescence. [They] ... represent a valuable information source not only for parents and those caring for children, but also professionals. They have been developed from research in conjunction with appropriate experts and are widely used throughout Australia. (Parenting SA. 'Parent Easy Guides', http://www.parenting.sa.gov.au/pegs/)

The ideal parent reader inscribed in these materials is the ideal pedagogical subject. Eager to learn how to assist children to remain physically healthy, and to learn to speak, read, write and count, he or she understands the need to be actively engaged in children's early learning (Nichols, Nixon & Rowsell, 2009). The mode of address of these pamphlets reinforces this attitude as normative. For example, readers are told that because 'children need words for thinking and learning', then 'one of the most important things you can do for your child is to talk with her and listen to her as she talks to you' ('Growing and learning in the family', PEG 51, Government of South Australia, 2001). Another explains to parents that 'learning to talk is one of the most difficult and important steps that young children take', and advises that they can assist children to learn to talk if they do things like 'help your child to notice road signs and billboards' ('Learning to talk', PEG 33, Government of South Australia, 2001).

That is, in health department materials, parents are inscribed not only as learners, but also as needing to *become pedagogues* themselves so that they can teach their children to learn. In particular, the normative behaviour described in clinic-disseminated talk and materials gives high value to the pedagogical dimension of the mother-child interaction (Vincent et al., 2010). As has been noted in relation to 'edutainment' magazines produced for preschool children, such double constructions of parents as both learners *and* teachers can be accounted for by a number of economic and social factors, including the increasing commercialisation of children's media culture and the expansion of niche markets alongside 'the growing competitiveness generated by government policy on education' (Buckingham & Scanlon, 2001, p. 298). This trend has increased over the last decade (Buckingham, 2011).

A book about and for reading to babies distributed free of charge by the health department is an intervention designed for this policy environment. Titled *Right from the Start: Loving Reading with Your Baby* (Department of Health, Government of South Australia, 2003/2009), the preface makes clear that the book is overtly pedagogical in nature; it explains to parents that reading to their babies is extremely important because it helps them to learn ('They start to learn about the world and develop their thinking skills from looking at pictures and hearing words with you', no page number). Designed as a board book similar to commercially produced 'early readers', *Right from the Start* has three main sections. First, it opens by explaining to parents the importance of the early weeks of life 'when the foundations for the baby's future are laid down ... [p]atterns of learning about the world, and being a person in it, begin at this time and form the basis for all future living and learning' (Department of Health, Government of South Australia, 2003/2009, no page number). The second section – 'How to Read with Your Baby' – employs the imperative mood to explicitly instruct parents about how to conduct themselves as they take on the dual role of learner-teacher.

Hold the book so you can both look at the pictures. Point to the pictures and say what they are. Try to change the tone of voice when you are looking at the pictures and sound really interested. 'Look, here is a ball'. You can use the words in the book or your own words about the picture. (no page number)

Finally, the third section replicates a young child's first picture book. Facing pages include a simple coloured and annotated image on the left-hand page (see Figure 10.2). Each right-hand page provides two resources: first there are suggested brief read-aloud 'starter sentences' for parents to use when reading (see top right, Figure 10.2), and second, there is an explanation of the

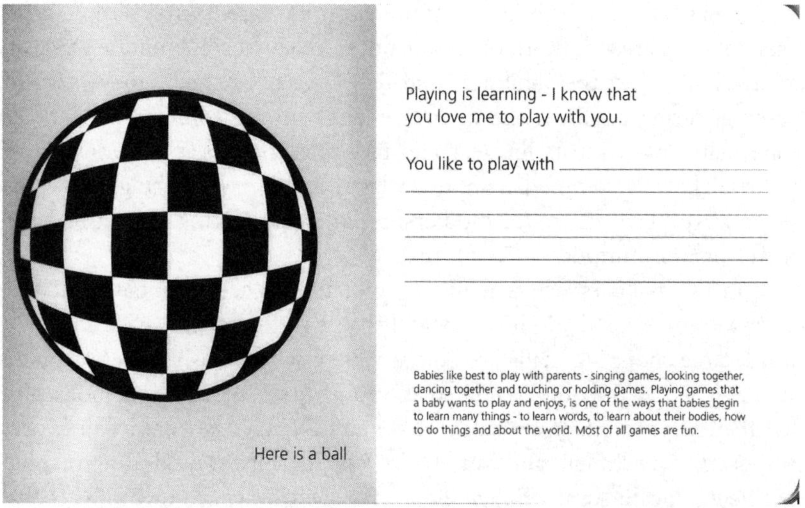

Here is a ball

Playing is learning - I know that you love me to play with you.

You like to play with _____

Babies like best to play with parents - singing games, looking together, dancing together and touching or holding games. Playing games that a baby wants to play and enjoys, is one of the ways that babies begin to learn many things - to learn words, to learn about their bodies, how to do things and about the world. Most of all games are fun.

FIGURE 10.2 Pages from a free book for parents from the health department

significance of the text and the practice it advocates (see bottom right, Figure 10.2). For example, text on the pages titled 'Here is a ball' explains that:

Babies like best to play with parents – singing games, looking together, dancing together and touching or holding games. Playing games that a baby wants to play and enjoys, is one of the ways that babies begin to learn many things – to learn words, to learn about their bodies, how to do things and about the world. (no page number).

In summary, parents are addressed throughout as pedagogic subjects who need to learn the connections between particular social contexts and practices (e.g. 'being with you', 'books and singing') and the literacy learning and development that is fostered by particular ways of approaching them. That is, in this context, the assumed reader is not only the middle-class aspirational parent but 'every parent', and he or she is simultaneously being taught *how* to take charge of children's early learning and that it is their *civic duty* to do so 'right from the start' of a child's life.

LEARNING WITH AND FOR YOUNG CHILDREN IN THE MALL

The commercial shopping centre or mall is another place routinely visited by parents with young children. For this reason, and because they constitute important niche markets, shopping complexes contain many different spaces deliberately designed to attract young families. Promising to inform and advise parents about matters that concern them is one commercial strategy. As Daniel Cook (2009) argues, even though some parents may wish to resist consumer culture, it is more-or-less inconceivable that contemporary parents can avoid it or raise their children 'outside' of it. As he notes, in today's world, 'parental caring practices entail engagement with the commercial world in some manner – with its imagery and meanings as well as material things' (p. 321). This is a routine part of everyday life and an increasingly powerful one in a world in which, for mothers in particular, 'caring cannot be extricated from consumption' (Cook, 2011).

From a spatial perspective, malls are configured to accommodate a mixture of civic, transactional and instrumental spaces (Goss, 1993, p. 19). Across the world, large shopping malls are both a recognisable transnational phenomenon and also slightly differentiated according to the particular demographic that they cater for (Salcedo, 2003). No matter where they are located, contemporary department and variety stores, pharmacies and supermarkets routinely allocate some of their floor and shelving space to products that target consumers as parents. In one mall we studied, located across a highway from the clinic described above, 18 of the 237 shops were either mainly or in part devoted to attracting parents of young children and stocked both parenting and early learning resources.[2] In this mall, we also regularly found mothers, older adults and young children in the vicinity of 'Playworld', a public area specifically designated as a play space for children up to the age of six who are supervised by adults (Nixon, 2011). This then is space that is both 'civic' (freely provided for adult rest and children's enjoyment) and 'instrumental' (allowing shopping breaks that help people to continue shopping rather than leave).

Playworld is designed so that carers can watch children play while adults sit nearby. In this mall, parents have the choice to either sit on public seats – like seats for resting and waiting placed throughout the mall – or on lounge chairs and at tables belonging to an adjacent cafe where adults can take refreshments while watching over children (see Figure 10.3). A large list of rules attached to the border of the play space informs parents that they are responsible for being vigilant and ensuring children's safety (see Figure 10.4); they 'must

FIGURE 10.3 Parents supervise children in a shopping mall play area

---

[2]   These shops were a large toy store, a bookstore, three newsagents, a department store, three supermarkets, three variety stores, two pharmacies, a post office, a games store, a computer software store and a shop run by the Australian Broadcasting Commission (ABC).

FIGURE 10.4 Rules for using Playworld play spaces in shopping malls

supervise children at all times'. Because children who use the space are
generally too young to read (0 to 6 years), such lists are in fact designed to
be read by parents even though, in grammatical terms, they appear to address
child patrons: 'Do not climb on the netting', 'No shoes, socks must be worn',
'No sharp objects' and 'No chewing gum'. That is, the rules perform an in situ
pedagogical function by specifying for parents what does and does not
constitute safe and socially approved behaviour for children to display in
such public spaces. In effect, the rules function not only to minimise the
public liability of the centre managers, but also to potentially teach parents
how to appropriately supervise and discipline their children when using play
equipment in public spaces. In this context, the parent is constructed simultaneously as consumer *and* learner within the pedagogisation of everyday life.

As in the case of the health department, the website of this global chain of shopping centres – one of the largest throughout Australia, the United Kingdom and the United States – plays an important role in reaching and teaching parents. A number of factors make online spaces most suitable for these purposes. First, websites have virtually unlimited space for text and images, enabling huge volumes of information to be attached to them. Second, web pages can easily be subdivided into sections that target niche audiences, designated as being 'for parents', 'for kids', 'for families' and so on. This enables adults to consult sections that address their specific needs as parents of 'newborns', 'toddlers' and so on. At the same time, this differentiated categorisation of web space builds a common-sense understanding that newborns, toddlers and so on are 'natural' categories of children that require different kinds of education and care. Second, hypertext has virtually unlimited potential to include intertextual referencing between editorial commentary, commissioned content and advertising. This is obviously attractive to corporations that need to market the physical spaces of malls as well as the online spaces devoted to products and services that the mall provides. The virtually limitless space, and the potential for hyperlinking to other sections and sites, greatly expands possibilities for reaching the diversity of people likely to visit each mall.

Another key function of websites is to encourage people to visit the mall using promotions and members' 'clubs' and by involving them in competitions, surveys, chat sites, online catalogue searching and so on. The retail objectives are to maximise the possibility of ongoing connection and information flows between centre management and households that will translate into brand loyalty and commercial transactions. Public mall spaces, such as customer enquiry desks, play spaces and parents' rooms (Australia) and family rooms (UK), are interesting in this regard. Although they have no obvious connection with product sales, they are key to attracting parents with children to visit and stay in a mall, thereby increasing the likelihood of commercial transactions. The way these 'civic' spaces are described online illustrates how the figure of the 'parent-as-consumer' is understood by mall owners, retailers and advertisers. First, because it is often difficult to shop with young children, parents are assumed to want some dedicated spaces that they can retreat to from the noise and gaze of other shoppers. Accordingly, they are assured that:

Meltdown moments are familiar to anyone shopping with kids. When a nappy needs changing, or a toddler needs taming, head to one of our three Family Rooms and enjoy the calm and peaceful environment. There you'll find an oasis of peace and tranquillity. (Westfield Group, 'Kids Services. Family Rooms', London UK, 2012a)

Second, it is acknowledged that parents shopping with children face significant physical challenges when trying to navigate vast expanses of space. In response, parents are invited to lessen this burden by taking advantage of free strollers or collecting 'a Kiddy Car to keep [children] entertained and they even get their own driving licence!' (Westfield Group, 'Kids Services. Kiddy Cars, London UK, 2012b). Here, the undeniable attraction for parents of having free access to toylike methods of transportation to help them move tired or recalcitrant children through these expanses has been well understood.

Finally, the fact that parents are also constructed in this context as consumer *and* learner is clearly illustrated with reference to play spaces. Indeed, online descriptions make very explicit how these spaces have been designed to assist parents to help children to develop, learn and socialise with others. As explained to parents, these play spaces have been designed with the knowledge that learning while playing happens when children engage in art-based activities and play, activities that engage the mind and the body and activities that include socialisation with other children. They make this kind of learning possible through the incorporation of slides, tunnels and climbing equipment, and interactive areas in which children can 'discover the life size pin screen, marvel at the mini-periscope, or play hide and seek in the tunnel and den' (Westfield Group, 'Kids Services. Playworld', London UK, 2012c). An authoritative mode of address is enlisted to explain the valuable educational connections between fun and play in the mall and the ongoing support from parents that is required to ensure children's timely learning and development. In this respect, the shopping complex inscribes the parent as a pedagogic subject in much the same way as the clinic described above. While it is children who are described as learners when active in play spaces, parents too are positioned as learners about why and how they should devote time and care to assisting children's development of motor skills, enquiry and social skills. In effect, children's learning in the early years is being 'sold' to parents as a valuable commodity, albeit a commodity that, in this instance, mall owners provide free of charge.

In the space available, I am unable to explore how the construction of parents as learners plays out in other spaces of the mall. However, parenting guides and advice books and 'educational' toys sold in a wide variety of stores provide rich examples of this process in action. Here, too, URLs promoted in magazines and on toy packaging potentially connect parents with websites where they will find other opportunities to learn about how to facilitate and monitor children's learning in the early years (Nixon, 2011). Web 2.0 environments conveniently make possible deeper explorations of parenting topics by way of the volume of information that can be referenced, the examples that can be illustrated in case studies and the anecdotes that can be solicited in forums. These environments are also attractive to some parents because they enable high levels of engagement and participation. While there is obvious potential for dominant conservative gendered and classed discourses about parenting to be reinscribed in these arenas (Madge & O'Connor, 2006), there is also some evidence that this is not always the case. For example, studies of online parenting communities show that virtual spaces can be used by mothers in particular to trouble romanticised constructions of motherhood (Madge & O'Connor, 2006) and construct nontraditional parenting identities (Wang, 2003). They can also provide a place for mothers who experience marginalisation in their nonvirtual lives to experience a sense of social inclusion and to 'call into question the foundations on which expert advice is based, validating experiential knowledges' (Mungham & Lazard, 2011). Apart from anything else, this highlights the ways in which people's learning lives are always situated 'intricately and intimately in a matrix of "trans-actions" . . . [and now] often mediated by a range of technologies' (see introduction, this volume).

SUMMARY

I have argued that, in the contemporary neo-liberal policy climate, people are being encouraged to take on the role of lifelong learners, beginning from birth and continuing throughout the life course. Further, they are being positioned to take on this responsibility as individuals, in whatever ways they can, and with lessening support from the state. This privatisation of the welfare state has seen a shift from an emphasis on *learning* to an emphasis on *the learner*, and a relocation of educational provision to the private rather than the public sector. It has also been accompanied by conceptions of learning as a 'lifestyle choice' (Featherstone, 1991) and a cultural commodity that, like all commod-ities, is not equally available to all (Griffin, 2000).

Parents and young children occupy an interesting position in this context. First, parents are increasingly required to assume economic and social responsibility for both their own and their children's education and welfare and with fewer social support mechanisms. As the state and the commercial world – today increasingly in 'partnership' – circulate discourses about 'proper' parenting, parents are constructed as needing to take on the identities of learners about parenting and about early-years learning in order to take on the role of teachers of young learners who are just setting out on their own course of lifelong learning. While policy discourses may be acting upon families 'through an unstable mix of support, exhortation and the threat of punitive action' (Vincent et al., 2010), consumer discourses construct the parent as learning to be a consumer in order to adequately care for the child. In this context, an important dimension of parental caring for children is connected with the consumption of goods and services that assist adults to bring forth the 'learning potential' of babies and infants, in order to ensure that they are competitive by the time they enter the life stage of formal education. In this high-stakes process, both parental and young children's learning is redefined as individual parents' private consumption of 'educational' commodities (Hughes, 2005, p. 35) that can be sourced from retail outlets or by taking up the learning opportunities provided on company websites.

As critiques of 'the learning society' have suggested, there are 'new and powerful inequalities' (Smith, 1996/2001) at work in a scenario in which people are left to fend for themselves in order to access the knowledge they need, throughout the life course, without support from the state:

The idea that learning is sited in everyday experience, and in the social relations of family, community and work, effectively distances it from public education and thus removes it from the realms of both policy and strategy. (Griffith, 2001, p. 12)

In short, the notion that learning 'happens anytime and anywhere' (e.g. in the play spaces of shopping malls), in a lifelong and lifewide ecology of informal learning, exacerbates both the difficulty of ensuring universal educational provision and the challenge for educational researchers of understanding how learning actually takes place in the spaces and moments of everyday lives.

REFERENCES

Buckingham, D. (2011). *The material child: Growing up in consumer culture.* Cambridge, UK: Polity.
Buckingham, D., & Scanlon, M. (2001). Parental pedagogies: An analysis of British 'edutainment' magazines for young children. *Journal of Early Childhood Literacy, 1*(3), 281–99.
Clegg, S., & McNulty, K. (2002). The creation of learner identities as part of social inclusion: Gender, ethnicity and social space. *International Journal of Lifelong Education, 21*(6), 572–85.
Commonwealth of Australia (2008, August). *A national quality framework for early childhood education and care.* Productivity Agenda Working Group: Education, Skills, Training and Early Childhood Development. Retrieved October 11, 2011, from http://www.deewr.gov.au/earlychildhood/policy_agenda/quality/pages/home.aspx

Cook, D. T. (2009). Semantic provisioning of children's food: Commerce, care and maternal practice. *Childhood, 16*(3), 317–34.

Cook, D. T. (2011). Through mother's eyes: Ideology, the "child" and multiple mothers in U.S. American mothering magazines. *Advertising and Society Review, 12*(2). Retrieved October 11, 2011, from http://muse.jhu.edu/journals/advertising_and_society_review/v012/12.2.cook.html

Department of Health, Government of South Australia. (2003/2009). *Right from the start: Loving reading with your baby*. Adelaide, SA: Parenting SA/Child Youth & Women's Health Services.

Featherstone, M. (1991). *Consumer culture and postmodernism*. London: Sage.

Gillies, V. (2005). Meeting parents' needs? Discourses of 'support' and 'inclusion' in family policy. *Critical Social Policy, 25*(1), 70–90.

Goss, J. (1993). The "magic of the mall": An analysis of form, function, and meaning in the contemporary retail built environment. *Annals of the Association of American Geographers, 83*(1), 18–47.

Government of South Australia. (2001). *Parent Easy Guides* (PEGS). Adelaide: CYWHS and Parenting SA. Retrieved September 21, 2011, from http://www.parenting.sa.gov.au/pegs/

Giddens, A. (1991). *Modernity and self-identity: Self and society in the late modern age*. Cambridge: Polity.

Griffin, C. (2000, July). *Lifelong learning: Policy, strategy and culture*. Working paper of the Global Colloquium on Supporting Lifelong Learning [online]. Milton Keynes, UK: Open University. Retrieved October 10, 2011, from http://www.open.ac.uk/lifelong-learning

Hall, S. (1996). Introduction: Who needs 'identity'? In S. Hall & P. Du Gay (Eds.), *Questions of cultural identity* (pp. 1–17). London, Thousand Oaks, CA, & New Delhi: Sage.

Hughes, P. (2005). Baby, it's you: International capital discovers the under threes. *Contemporary Issues in Early Childhood, 6*(1), 30–40.

Kenway, J., & Bullen, E. (2001). *Consuming children: Education-entertainment-advertising*. Buckingham, Milton Keynes: Open University Press.

Luke, C. (1994). Childhood and parenting in popular culture. *Journal of Sociology, 30*, 289–302.

Lyotard, J.-F. (1979/1984). *The postmodern condition: A report on knowledge* (G. Bennington & B. Massumi, Trans.). Manchester: Manchester University Press.

Madge, C., & O'Connor, H. (2006). Parenting gone wired: Empowerment of new mothers on the internet. *Social & Cultural Geography, 7*(2), 199–220.

Martens, L., Southerton, D., & Scott, S. (2004). Bringing children (and parents) into the sociology of consumption: Towards a theoretical and empirical agenda. *Journal of Consumer Culture, 4*(2), 155–82.

Millei, Z., & Lee, L. (2007). 'Smarten up the parents': Whose agendas are we serving? Governing parents and children through the Smart Population Foundation Initiative in Australia. *Contemporary Issues in Early Childhood, 8*(3), 208–21.

Mungham, S., & Lazard, L. (2011). Virtually experts: Exploring constructions of mothers' advice-seeking in online parenting communities. *Radical Psychology, 9*(2). Retrieved September 20, 2011, from http://www.radicalpsychology.org/vol9-2/mungham.html

Nichols, S., & Jurvansuu, S. (2008). Partnership in integrated early childhood services: An analysis of policy framings in education and human services. *Contemporary Issues in Early Childhood*, 9(2), 118–30.

Nichols, S., Nixon, H., Pudney, V., & Jurvansuu, S. (2009). Parents resourcing children's early development and learning. *Early Years: An International Journal of Research and Development*, 29(2), 147–61.

Nichols, S., Nixon, H., & Rowsell, J. (2009). The "good" parent in relation to early childhood literacy: Symbolic terrain and lived practice. *Literacy*, 43(2), 65–74.

Nichols, S., & Rainbird, S. (2012). The mall, the library and the church: Inquiring into the resourcing of early learning through new spaces and networks. *International Journal of Qualitative Studies in Education*. Retrieved from iFirst online paper at http://www. tandfonline.com/action/showCitFormats?doi=10.1080%2F09518398.2012.666285

Nixon, H. (2011). 'From bricks to clicks': Hybrid commercial spaces in the landscape of early literacy and learning. *Journal of Early Childhood Literacy*, 11(2), 114–40.

Organisation for Economic Cooperation and Development (OECD). (2000). *Knowledge management in the learning society*. Paris: OECD Publishing.

Raggatt, P., Edwards, R., & Small, N. (1996). Introduction: From adult education to a learning society? In P. Raggatt, R. Edwards, & N. Small (Eds.), *The learning society: Challenges and trends* (pp. 1–9). London: Routledge.

Salcedo, R. (2003). When the global meets the local at the mall. *American Behavioral Scientist*, 46(8), 1084–103.

Seiter, E. (1995). *Sold separately. Parents and children in consumer culture*. New Brunswick, NJ: Rutgers University Press.

Scollon, R., & Scollon, S. (2003). *Discourses in place: Language in the material world*. London: Routledge.

Smith, M. K. (1996/2001). *'Lifelong learning', the encyclopedia of informal education*. Retrieved October 11, 2011, from http://www.infed.org/lifelonglearning/b-life.htm

Sunderland, J. (2000). Baby entertainer, bumbling assistant and line manager: Discourses of fatherhood in parentcraft texts. *Discourse and Society*, 11(2), 249–74.

Vincent, C., Ball, S., & Braun, A. (2010). Between the estate and the state: Struggling to be a 'good' mother. *British Journal of Sociology of Education*, 31(2), 123–38.

Wang, G. (2003). 'Net-Moms' – a new place and a new identity: Parenting discussion forums on the Internet in China. *Provincial China*, 8(1), 78–88.

Westfield Group (2012a). *'Kids Services. Family Rooms'*, Westfield London, UK. Retrieved May 12, 2012, from http://uk.westfield.com/london/kids/kids-services/ london-family-rooms

Westfield Group (2012b). *'Kids Services. Kiddy Cars'*, Westfield London, UK. Retrieved May 12, 2012, from http://uk.westfield.com/london/kids/kids-services/london- kiddy-cars

Westfield Group (2012c). *'Kids Services. Playworld'*, Westfield London, UK. Retrieved May 12, 2012, from http://uk.westfield.com/london/kids/kids-services/playworld

Chapter 11

Participant Categorisations of Gaming Competence: *Noob* and *Imba* as Learner Identities

Björn Sjöblom and Karin Aronsson

Computer gaming has become an important part of young people's lives. Moreover, it constitutes a novel arena for the display and negotiation of identities and social positionings (Arnseth & Silseth, Chapter 2, this volume). In this chapter, we argue that such *identity work* is intimately related to peer assessments and membership categorisation practices (Sacks, 1974; Benwell & Stokoe, 2006), and this has implications for how games function as arenas for learning in children's everyday lives. Even though computer games are played by school-aged students daily and for many hours a week (Medierådet, 2010), studies of actual game play as situated activities are still scarce (but see Stevens, Satwicz & McCarthy, 2008; Aarsand & Aronsson, 2009; Piirainen-Marsh & Tainio, 2009; Fields & Kafai, 2010; Keating & Sunakawa, 2010).

In a recent paper, Reeves, Brown and Laurier (2009) discussed how players may display expertise in computer gaming, for example, by learning how to negotiate the terrain of the game through refined embodied attunement to the game environment. Game play may also involve distinct ways of measuring progress (such as levels); that is, indications of how a player has advanced from novice to expert gaming. This chapter will show how it is not only through such measures of in-game actions that players show expertise, but also through their ways of *talking* about their own and others' gaming. Demonstrating proficiency in computer gaming therefore also involves discursive actions: expert game play is often accompanied by ways of speaking competently *about* and *in* the game (see also Steinkuehler, 2006). In line with work on indexing and positioning (Davies & Harré, 1990; Ochs, 1992; Sparrman & Aronsson, 2003), it is expected that players will discursively position themselves and others as experts or novices.

The social dimensions of learning and identity have been discussed by Ito (2006). In an article highly critical of edutainment software, she shows how players, in an after-school club, were remarkably disinterested in the games' educational content. However, they were clearly oriented towards progressing in the games. What could be seen was that a 'habitus of achievement' (Ito, 2006, p. 150) was much more important than the educational content. Despite the presence of adult tutors, the children sought quick solutions to the in-game problems, and thereby the right to show this in front of their peers. Identity as publicly performed actions in a peer-evaluated activity had implications for what was valued as important knowledge, and thereby for learning in the first place. Identities are displayed and communicated in relation to in-game achievements, which is, in turn, related to learning efficient routes through the games (cf. Linderoth, 2004).

In the work of Gee (2008), players' identities are discussed in relation to how specific games facilitate certain ways of seeing and acting in the game world that are related to the projected role of the player's avatar (i.e. his character). In terms of public displays of learning and identity, sites based on popular culture provide excellent arenas for learning, what can be called 'affinity spaces' (Gee, 2005). These are abundant in relation to computer games, where websites, online gaming space and physical gatherings of players (such as local area network [LAN] parties) facilitate the distribution and dissemination of knowledge between participants in quite an egalitarian fashion. Players may acquire status and reputation in a number of different ways, or they may refrain from doing so.

Both Ito's and Gee's approaches differ somewhat from the present one. In our research, identity is understood as both the outcome of and a resource for participating in game activities (cf. Antaki, 1998). This chapter discusses the detailed practices in which participants make themselves available to each other as skilled and knowledgeable players in a specific site and medium, but also how these negotiations of status and central positions within a community of players are essential for understanding young people's orientations towards learning and identity in relation to a specific field of practice. Whereas Gee explored learning properties in games (Gee, 2008), we have primarily studied in detail how participants interactionally position themselves as players of different skills.

Becoming a competent multiplayer gamer involves both learning about the game's formal structures (such as levels) and recognising fine distinctions in co-players' and opponents' characters, equipment and actions, as well as in the 'terrain' of the virtual world (Reeves, Brown & Laurier, 2009). In school contexts, learning within collaborative projects obviously involves joint success or failure. In gaming, the lives of the players' avatars might be in danger. This means that learning is a matter of life and death. In collaborative gaming, a player (e.g. a novice) who does not recognise and foresee distinct moves will be a burden to his team as his lack of foresight might lead to a player death and to the failure of the team. In multiplayer gaming, the stakes are high, and learning is crucial for the collective performance of a team.

Evaluations of ongoing game play should be studied with a focus on specific situated interactional practices. In a paper on action aesthetics and children's gaming in an out-of-school context, Aarsand and Aronsson (2009) found that the players' spontaneous assessments of their own and co-participants' skills were often embedded in affect displays that took the form of response cries (e.g. 'wow!', 'no!': Goffman, 1981), code switching, sing-song performance and other indices of affects, such as surprise, glee or disgust at the way the game progressed. In line with Goodwin (2007), players' public displays of affect are important ways of coordinating and calibrating joint action, indicating what is the preferred or dispreferred course of action in a specific situation. Moreover, players often use specialised terminology infused with *leetspeak argot*, such as netspeak abbreviations and hybrid constructions, as important features of the shared repertoire of a community of gamers (Blashki & Nichol, 2005).

Multiplayer computer gaming at internet cafés can be analysed as a type of participation in a community of practice (Lave & Wenger, 1991) where players move from peripheral to central positions. Lave and Wenger did not draw on analyses of membership categorisations, but our data indicate that such analyses would make sense. In accordance with ethnomethodology's strong insistence on detailed analyses of members' orientations to (and reflexive constitution of) social phenomena, praise and blame are just some of the actions accomplished in and through the participants' skilful invocations of social categories and category-bound actions (Sacks, 1974; Watson, 1978). Through categorisations, members may position themselves as, for example, 'competent', while excluding others from such a position. Similarly, they may draw on contrastive devices (e.g. 'us and them'), creating various sorts of boundaries and normative orders (Jayyusi, 1984; Housley & Fitzgerald, 2009). Such polar categorisations can, for instance, be used for making status degradations or for placing others in 'downgraded positions of identity' (Housley & Fitzgerald, 2009, p. 354). We would argue that the notion of communities of practice is often used in somewhat idealistic ways, ignoring members' power struggles, local hierarchies and phenomena like exclusion or marginalisation (but see, for example, Davies, 2005; Tusting, 2005). In order to understand young people's learning in informal contexts, we would advocate detailed work on gaming within specific communities of practice, including situated analyses of competition and disputes. It is our belief that such analyses may shed light on informal learning, thus broadening our understanding of learner identities.

METHOD

Internet cafés (or cybercafés) were chosen as suitable sites for analyzing participants' assessments of gaming competence as they provide settings for informal learning where the participants spontaneously produce public evaluations of players' performances. The cafés are places where predominantly young people gather to play multiplayer games. Some may house more than a hundred players at a time who play with other co-present players and/or with players on the internet. The cafés are highly sociable places; participants will often go there after (or during) school hours to play, buy soft drinks, use the internet or watch other people play, all the while interacting on and off screen with their peers.

The games played include *World of Warcraft*, *Counter-Strike*, *Warhammer Online* and *DotA*, all of which are possible to play over the internet. Usually, players have access to at least some of the games at home, but the off-screen social interaction seems to be part of the attraction of gaming at cafés.

Video Recordings

The analyses primarily draw on video recordings[1] of game-play activities at internet cafés in Stockholm. During thirty visits – over a year – the first author (BS) video recorded around thirty hours of gaming among young people aged between 15 and 18, all of them boys. Internet cafés in Sweden are highly gendered places, a rough estimate being that 95 per cent of players at the cafés studied were male (on the gendered aspects of internet cafés, see Lazzaro, 2008). Ethnographic observations and informal interviewing were other features of the data collection.

The analytical focus concerns the participants' own assessments of gaming competence (or a lack thereof), recorded as parts of game-play conversations, covering rounds of games or talk on past games. The players usually played games in groups of two or more (sometimes in the presence of a bystander). The present data reflect typical player configurations.

---

[1] Thanks are due to the Swedish Research Council for economic support to K. Aronsson's project 'computer gaming as an aesthetic practice and informal learning' (VR-2007-3208). The video-taped interactions were transcribed in Swedish, marking gaze patterns, body posture, locomotion and other types of embodied actions. The Swedish transcripts have then been translated into English, with the ambition of rendering a version that captures some of the original Swedish language constructions (e.g. hybrid constructions). In a few relevant cases, Swedish originals are presented within parentheses.

The conversations were filled with leetspeak terminology, gaming jargon and youth language register, including code switching into English and hybrid Swedish-English constructions (cf. Piirainen-Marsh & Tainio, 2009). All this, of course, makes interaction somewhat opaque to an unfamiliar reader, as well as notoriously difficult to translate.

ANALYSIS

During the game sessions, computer games were continuously played and discussed, both in between and during game play. The players' gaming competence was publicly displayed, and onlookers and other bystanders gathered around the computers, evaluating other players' performances and creating highly dynamic participation frameworks (Sjöblom, 2008; Keating & Sunakawa, 2010). Through the public nature of the café settings, the players' in-game actions were under constant peer scrutiny, and the players worked hard to show their gaming prowess and expertise. In our data, both novice and experienced players often oriented to their co-players or bystanders, accounting for poor moves or celebrating successful ones in various sorts of assessment sequences.

In such assessment sequences, social categorisations formed important resources for evaluating one's own or other players' gaming skills and thereby for doing social positionings and situated identity work. In many cases, the leetspeak terms *noob* and *imba* were used as labels for different categories of players, ranging from poor performers to expert gamers. In leetspeak jargon, *noobs* refer to newcomers or novices (sometimes also referred to as *newbies*). Conversely, the players used the term *imba* for categorising skilful moves, finesse and panache. The categories of noob and imba thus define a scale of player assessments ranging from novice to excellence (see Figure 11.1).

It is to be noted that social categories often involve *category-bound activities* (Sacks, 1974); for instance, a skilful (imba) player is likely to engage in activities that ingeniously lead to the death or wounding of monsters and opponents. Conversely, a noob has neither learnt how to attack, nor how to avoid actions that lead to the immediate death or wounding of his own or his co-player's avatar. A player's learning trajectory (from novice to expert) is, in many games, partly bound to the gradual development of a virtual character. For example, a character in *WoW* develops over weeks, months or years.

noob ←   → imba

FIGURE 11.1 Categorisations of player performance

The following two excerpts are examples of how players, in assessments of their game play, rank themselves, ascribing different player identities to themselves and to others through categorisation practices.

Positioning Someone as a *Noob*

In the first episode to be discussed, *noob* was used as a categorisation of a co-player in allocating blame for a mishap, here a premature player death (on blame allocation, see also Watson, 1978). The sequence was embedded in a larger discussion in which two players and a bystander argued about what had led to the player death. In his conversation with the bystander, one of the players accounted for it by complaining about his co-player's incompetence, positioning him as a noob.

Example 1

Participants: Two players: Player R (R) and Player L (L), as well as a bystander (BY), a staff member who happened to pass by.
Game: *World of Warcraft* (2 v 2 Arena: the two players at the café against two others on the internet)

1	R		But not greater heal!
2	L		What (h)? ((faces R, then quickly faces the screen again))
3	R		Not greater heal=
4	L		=Yeah, 'cause you had 4,000 [HP=
5	R		[Yeah.
6	L		=Then I can use greater heal.
7	R		No, but you're not supposed to use greater heal.
8			'cause the cast time is too long
9	L		>Come on, come on, come on<
10			Manaburn ((continues to play))
11	R	→	He's a noob ((turns towards BY, pointing at co-player L
12			with his thumb))
13	BY		xxx
14	R		I had this much hp and instead of (x) you get a
15			greater heal ((showing how much using his hands))
16	BY		Then you're^{IMPERSONAL} good ((ironic voice))
17	R		Yeah (.) it is (xx) ((R faces the screen))
18	BY		Is it three v three?
19	R		No, it's two versus two.
20	BY		What classes 're you running?
21	R		Warrior priest versus paladin priest ((facing BY))
22	BY		Then you^{PLURAL} should [really get them.
23	L		[No:: ((BY leaves))

24	R	→	We did it the last time but I told you he's a noob
25			((facing the screen))
26	L		But see, we're not supposed to take them, not when
27			he is retri= ((facing R))
28	R		=Yes, we should.

The initial part of this round involves an exchange in which the two players analyse the game and the factors leading up to the death of Player R's avatar, that is, his game character. (See Figure 11.2 for transcription coding of the sessions.) Player R complains about his noob co-player to a bystander. This person is also an accomplished *WoW* player, and he is well qualified to judge whether player L is indeed a noob. Player R draws on a range of resources that underpin his categorisation of his co-player as a noob. First of all, he goes public when he presents his complaint to a party outside the activity at hand (line 11). Doing this is one method of validating your arguments, aligning with someone who apparently has no stake in the outcome of the ensuing argument and who can thus make an 'objective' judgement. Second, he recounts his version of the game leading to the player death (lines 14–15). His blame account is supported by the bystander, who responds in a notably ironic voice, 'then you're good', indirectly ridiculing player L's lack of skills. The bystander is thereby aligning with him in endorsing 'the teller's perspective' (Stivers, 2008, p. 32).

The bystander then asks a few questions in order to clarify the circumstances (lines 18–20). Every player in this game has a *class* which determines the kinds of abilities that the pair of players has at their disposal (for attacks, defence, movements, etc.). Certain combinations of classes are seen as stronger than others, and, all other things being equal, a team with a superior combination of classes should defeat a team with an inferior composition. Ultimately, the bystander formulates an evaluation of both players' performance ('Then you^{PLURAL} should really get them'), which can, in fact, be seen to involve a disalignment (cf. Goffman, 1981; Goodwin & Goodwin, 1992; Aronsson, 1998) that is a negative assessment of both players' performance (line 22). In view of their 'class composition', the players should have defeated their two opponents. The bystander audibly addresses both players, in that he uses the plural 'you', and thereby attributes responsibility for the mishap to both of them. This subtle shift is face threatening to both players.

Player R restates his prior categorisation of L as a noob, adding 'I told you' (line 24) in an apparent attempt to get the bystander to realign with his perspective on the events. Player R's initial blame account was based on his co-player's use of the wrong spell at the wrong time, but this complaint was soon reformulated as a general categorisation of his co-player's incompetence (a noob). The initial account can be seen as a correction of erroneous behaviour, but the category of noob creates identity, something that player L *is*, rather than something he has *done*. This is part of what constitutes the face-threatening aspects of ascriptions of identity categories. They are bound to a whole range of negative characteristics of the incumbent of the category (e.g. 'a noob is a person who …'), and they thus go far beyond the assessment of a singular (misfortunate) action.

In his response, player L accounts for their failure (lines 26–7) by referring to the strength of one of their opponents: a *retri* (a special type of *paladin*), trying to renegotiate the terms under which the bystander's assessments were made. He attempts to avert this threat to his identity as a competent gamer by appealing to 'objective' characteristics of categories (in this case, that *retris* are difficult to beat), thereby deploying a strategy for decoupling the association between their (substandard) performance and poor skills. In their joint attempts to account for the prior situation, both participants thus try to renegotiate blame and to attribute responsibility for it to another party (R, to his co-player; L, to their opponent).

By categorising his co-player as a noob, player R is simultaneously displaying his own competence, establishing a local hierarchy where he is seen as superior. This is done sequentially through making a first assess-ment, a common way of demonstrating your own epistemic access to relevant features of the event (Heritage & Raymond, 2005). The comparison between himself and player L is not done explicitly by, for example, saying (in one way or another) that 'I am better than L'. However, by making a public 'correction' of his co-player, and by enlisting an outsider's support, he shows that he, unlike his co-player, is aware of the 'correct' action to take in a critical situation. Through his denunciation of his co-player, he saves his own face, as it were. In so doing, he temporarily manages to present himself as someone who has advanced to full participation within the local community of practice. As in most classroom contexts, grades are relative affairs.

Positioning Someone as *Imba*

The next excerpt involves the same two players. This time, player R engages in explicit self-praise, categorising his own actions as imba. As seen, he again positions himself above his co-player, as it were.

Example 2

Participants: R and L
Game: World of Warcraft (2 v 2 Arena)

1	L		Do you know how close you were to dying there=
2	R	→	=Yeah, but I got the paladin down 'cause I'm <u>imba</u>.
3			(2.)
4	R	→	Oh ho ho, so fuckin' owned.
5			((*The last on-screen opponent stops defending*))
6	L		Oh, God↓da:mn ((exhaling))
7			(2.)
8	R		He's given up.
9	L		Godda:mn, I mean [I was like
10	R	→	[Yeah, Goddamn, how imba.
11	R		((R leans back))
12			I mean, I had like a hundred hp, I mean like three
13			times ((R turns towards L and they touch fists,
14			facing each other, celebrating the end of the game))

Player L's initial comment could be seen as a mild complaint. In any case, his co-player, R, produces a defensive account (line 2) where he points out that he has indeed just successfully defeated one of their opponents (the paladin). Being able to do this, despite the dire circumstances, shows that he is imba. Here, the preference organisation of blame and praise is radically different from other types of conversational contexts (cf. Pomerantz, 1984), and self-attributions of praise are indeed not uncommon in these sorts of computer gaming. In the present context, 'playing well and thereby succeeding despite difficult circumstances' is precisely one of those activities that incumbents of the category imba are known to be doing. To be able to engage in self-praise, that is, positioning oneself as imba, rests on the associations between that category and the activities connected to it.

Player R then exclaims, 'Oh ho ho, so fuckin' owned' (line 4). Through this response cry (Goffman, 1981; Aarsand & Aronsson, 2009), a brief public display of affect, he can be seen to display glee, mocking his defeated opponent. Such response cries coordinate players' attention and attitudes towards the game through expressions of delight, fear or revulsion in response to game events. Moreover, the player invites his co-player's alignment (Goodwin & Goodwin, 1992; Aronsson, 1998) with the type of affects and attitudes involved. To *own* someone is directly connected to a player's skilful performance (conversely, someone who is *owned* is an inferior player, on a par with a noob). He thus positions himself as an advanced learner, someone who fully masters the game. At this point, his co-player, L, aligns with him, celebrating or at least validating his self-assessment of superior skills by saying, 'Oh, Godda:mn' (line 6). By now, the last opponent has indeed given up, which is pointed out by player R in his next move, which, of course, further underpins his positive self-assessment. He again receives affiliative support from player L ('Godda:mn, I mean I was like-': line 9). At this point, our imba player engages in format tying (Goodwin, 1990), in that he partly repeats player L's utterance, 'Yeah, Goddamn, how imba': line 10).

The game thus ends in a series of affiliative moves in which the two players align around player R's imba performance, and ultimately they touch fists, facing each other, celebrating their successful end to the game. As they are playing a cooperative game, it is their joint performance that is ultimately celebrated. However, it is interesting to see how player R tries to differentiate his performance from his co-player's, justifying his self-praise (and identity as an imba player) by explicating specific in-game circumstances (lines 12–13). By doing this, he not only *claims* that he is a competent player and the creator of their victory, he also provides supporting evidence that this is the case. Hierarchical rankings of participants may indeed take place also in contexts of success and celebration.

Using Game Rankings as Social Metrics

In this volume, one of the ambitions is to show how local learner identities are connected to learning trajectories and the building of lifeworlds over time. In the gaming careers of novices, learning trajectories may be graded in very precise ways (e.g. from level 1 to level 70). Many games, notably role-playing ones (such as *World of Warcraft*), measure the player's development of his character through the use of *levels*, which roughly reflects the amount of work and skills invested in developing a character. In gaming, the distinct levels of the player's characters may, at times, reflect weeks, months or years of time investment. The same is true of *gear* (the character's equipment), which is the second metric regularly used by players. These are important metrics in these games, as they will determine what sorts of actions and activities are available to the player. They are also important resources for creating a hierarchical order of more- and less-experienced players. Moreover, the number of high-level characters a player has is another metric that may indicate experience (i.e. his prior life story, as it were). The next two data fragments show how in-game metrics are utilised as a resource for discussing and grading players' progress in a game.

Example 3

Participants: A (player) and BY (a bystander)
Game: World of Warcraft (played solo)

1	A		Hey (.) check this out (.) now I'm gonna fuck
2			out my character. ((Swedish: *fakka ur min gubbe*))
3			((looking at BY))
4			Hey, chill, I'm gonna deal with this one, I'm
5			just gonna deal with the trinket, you're gonna
6			see now (.) he's running amok *((arranging his*
7			*gear and starting to run towards some monsters))*
8			Look, now I'm gonna kill ALL of these
9			(.) you think I'll succeed?
10	BY	→	You're already dying *((A is fighting with*
11			*several monsters))*
12	A		Ok, I'm not gonna die (.) I dragged four level
13			70s on me so that was perhaps a bit stupid.
14	BY	→	Level sixty-five.
15	A		No, but some are seventy (.) sixty-nine mm (5 sec.)
16			*((running towards new monsters, kills monsters))*
17			I'm just killing (.) can you start playing your
18			druid again so we can do it together?

Player A is just starting to arrange his character's gear, telling the bystander to wait so that he will be able to see when he runs amok with his avatar, using the Swedish term *dampa*. The colloquial verb *dampa* is actually part of a youth register, derived from a psychiatric diagnosis of hyperactivity, DAMP. Here, it refers to working to the maximum of his strengths, that is, attacking several monsters. All of this can be seen as a prelude to the upcoming game performance, where he is highlighting to the bystander what he should look for, namely, him attacking monsters and defeating them by using all of his available abilities to the maximum. What is analytically interesting is that his account requires that he will succeed in defeating the monsters. As in excerpt 2, 'being successful in dire circumstances' is a type of action that is bound to the category of 'competent player'. However, the converse is also true: failing to complete his stated mission means that he will be seen as incompetent. This means that the stakes are high. In this case, the bystander, in fact, repeatedly questions player A's performance, pointing out that he is about to lose (line 10) and the task is not as difficult as suggested (line 14), the first challenging the performance and the second the premises for that very performance.

In the following excerpt, player P is playing *DotA* (a cooperative strategy/action game). He is also talking to a bystander (BY) about his own and the bystander's *WoW* characters and about their game metrics, that is, indirectly also about their own development as players, the curriculum vitae of their learning lives as gamers, as it were. The two boys are acquainted, but have not met for some time.

Example 4

Participants: Player P, playing the game, and BY, a bystander
Game: Warcraft III – DotA

1	BY		Are you – are you playing *WoW*, Per?
2	P		Ye:ah, wait, is that good or this one?
3	BY		Well, I dunno (.) I've no idea about *DotA*.
4	P		Ah, I'm still playing- I've a rogue (.) chilling
5			with that.
6	BY	→	Level?
7	P	→	Seventy!
8	BY		Yeah, you've got it now?(.) what server (.) is it
9			Dentarg?
10	P		No, Mazrigoz ((turns towards BY)).
11		→	One T5, one T4, well, quite ok (.) how about you?
12	BY	→	Yeah, things are going quite well. I <'ve a- e:h
13			priest 70, eh warrior 70 (.) one mage and a
14			paladin of 40.
15	P	→	Abo! ((P turns towards BY)) (1 s.) oh yeah, by
16			the way, I've also got a level-60 <hunter> -56
17			warrior.
18	BY		Yeah, okay.

Initially, the player tells the bystander what class of character he plays in *WoW*: *rogue*, that is, one of the ten playable classes of characters in *WoW*. The bystander's next question is key, in that he asks about the level of the rogue (line 6). This will reveal a lot about the player's progression in the game. It is like asking about someone's test results. At this point in the game's history (autumn of 2008), 70 is the maximum level, and his answer thus shows that he has taken his character's level as far as he could possibly advance.

The player's report, 'One T5, one T4, well, quite ok' (line 11), constitutes another metric for how far he has progressed in the game (referring to the level of gear he has obtained). To someone in the know, these numerical indices rank his equipment in relation to other players' equipment levels. At this point, player P reciprocates, asking the bystander about his game status ('how about you?': line 11). The bystander turns out to have *two* characters at the maximum level of 70, as well as a few mid-level characters. This is testament to his gaming strength and endurance. Apparently, his modest self-assessment, 'Yeah, things are going quite well' (line 12), is thus something of an understatement. This can be seen in the player producing a response cry ('Abo') of surprise or admiration (line 15); he is code switching to colloquial youth jargon ('Rinkeby Swedish', a hybrid variety of Swedish linked to a multiethnic urban area in Stockholm). Goffman (1981) originally discussed changes of footings in terms of code switching. By code switching, the player here highlights the bystander's achievements, aligning with him through a positive affective stance.

The player then immediately produces more information about his own achievements: in fact, he also has a level-60 hunter and a level-56 warrior; that is, he also boasts some prior achievements (lines 15–17). By listing his achievements, he demonstrates that he indeed has some high-level characters, and he is not only 'chilling with his rogue'. By listing their own achievements, both players thus announced their relative ranks, positioning themselves as experienced players. The metrics with which they do this are through speaking about their characters and their progression. The in-game metrics of *level* and *gear* are thereby used as recourses for the players in positioning themselves in relation to each other. The level, the number of high-level characters and the development of their gear become the 'objective' standards with which to measure local forms of expertise or learner identities in the game in terms of inexperienced or more-experienced (expert) learners.

SUMMARY

In this chapter, it has been shown that it is not only through the gaming as such that players may display their skills, but also through their ways of reflecting on that very gaming and on evaluating and grading their own and others' performances. An onlooker may, for example, position himself as a competent gamer, without actually displaying in-game skills, by how he *talks about* games and specific ways of playing the game (Examples 1 and 4). Game talk is, therefore, an integral part of manifesting your identity as a competent player, which is in line with positioning, performativity and identity theories (Goffman, 1981; Bucholtz, 1999). This has rarely been explored in relation to displays of skills and progression in computer games.

The present players strived for central positions in their community of practice, but would often do so at the expense of their peers. Even though (or perhaps because) the games were collaborative, the players positioned themselves as competent by downgrading their co-players' or opponents' competence. In collaborative gaming, player failures are literally a matter of life and death (excerpts 1 and 2). This means that the stakes are high, and affect displays, self-praise, denunciations and blaming the co-player have to be understood against this background. Our findings thus extend prior work on informal collaborative learning (e.g. Lave & Wenger, 1991; Rogoff, 2003) in showing that a community is not only a haven of peer support; it is also an arena for blame, criticism and downgradings.

As seen, the rules and structure of the game established some sort of 'objective' standard by which performance could be evaluated. This could be seen most clearly in Examples 3 and 4, where the participants engaged in very precise metrics using concepts such as level and gear. Moreover, the very fact that someone did or did not succeed in defeating monsters or opponents established rankings of expertise (Examples 1 and 2). Yet, this was in itself not enough. The participants traded insults and took on challenges regardless of the skills displayed and worked hard to display themselves as competent players both in the game and within their communities of practice at the cafés. The local hierarchies that were reflexively constructed and created through these assessment practices were important features of computer gaming.

In sum, the present analyses of communities of gaming show that the participants constantly work at assessing and ranking their own and their co-players' knowledge, skills and game performance. Peer assessments were ways of positioning co-players and ascribing to them specific learner identities, such as novices (noobs) or experts. This was done both in terms of the precise metrics of levels or opponents killed, or other ways of marking players' competences in relation to their actions. Conversations about these metrics, and the implicit rankings that they involved, were recurrent features. Moreover, the participants themselves created rankings, in that they constantly struggled for others' positive assessments of their performance. Local hierarchies were thus pervasive features of informal learning in gaming situations. If games are understood to be played and discussed within certain 'affinity spaces' (Gee, 2005), we must also understand how such spaces provide ways for players to establish hierarchies and dichotomies. These findings indicate that we need to reappraise and extend models of participation (e.g. Lave & Wenger, 1991; Rogoff, 2003; Gee, 2005) to include notions of examination, rankings and competition.

Understanding how identity work is part of how games are played, taught and learnt in informal contexts has implications for their possible inclusion in contexts of formal schooling. The establishment of hierarchies is, we argue, part of what makes co-located gaming attractive and motivating for the players. The risk taking involved (marginalisation and player death) is part of the allure. Moreover, there is excitement in the possibility not only of winning and losing the game, but also of winning and losing social standing among peers. Gaming thus has real-world consequences. While online gaming may also include these sorts of identity work (cf. Steinkeuheler, 2006), it is our contention that co-located settings may increase this type of motivation for gaming.

Our findings indicate that models of participatory learning (which are often somewhat idealistic) should take into account local stratifications and their implications for identity and learning. Future research should also explore gaming among players of different age groups or experience levels, as well as gaming in distinct settings. Such work would inform us about how learner identities are formed and performed.

:	: prolonged syllable
[ ]	: overlapping utterances
(.)	: micropause, i.e., shorter than (0.5)
(2)	: pauses in seconds
x	: inaudible word
(xx)	: unsure transcription
YES	: relatively high amplitude
(( ))	: comments
?	: rising terminal intonation
.	: falling terminal intonation
=	: latching between utterances
no no	: sounds marked by emphatic stress
hehe	: laughter

FIGURE 11.2 Transcription notations

REFERENCES

Aarsand, P. A., & Aronsson, K. (2009). Response cries and other gaming moves: Building intersubjectivity in gaming. *Journal of Pragmatics, 41*, 1557–75.

Antaki, C. (1998). Identity as an achievement and as a tool. In C. Antaki & S. Widdicombe (Eds.), *Identities in talk* (pp. 1–14). London: Sage.

Aronsson, K. (1998). Identity-in-interaction and social choreography. *Research on Language and Social Interaction, 31*, 75–89.

Benwell, B., & Stokoe, E. (2006). *Discourse and identity*. Edinburgh: Edinburgh University Press.

Blashki, K., & Nichol, S. (2005). Game geek's Goss: Linguistic creativity in young males within an online university forum. *Australian Journal of Emerging Technologies and Society, 3*(2), 77–86.

Bucholtz, M. (1999). Why be normal? Language and identity presentations in a community of nerd girls. *Language in Society, 28*, 203–23.

Davies, B. (2005). Communities of practice: Legitimacy not choice. *Journal of Sociolinguistics, 9*(4), 557–81.

Davies, B., & Harré, R. (1990). Positioning: The discursive production of selves. *Journal for the Theory of Social Behaviour, 20*(1), 43–63.

Fields, D. A., & Kafai, Y. B. (2010). Knowing and throwing mudballs, hearts, pies, and flowers: A connective ethnography of gaming practices. *Games and Culture, 5*(1), 88–115.

Gee, J. P. (2005). Semiotic social spaces and affinity spaces: From the age of mythology to today's schools. In D. Barton & K. Tusting (Eds.), *Beyond communities of practice: Language, power and social context* (pp. 214–32). Cambridge: Cambridge University Press.

Gee, J. P. (2008). *What video games have to teach us about learning and literacy*. Basingstoke: Palgrave Macmillan.

Goffman, E. (1981). *Forms of talk*. Philadelphia: University of Pennsylvania Press.

Goodwin, C. (2007). Participation, stance and affect in the organization of activities. *Discourse & Society, 18*(1), 53–73.

Goodwin, C., & Goodwin, M. H. (1992). Assessments and the construction of context. In A. Duranti & C. Goodwin (Eds.), *Rethinking context: Language as an interactive phenomenon* (pp. 147–90). Cambridge: Cambridge University Press.

Goodwin, M. H. (1990). *He-said-she-said: Talk as social organization among black children*. Bloomington, IN: Indiana University Press.

Heritage, J., & Raymond, G. (2005). The terms of agreement: Indexing epistemic authority and subordination in assessment sequences. *Social Psychology Quarterly, 68*, 15–38.

Housley, W., & Fitzgerald, R. (2009). Membership categorization, culture and norms in action. *Discourse & Society, 20*(3), 345–62.

Ito, M. (2006). Engineering play: Children's software and the cultural politics of edutainment. *Discourse: Studies in the Cultural Politics of Education, 27*(2), 139–60.

Jayyusi, L. (1984). *Categorization and the moral order*. London: Routledge and Kegan Paul.

Keating, E., & Sunakawa. C. (2010). Participation cues: Coordinating activity and collaboration in complex online gaming worlds. *Language in Society, 39*, 331–56.

Lave, J., & Wenger, E. (1991). *Situated learning: Legitimate peripheral participation*. Cambridge, MA: Cambridge University Press.

Lazzaro, N. (2008). Are boy games even necessary? In Y. B. Kafai, et al. (Eds.), *Beyond Barbie and Mortal Kombat: New perspectives on gender and gaming* (pp. 199–216). Cambridge, MA: The MIT Press.

Linderoth, J. (2004). *Datorspelandets mening: Bortom idén om den interaktiva illusionen.* Göteborg: Acta Universitatit Gothenburgensis.

Medierådet. (2010). *Ungar & medier 2010:* Fakta om barns och ungas användning och upplevelser av medier. Stockholm: Medierådet.

Ochs, E. (1992). Indexing gender. In A. Duranti & C. Goodwin (Eds.), *Rethinking context: Language as an interactive phenomenon* (pp. 335–58). Cambridge: Cambridge University Press.

Piirainen-Marsh, A., & Tainio, L. (2009). Collaborative game-play as a site for participation and situated learning of a second language. *Scandinavian Journal of Educational Research, 53*(2), 167–84.

Pomerantz, A. (1984). Agreeing and disagreeing with assessments: Some features of preferred/dispreferred turn shapes. In J. M. Atkinson & J. Heritage (Eds.), *Structures of social action: Studies in conversation analysis* (pp. 57–101). Cambridge: Cambridge University Press.

Reeves, S., Brown, B., & Laurier, E. (2009). Experts at play: Understanding skilled expertise. *Games & Culture, 4,* 205–27.

Rogoff, B. (2003). *The cultural nature of human development.* New York: Oxford University Press.

Sacks, H. (1974). On the analyzability of stories by children. In R. Turner (Ed.), *Ethnomethodology: Selected readings* (pp. 216–32). Harmondsworth: Penguin.

Sjöblom, B. (2008). Gaming as a situated collaborative practice. *Human IT, 9*(3), 128–65.

Sparrman, A., & Aronsson, K. (2003). Pog game practices, learning and ideology: Local markets and identity work. In G. Walford (Ed.), *Investigating educational policy through ethnography* (pp. 169–92). Amsterdam: Elsevier.

Steinkuehler, C. A. (2006). Massively multiplayer online video gaming as participation in a discourse. *Mind, Culture, and Activity, 13*(1), 38–52.

Stevens, R., Satwicz, T., & McCarthy, L. (2008). In-game, in-room, in-world: Reconnecting video game play to the rest of kids' lives. In K. Salen (Ed.), *The ecology of games: Connecting youth, games, and learning* (pp. 41–66). Cambridge, MA: The MIT Press.

Stivers, T. (2008). Stance, alignment, and affiliation during storytelling: When nodding is a token of affiliation. *Research on Language and Social Interaction, 41*(1), 31–57.

Tusting, K. (2005). Language and power in communities of practice. In D. Barton, & K. Tusting (Eds.), *Beyond communities of practice: Language, power and social context* (pp. 36–54). Cambridge: Cambridge University Press.

Watson, R. (1978). Categorization, authorization and blame-negotiation in conversation. *Sociology, 12,* 105–13.

Chapter 12

Making a Filmmaker: Four Pathways Across School, Peer Culture and Community

Øystein Gilje

Youthful media production has become a celebrated phenomenon over the last two decades. The relative ease of availability and affordability of filmmaking facilitates new forms of uptake and creative content production across a wide range of genres and contexts. However, the majority of young people engage in moving image production primarily as a social activity (Lenhart et al., 2007; Ito, 2009a). In addition, there are also a growing number of youngsters aspiring to be professionals and even to become famous through their creative work in the film and TV sector. In the United Kingdom, the absence of professional licenses to practice is dominant and, due to structural changes in this sector over the last two decades, skills development has undergone dramatic changes, producing new and shifting career paths and learning trajectories (Grugulis & Stoyanova, 2009). The Norwegian film and TV industry resembles in many ways the situation in United Kingdom, with a wide range of small independent production companies. Second, internet and digital media have opened up opportunities for economic activity for young people beyond the existing ghettos of youth labor (Ito, 2009b). Thus, producing and working with moving images is now made easier for young people outside the big hubs of the film and TV industry. As a part of the wider research field on digital media and learning, there is a growing interest among scholars in looking into the growth of creative workers who are making their way into the sector.

This chapter explores how four young men (aged 17–20 when interviewed in 2008) seek to position themselves as aspiring young filmmakers trying to establish themselves as freelancers. In the review of literature, the chapter illuminates the blurring boundaries between youthful media production (as we know it from case studies in schools and after-school programs), towards studies that describe freelance careers in the cultural and creative sector. By providing four portraits of aspiring young filmmakers in the transition between media education in upper secondary schools and further work with moving images, the chapter gives new insight into our understanding of the available roles young filmmakers can acquire as part of their learning trajectories in their early careers. In order to explore these roles and conduct an analysis of empirical material, the notions of identity and learning trajectory are further elaborated in line with the overall issues in this book. The analysis places emphasis on how these youngsters establish an identity as young filmmakers within their own individual learning trajectories (Biesta, Hughes & Ecclestone, 2010; see also Erstad et al., 2009) through their engagement in filmmaking. By drawing on approaches to identity as a narrative (Moje & Luke, 2009), the chapter explores different aspects of the roles available for young filmmakers in the new landscape of creative work in Norway.

The chapter starts by examining what it means to be an aspiring filmmaker in a creative labor market. By referring to the two aforementioned bodies of research, it provides a lens to understand the transition between playful media production and more professionally oriented practices. The argument is that the changing societal and cultural conditions for filmmaking have provided young filmmakers with a number of different positions to take as freelancers in what scholars have termed 'tournament careers', insecure and risky jobs in the cultural and creative sector (Stoyanova & Grugulis, 2012). By looking at these positions through the lens of an identity, the analysis in the second part of the chapter draws attention to how four young filmmakers play and perform the role of an aspiring filmmaker by positioning them-selves towards the resources found in the educational context, but also towards their understanding of styles and genres. The perspective taken pays particular attention to how young people play out their role as aspiring filmmakers in a variety of different contexts. Much of this discussion is based on data drawn from interviews. I will integrate use of forms of conversational analysis in discussion as I show how the presentation of 'self in talk' is a key way that learning identity is produced. Following this line of thought, the final section closes with a call for a more systematic and empirically grounded analysis of how young filmmakers develop in the transition from working with moving images in playful ways towards a more professionally oriented approach.

CREATIVITY AND IDENTITY IN CULTURAL WORK

Playful media production has, since the mid-1990s, been explored in a grow-ing number of studies, examining young people's learning about and the creation of moving images (Buckingham & Sefton-Green, 1994; Burn &

Parker, 2003; Burn, 2009; Gilje, 2010). Although interesting in themselves, these studies are primarily oriented towards the ways in which kids learn and engage in moving image production in a formal learning context. This body of research has been extended with studies looking at young people's engagement with moving images in after-school programs, as well as in online communities (Drotner, 1991; Hull & Nelson, 2005; Peppler & Kafai, 2007). On a larger canvas, Drotner (2011) illuminates how, over the last twenty years, new roles and positions have become available to youngsters in different ways in creative learning processes. These roles are available in formal schooling, as well as in informal or nonformal communities of learners, in online communities as well as after-school programmes. In this sense, filmmaking makes a wide range of roles available for young people and makes clear that young filmmakers' agency can be oriented towards these positions, which were not available two decades ago.

A slightly different kind of perspective on young people's engagement with moving images is found in the large field of studies which examines creative work as a driving force in the cultural and creative sector in the Western world (see for instance Banks, 2007; Brabazon, 2008; Grugulis & Stoyanova, 2009; Guile, 2010; Hesmondhalgh, 2007). From the perspective of economic geographical research, for instance, creative work is seen as the driving force of a new economy (Thompson, Jones & Warhurst, 2007). Moreover, based upon larger surveys of students in creative studies, scholars have identified that a surprisingly large number of aspiring artists manage to earn their major income from jobs related to studies in creative educational programs (Hearn & Brow, 2008; Cunningham, 2011; Hartley, 2010). Looking at the creative sector–based analysis at the level of the individual, this new type of media 'entrepreneurism' is also identified by other scholars (Lessig, 2008; Stavrum, 2009; Guile, 2010). In the same vein, Leadbeater and colleagues suggest the term *pro-am* – a professional amateur – in order to describe how aspiring practitioners offline as well as online constitute new roles, but they do not provide concrete analysis of how such a role is played out in practice (Leadbeater & Miller, 2004). Cunningham (2006) argues that new pathways between these (online) communities of practice and the commercial industry should be established by suggesting that the new, emerging culture of professional amateurs is as much about the creativity invested in the distribution (as well as in the potential afforded by new communication platforms), as it is about content. Although these studies give fresh insight into the changing nature of the cultural industries, they do not offer a close look at how aspiring young filmmakers use their learning and education as a way into their role as freelancers.

Using ethnographical approaches, Ito and colleagues (2009a) have addressed other kinds of creative work, including filmmaking, describing how young people create their learning pathways across different contexts. In these studies, meaning making in creative work is understood on the level of the learner. With a particular focus on informal learning, the researchers identified a new set of jobs that relied on digital media and small economic ventures that were started by youth (Ito, 2009b; Brice Heath, Chapter 9, this volume). This form of new media 'entrepreneurism' involves young people's mobilisation and hustling to market their new media skills: 'The vast majority of these engagements do not translate to paying jobs and successful careers in the creative class' (Ito, 2009b, p. 334). In these studies, researchers were concerned about how, even among the most privileged kids, these forms of entrepreneurism with new media were more serious hobbies and not directly related to their real-life trajectories. Barron (2010) analyses the role of distributed resources such as books or internet-based communities in two learner networks, describing how these support learning interactions. This small study illuminates how two boys with an interest in technology had different social support and interest. The differences between the two learning trajectories in Barron's study correlated with 'the accumulation of expertise, opportunities for learning and the possibilities for future learning' (Barron, 2010, p. 118). In both cases, formal instruction and classes in technology were important, although the resources provided from the informal learning context – family members – were dramatically different. This factor restricted one of the boy's opportunities for expertise development. Focusing more on identity and the positioning of the self, Stavrum identified how eight freelancers in the Norwegian film industry (2009) oriented themselves towards discourses on art and filmmaking. In the interviews with filmmakers, older and more established than in the present study, she identified 'artistic' filmmakers as well as 'business' filmmakers, and these positions include question of style and genre.

These latter studies, with their analysis of personal learning trajectories, relate to questions about identity and agency in different ways than do the studies that examine the creative economies at a macro level. The portraits provided by Ito and colleagues provide us with an analysis of how digital means of expression may facilitate future developments and the organisation of creativity. Findings in the studies by Barron and Stavrum suggest that research on new media entrepreneurism should 'expand its focus to include examination of engagement as an outcome and to consider how engagement develops across different settings, timescales, and networks of support' (Barron, 2010, p. 114). The *Making a Filmmaker* project provides four portraits of young filmmakers between the age groups studied in Barron and Stavrums' studies, as these four young men are establishing themselves as freelancers and, through their hustling, beginning to turn their filmmaking into real-life trajectories.

UNDERSTANDING YOUNG FILMMAKERS: IDENTITY AND TRAJECTORIES

In studies about identity, agency and film/video production, a number of researchers have explored how youngsters play with digital editing tools, as well as work with moving images (Burn, 1999, 2007; Niesyto, Buckingham & Fisherkeller, 2003). These studies analyse issues of identity and learning in relation to media production in formal learning contexts: questions of identity are usually explored in relation to the work produced and not on how available roles interrelate with learning trajectories in young filmmakers' everyday lives. Issues of learning trajectories and identity across contexts are seldom questioned or problematised. Only a few of the aforementioned studies provide insight into how the filmmakers reflect upon their learning pathways across contexts. In other words, our knowledge is restricted when it comes to understanding the learner's view of his or her learning trajectory across contexts (see Arnseth & Silseth, Chapter 2, this volume). In order to understand the filmmakers' view, we need studies that take an emic perspective on identity and agency.

Emic perspectives on individual learning trajectories build on specific understandings of identity. Indeed, one of Luke and Moje's five metaphors of identity is particularly helpful for our argument. In their article *Literacy and Identity: Examining the Metaphors in History and Contemporary Research*, they focus on identity as a narrative and identity as position (Moje & Luke, 2009). With reference to Wortham (2004), they point out that identity in a narrative may take two different forms: narrative as a representation and/or narrative as enactment in interaction. It is important to emphasise that it is the interaction itself, whether with other peers or in an interview, that shapes the narration of self in particular ways (Moje & Luke, 2009, p. 428). The study, *Making a Filmmaker*,[1] upon which this chapter draws, involved the invitation of 29 young Scandinavian filmmakers to reflect

---

[1] The *Making a Filmmaker* project was collaboration among four researchers in Denmark, Sweden and Norway. The overall objective was to investigate how young, aspiring filmmakers established their personal learning trajectories, drawing on a wide range of different resources across contexts.

upon their learning over time as a narrative about themselves as aspiring filmmakers. The interviews with the young filmmakers revolved around informants' views on how different contexts provided them with resources for developing as filmmakers. Moreover, the interaction in the interviews explored the main stages in their educational trajectories and how they legitimated and made filmmaking relevant across these contexts. My approach draws on conversational analysis, where the relationship between the interviewer and interviewee must be accounted for in methodology and analysis (Edwards & Potter, 1992; Jordan & Henderson, 1995).

Of particular interest here is also the context for the interviews. By conducting them online as an MSN chat, I suggest that the filmmakers were able to reflect and elaborate more freely compared to the restrictions often found when interviews are conducted in school. As in all cases in which interviews are used as a way of collecting and constructing data, I do consider the fact that statements and answers given by participants are discursively formed and highly dependent on social dynamics and other aspects related to the contexts of the interview. This is what Silverman (2001) refers to as *emotionalism*, in which both the interviewer as well as the interviewee are characterised as emotionally involved subjects. The online interviews created narratives and life trajectories about filmmaking in which the interviewees reflected upon their roles as learners in the past. By obtaining an intersubjective depth between both sides – the interviewer and the interviewee – we can find an emic, or insider, perspective on learning trajectories. In this sense, the interviews can be understood as a 'created interview context' working on shorter timescales, but related to events and episodes in the filmmakers' personal learning trajectory over longer timescales (see Lemke, Chapter 4, this volume), as youngsters develop as filmmakers across places and times. In addition, by conducting an interview in a virtual space rather than in the classroom or in after-school contexts, the study is differentiated from the studies discussed above.[2]

In the analytical work with the material, issues related to filmmaking in a particular context and as a process emerged as interesting topics in terms of understanding how the filmmakers constructed their identity throughout the MSN conversation. An overall issue among the majority of informants in the

---

[2]   As Hine points out, qualitative interviews online pose a number of challenges to how 'we perform our identity as a researcher' (2000, p. 74). In the online interviews, the young filmmaker becomes more of the expert, while the researcher is the one who listens and asks questions. Moreover, online interviews give the interviewee respondent new ways of making inscriptions and texts relevant throughout the talk by copying in links that are shared in the context of the online conversation.

study concerns how they addressed the formal learning context in terms of its importance, or lack thereof, for their development as filmmakers. Some young filmmakers found it extremely valuable to learn about film and film-making in school or at college, while others downgraded the role of formal learning and the resources found there. In general, female filmmakers inter-viewed in the project appreciated the formal learning context to a greater degree than did the males (see Gilje et al., 2010). Moreover, the material showed in general the importance of online resources for the young film-makers, both in terms of networking and in finding communities to share their work and experience, as well as to learn from other more established filmmakers. These findings are in line with other ongoing studies on this subject (Grugulis & Stoyanova, 2009, 2011). In order to provide an analytical perspective on four filmmakers within the limits of this chapter, I examine in detail how the boys position themselves by downgrading the role of formal education, as well as how they define themselves in contrast to their peers in school settings. In addition, I point to the role of genre and style, and how these means are used to construct a subject position as a filmmaker through-out the interviews.

PERFORMING IDENTITY AS YOUNG FILMMAKERS

A large number of young filmmakers in the *Making a Filmmaker* study were between upper secondary school and higher education at the time the online interviews were conducted. In terms of formal education, they had all joined a formal media programme at upper secondary school in their country.[3] Many of them had applied to film schools or media programmes in higher education institutions as a next step in their learning trajectory about film and filmmaking. The four filmmakers were all owners of a digital video camera and editing suite, worth more than 2,000 Euro apiece, and had been working with moving images for more than six years (at the time of interview, 2008); all four had all been nominated, or even won an

---

[3]   In the last 8–10 years, media and communication as a vocational programme, but with an opportunity to qualify for university and university college, has become very popular at upper secondary schools in Sweden, Norway and Denmark. In particular, this subject has become very popular in Norway, attracting more than 5 per cent of the youngsters in the age group of 16–19 years, which means that pupils required good marks to qualify for the programme. All the informants described in this chapter have attended a formal media programme in upper secondary school.

award or prize, for one or more films at a national or international film festival for youngsters.[4]

I first present two of the filmmakers who were interviewed together as they are collaborating on a small business they developed after finishing the media programme in upper secondary school. At the time they finished lower secondary school (age 16),[5] these boys did not have good enough marks to participate in the media programme. But, by being eager and arguing their way into the media programme in upper secondary school, they won themselves places. In the following excerpt, the boys have been asked about their view on the media programme, and they begin by talking about their peers in the class:

ANDREAS: Seems like 90 per cent of the media students are not that interested in the subject of media and communication as such. But they have good enough marks to choose what they want. They choose the subject because they suppose that it is more fun than doing the academic course,[6] which means that the milieu for learning is not that stimulating [for us].

INTERVIEWER: So, about schooling, you both state [in the online questionnaires] that you did not acquire that much knowledge in the media and communication classes. In what sense were those classes irrelevant for you?

MARIUS: We have both been very dedicated to film and filmmaking, and we hoped that media and communication [as a school subject] would give us a good chance to work and elaborate this interest as part of our time at school, but this was not a place for personal development.

ANDREAS: This has to do with the special issues we had to focus on in depth. Moreover, the different subjects and issues within this course are much too fragmented.

MARIUS: In addition, the milieu among the teachers at the school was dreadful and alarming.

---

[4] The Nordic countries have a long tradition for arranging film festivals for young people. More than thirty film festivals are arranged on an annual basis. The national festivals receive more than 300 short films, music videos and documentaries from aspiring filmmakers and media and education students in the age group 15–21 years.

[5] In Norway, nearly 98 per cent of the students apply for upper secondary school after lower secondary school (14–16 years old).

[6] By adding several subjects to your plan of study in the third year in upper secondary school, media and communication students are allowed to apply for university and university college, although the programme in itself is vocationally oriented.

INTERVIEWER: So, in that sense, the environment at the school did not mean that much for your development as filmmakers – is that correct?

ANDREAS: Yes, but having said that, we did get some good experience from a few projects. But, three years in media and communication should, for our sake, have been reduced to just three months.

There are a number of different ways that Andreas and Marius position themselves as learners when talking about and criticising the formal learning context of which they have been a part for three years. On one level, they accuse most of the students of joining the media programme just 'for fun'. More to the point here, they use the phrase 'is more fun than doing the academic course'. This implies two issues. First, they suggest that most of the students in media and communication would rather join the academic stream in upper secondary school because this is the default trajectory when applying for upper secondary schools. In this sense, they are also positioning themselves as students with little to no academic interest, but rather as aspiring filmmakers focusing on film as a form of craftsmanship. Andreas further confirms this issue: 'we have both been very dedicated to film and filmmaking'. This last utterance indicates a need to justify their specialness. In doing this, they position themselves against their middle-class peers who work with film for fun and as a hobby (cf. Ito, 2009a). Andreas and Marius are, in this part of the interview, putting an emphasis on filmmaking as a real-life career choice. However, they do not find the resources to develop as filmmakers in the formal educational setting, and, consequently, they downplay the role of this learning context.

The description of the programme, as well as their opinions about the teachers, underlines how they found this formal learning context to be of little interest for their development. In general, these two filmmakers position themselves as 'competent' – and at the same time, they exclude others from such a position. This process is somewhat similar to Sjöblom and Aronsson's argument about game players as 'noobs' and 'imba' (see Sjöblom & Aronsson, Chapter 11, this volume). By doing this, the two filmmakers are placing others in 'downgraded positions of identity' (Housley & Fitzgerald, 2009, p. 354).

Another boy in the *Making a Filmmaker* study is Martin, a 19-year-old filmmaker from the northern part of Norway. He started out by making small films on his cell phone. These spoofs became notorious among his mates, and, in lower secondary school, students and teachers referred to him as 'the filmmaker'. He subsequently joined a multimedia design programme at a university college in a city close to his hometown, with high expectations of becoming a professional filmmaker. When participating in the filmmaker project, he had made more than fifteen films, including a thirty-minute documentary on the world championship in the *stone, scissors and paper game*, where he and two peers travelled to Canada and Svalbard to research and shoot footage. This was basically a school assignment, for which he also received local funding. Martin did not appreciate the formal learning context or the school subject media and communication. Although he enjoyed working with other students, he found the school context to be irrelevant to his self-defined learning trajectory.

MARTIN: The teacher has no competence, bottom-line. Of course I have learned a lot, but not as much as expected after three years of training in this subject. Film was not prioritised as an issue, compared to working with journalism ... I have learned most of the things on my own, after a little help in the particular context [the teachers and other students].

In line with Marius and Andreas, Marius says he found the media programme quite poor. He was concerned with the lack of interest among the teachers about issues relating to film and describes himself as an autodidact when it comes to filmmaking. Trond, another 17-year-old filmmaker in Norway, pushes this argument further by making the process of collaborative work in the media classes relevant to the interview.

TROND: When doing collaborative work in groups, some people are less enthusiastic.

INTERVIEWER: So, then you realise that you have to do the job in order to make the film you really want, and you have to work late at night, in opposition to the others in the group?

TROND: He he. Yes, exactly, quite often.

INTERVIEWER: Is there anyone else that seems to enjoy working a bit extra sometimes? In other words, is it a couple of you who occasionally stay late at school?

TROND: Yes, there are others ('film souls') as well. Absolutely, but not that many. Others, again, are more into photography, and they work with such production [in the evenings] (...) It is not necessarily so that it's the same people who work late, but it is always some of us that have to do something extra in order to get things done.

The formal learning context in school provides only a few resources for these young filmmakers. But there are also other means used in order to take a role as a learner in the process of positioning themselves. As pointed out above, Andreas and Marius take a nonacademic approach to filmmaking. They emphasise the craftsmanship of filmmaking in contradistinction to how the middle-class kids take media classes for fun. This point is further elaborated in my interview with them:

INTERVIEWER: So, to follow up in the same line of thought, it seems to me that working with practical filmmaking is more important than [now] applying to film schools – can you elaborate on that issue?

ANDREAS: For us, [practical experience] has been crucial. Of course, our view is problematic; because we can't compare it with being a student on a film school [we haven't tried this]. However, we have the impression that the teachers [at these schools], peer students and their opinions and beliefs can influence our development [as filmmakers] in both ways [both negative and positive].

MARIUS: Or, I feel pretty strongly that you actually need some experience in order to improve as a filmmaker, and not only listen to others' experiences. In any case, that is our belief.

ANDREAS: I mean, I think we develop our own approach to working with film when we base it on our own criteria; our own understanding of 'quality' [in filmmaking]. In other words, I mean that those experiences you get as a student in a specific film education do not always push you in the pathway that is best for YOU [sic]. Education is, in one sense, equal to anyone. However, as pointed out, I think it is a bit silly of us to say too much about things we don't actually know anything about – and do not have experience with. But, in our case, we have not been interested in getting education in 'that' particular way.

INTERVIEWER: I think I understand. You both seem concerned with developing your own criteria for the filmmaking process, which means that you also have a particular understanding of quality [in filmmaking]. Would you say that these criteria and the understanding of quality are in conflict with conventions [and genres] in filmmaking as such?

MARIUS: Not necessarily, but I think our criteria and understanding of quality are related to the fact that we try to avoid more ordinary resources in filmmaking (or, we try to make ordinary approaches in filmmaking in an alternative way). When I read my answer here [referring to the chat on MSN], I do admit that it seems a bit pretentious, but anyhow, we prefer to create something that is different 'from scratch'. In any case, we aim at making something that is a bit different from anything else, but not necessarily 'narrow' and inaccessible.

There are indeed a number of different points to be taken up here. However, I will restrict the discussion to one utterance in the interview. When asked about why they work with their small company instead of applying to film schools, Andreas says:

ANDREAS: I mean, I think we develop our own approach to working with film when we base it on our own criteria; our own understanding of "quality" [in filmmaking]. In other words, I mean that those experiences you get as a student in a specific film education do not always push you in the pathway that is best for YOU [sic].

This utterance indicates that their ways of working with film are based on other criteria and understanding of quality than those found in the formal learning context. In this sense, they are linking *film as art* to a particular learning context, a formal institution, with implicit rules and norms about film language, genre, style and so on. As Stavrum (2009) argued, this positioning relates to broader discourses around being an artist or following a more commercial approach to filmmaking. Andreas and Marius are locating themselves outside of more formal learning trajectories to evade any restrictions in their development as filmmakers. We might also suggest that this implies that they position themselves as being more experimental or innovative in terms of style compared to the kind of mainstream found in the commercial industry, as well as at film school. This assumption is somewhat confirmed by looking at their short films and 'trailers'. As filmmakers, they are establishing a narrative about themselves as 'free souls', unrestricted by traditions and the language of film, as well as by genres that may be 'forced on them' within the more formal educational programmes.

This approach is also found in the interview with Martin. He addresses these issues by reflecting upon what it means to make movies just for fun. However, he frames this reflection within a long answer on norms and rules in online communities versus formal educational settings:

INTERVIEWER: Can you say something about internet, what works, how can you use it to learn, and which sites are ok or not?

MARTIN: www.norskfilmforum.com is the site I have used the most. I upload manuscripts and ideas, and get feedback on what works and what does not work. I have also used dvoted, but not that much, maybe because I feel the site is unfamiliar to me and, also most of the language there is in English and boring design. In addition, I keep in contact with my film mates, now when we have travelled in diverse directions after upper secondary school. Via norskfilmforum I have also found expert help I have needed for particular challenges in relation to my filmmaking.

INTERVIEWER: For how long have you participated in norskfilmforum, which I am not familiar with, but seems to be quite similar to the forum foto.no – is that correct?

MARTIN: Yes, I have been part of that community since my first year of upper secondary school, maybe until my last year in upper secondary school. The site is like a forum, where you can communicate with other 'film souls'. The site is more 'free' than foto.no, more youthful so to speak. On foto.no, which I have only used a couple of times, is it more professional (?), that's my opinion. While here (on norskfilmforum.no) I find the whole range of users – from amateurs to professionals. I think it is the plurality that attracts me. Amateurs usually don't follow the norms and rules and by that they are more creative with their suggestions compared to established and professional users, who seek to work according to some stricter rules, if you understand what I mean. When it comes to me, I used to be much more creative and spontaneous at secondary school compared to how I work now. Then, I could grab my camcorder, call my friend and go shooting. Now, everything must be planned, the manuscript must be written, the proposal must be sent and I must get some actors.

Although this online community as a learning context is interesting in itself, I want to focus on one particular utterance. In the last two paragraphs, Martin here draws on his narrative as a filmmaker in the past and now:

When it comes to me, I used to be much more creative and spontaneous at secondary school compared to how I work now. Then, I could grab my camcorder, call my friend and go shooting. Now, everything must be planned, the manuscript must be written, the proposal must be sent and I must get some actors.

One possible interpretation is that the first years of filmmaking attracted him in other ways. It seems that the more professional orientation he talked about in the present, in respect of planning and writing, seemed to bore him and constrain his ideas. Or, at least, this is the way in which he would like to position himself as a filmmaker in the MSN conversation. Following this line of thought, we might suggest that Martin appreciated working with film in a playful and not so organised way, although he knows that the latter is the case if you are going to develop as a filmmaker and make it your living. Again, these ways of positioning filmmaking draw on wider discourses about being an artist and making a living as one. For Martin, this is implied in his distinction between what it means to be an amateur and a professional. As an aspiring and young filmmaker, he is still negotiating his own identity between these two positions in his struggle of having fun as an artist and trying to earn some money alongside his studies of design and communication at the university college.

SUMMARY

My aim here was to give insight into how young, aspiring filmmakers draw on a narrativised sense of themselves constructed through forms of educational identification (either though affirmation or rejection) when they enter into a committed and professionalised stage in their lives. The four portraits do provide us with an understanding of how young men position themselves as learners at a very early stage in their career as young filmmakers. As noted in my opening sections, aspiring practitioners constitute a significant sector of the creative industries. By positioning themselves against the formal learning context and seeking to make this irrelevant for their development as filmmakers, the four young men here demonstrate an agency in their learning process. They elaborate a particular learning style, which we might identify as independent and real-world. They all describe themselves as being critical of formal education, expressing the ways in which it can restrict their role as aspiring filmmakers. At the same time, they are also aware of how working with film changes across time in the transition from being 'the filmmaker' in school towards the role of being a freelancer in the real labor market, in the cultural and creative sector. In order to position themselves in this process, the filmmakers sketch out a taxonomy of genres of participation among young people and how they engage in filmmaking. In this taxonomy, they all position themselves as being at one of the top levels, downgrading the engagement and competencies among teachers as well as of their peers. Such findings are in line with findings from ethnographical research on youngsters within other domains in the creative and cultural sector (Ito, 2009b). Moreover it reflects findings in other studies, where being an artist is not something you can do for fun but is constructed as a choice with real-life implications (Stavrum, 2009).

One of the aims of this chapter, as well as of this edited volume, is to work across disciplines to formulate a distinctive, but holistic, approach to how learners position themselves and build a learning identity across time and a wide range of contexts. By positioning themselves in respect of taste preferences, towards a like and dislike of 'commercial' film genres, towards peers and teachers alike, as well as in terms of preferring curriculum emphases, the informants explicitly created an individual learning trajectory. This positioning is framed by two groups of filmmakers we can find in the sector: the artist and the commercial filmmaker.

The study presented here has several limitations. One of them is the short period of time the filmmakers were followed, even though I had access to interviews and films themselves as part of the project. In order to understand more of these processes over time, these portraits should be elaborated through a longitudinal case study. Only by conducting such a study over time is it possible to see how biographies of learning have any potential to inform our enquiry into learning and how they relate to issues of identity over time. In this case, the twenty-nine young filmmakers in the *Making a Filmmaker* project will now be revisited in order to understand how they have, or have not, elaborated their role as filmmakers in 'real-life' learning trajectories.

ACKNOWLEDGEMENTS

The *Making a Filmmaker* project is a joint work conducted by four researchers in Denmark, Sweden and Norway. I would therefore like to thank Lisbeth Frølunde (Roskilde University), Fredrik Lindstrand (Gävle University) and Lisa Öhman (Konstfack in Stockholm) for their collaboration and collecting of data, as well as for their collaborative writing at previous stages of the project. Moreover, gratitude is owed to all the twenty-nine young filmmakers who spent many hours in the evenings chatting with us during the project, as well as sharing their films and thoughts. Finally, I would also like to thank the Norwegian Media Authority for funding the first part of the project.

REFERENCES

Banks, M. (2007). *The politics of cultural work.* Houndmills: Palgrave Macmillan.

Barron, B. (2010). Conceptualizing and tracing learning pathways over time and setting. *Learning research as a human science. National Society for the Study of Education Yearbook, 109*(1), 113–27.

Biesta, G. J. J., Hughes, M., & Ecclestone, K. (2010). *Transitions and learning through the lifecourse.* London: Routledge.

Brabazon, T. (2008). *Thinking popular culture: War, terrorism and writing.* Farnham: Ashgate.

Buckingham, D., & Sefton-Green, J. (1994). *Cultural studies goes to school: Reading and teaching popular media.* London; Bristol, PA: Taylor & Francis.

Burn, A. (1999). Grabbing the werewolf: Digital freezeframes, the cinematic still and technologies of the social. *Convergence, 5*(4), 80.

Burn, A. (2007). The place of digital video in the curriculum. In R. Andrews & C. Haythornthwaite (Eds.), *The Sage handbook of e-learning research* (pp. 504–524). London: Sage.

Burn, A. (2009). *Making new media: Creative production and digital literacies.* New York: Peter Lang.

Burn, A., & Parker, D. (2003). *Analysing media texts.* New York: Continuum International Publishing Group.

Cunningham, S. (2011). Developments in measuring the "creative" workforce. *Cultural Trends, 20*(1), 25–40.

Cunningham, S. (2006). Australia – a creative economy? *Creating Value: The Humanities and Their Publics, 26,* 33–41.

Drotner, K. (1991). *At skabe sig – selv: Ungdom, æstetik, pædagogik.* København: Gyldendal.

Drotner, K. (2011). The cult of creativity – Opposition, incorporation, transformation. In J. Sefton-Green (Ed.), *Sage handbook of creative learning* (pp. 72–80). London: Sage.

Edwards, D., & Potter, J. (1992). *Discursive psychology.* London: Sage.

Erstad, O., Gilje, Ø., Sefton-Green, J., & Vasbø, K. (2009). Exploring 'learning lives': Community, identity, literacy and meaning. *Literacy, 43*(2), 100–6.

Gilje, Ø. (2010). *Mode, mediation and moving images: An inquiry of digital editing practices in media education.* Ph.D. thesis written as a collection of articles, Faculty of Education, University of Oslo, Oslo.

Gilje, Ø., Frölunde, L., Lindstrand, F., & Öhman-Gullberg, L. (2010). Scandinavian filmmakers across contexts of learning. In B. Arnolds-Granlund et al. (Eds.), *Media literacy and education: Nordic perspectives* (pp. 95–108). Göteborg: Nordicom.

Grugulis, I., & Stoyanova, D. (2009). I don't know where you learn them: Skills in film and TV. In A. McKinlay & C. Smith (Eds.), *Creative labour: Working in the creative industries* (pp. 135–155). Basingstoke: Palgrave Macmillan.

Grugulis, I., & Stoyanova, D. (2011). *Social capital and networks in film and TV: Jobs for the boys?* Paper presented at the Conference on Working in the Creative Industries, Durham Business School.

Guile, D. J. (2010). Learning to work in the creative and cultural sector: New spaces, pedagogies and expertise. *Journal of Education Policy, 25*(4), 465–84.

Hartley, J. (2010). Whose creative industries? In L. Montgomery (Ed.), *China's creative industries : Copyright, social network markets and the business of culture in a digital age* (pp. vi–xxvii). Cheltenham: Edward Elgar Publishing.

Hearn, G. N., & Brow, J. (2008). 60Sox: An experiment in building digital literacies for emerging professionals in the digital content industries. *Media International Australia: Incorporating Culture and Policy,* pp. 104–111. Report. University of Queensland.

Hesmondhalgh, D. (2007). *The cultural industries.* Los Angeles: Sage.

Housley, W. & Fitzgerald, R. (2009) Membership categorization, culture and norms in action. *Discorse Society, 20*(3), 345–362.

Hull, G., & Nelson, M. (2005). Locating the semiotic power of multimodality. *Written Communication, 22*(2), 224–61.

Ito, M. (2009a). *Hanging out, messing around, and geeking out: Kids living and learning with new media.* Cambridge, MA: The MIT Press.

Ito, M. (2009b). Work. In M. Ito (Ed.), *Hanging out, messing around, and geeking out: Kids living and learning with new media* (pp. 295–337). Cambridge, MA: The MIT Press.

Jordan, B., & Henderson, A. (1995). Interaction analysis: Foundations and practice. *The Journal of the Learning Sciences, 4*(1), 39–103.

Leadbeater, C., & Miller, P. (2004). *The Pro-Am revolution: How enthusiasts are changing our economy and society.* London: Demos.

Lenhart, A., Madden, M., Macgill, A., & Smith, A. (2007). Teens and social media. *Pew Internet & American Life Project.* Retrieved from www.pewinternet.org

Lessig, L. (2008). *Remix: Making art and commerce thrive in the hybrid economy.* New York. Avery Pub.

Moje, E., & Luke, A. (2009). Review of research: Literacy and identity: Examining the metaphors in history and contemporary research. *Reading Research Quarterly, 44*(4), 415–37.

Niesyto, H., Buckingham, D., & Fisherkeller, J. (2003). Video culture: Crossing borders with young people's video productions. *Television & New Media, 4*(4), 461–482.

Peppler, K., & Kafai, Y. (2007). From supergoo to scratch: Exploring creative digital media production in informal learning. *Learning, Media and Technology, 32*(2), 149–66.

Stavrum, H. (2009). Filmskaping i Norge – tivoli, kunst eller næring? In P. Mangset & S. Røyseng (Eds.), *Kulturelt entreprenørskap.* Bergen: Fagbokforlaget.

Stoyanova, D., & Grugulis, I. (2012). Tournament careers: Working in UK television. In C. Mathieu (Ed.), *Careers in creative industries.* London: Routledge.

Thompson, P., Jones, M., & Warhurst, C. (2007). From conception to consumption: Creativity and the missing managerial link. *Journal of Organizational Behavior, 28* (5), 625–40.

Wortham, S. (2004). The interdependence of social identification and learning. *American Educational Research Journal, 41*(3), 715.

Chapter 13

Portrait of the Artist as a Younger Adult: Multimedia Literacy and 'Effective Surprise'

Mark Evan Nelson, Glynda A. Hull and Randy Young[1]

'A day of dappled seaborne clouds' is the poetic phrase that the young Stephen Dedalus whispers to himself while standing beside the Irish Sea, contemplating a life in the priesthood. Thus putting words to his world, Dedalus, the protagonist of James Joyce's semi-autobiographical masterwork *A Portrait of the Artist as a Young Man* (1916/1988), experiences a moment of epiphany and resolution. With this quiet utterance, the direction of his adult life is determined: it is to be the life of an artist (or 'artificer' in Joyce's phrase), not that of a Catholic priest. Young Stephen at once hears, sees, feels and thus comprehends, the contents of his own mind and heart in this singular expressive instant. 'The phrase, and the day, and the scene,' Joyce writes, 'harmonized in a chord' (p. 166). And the musical metaphor is an apt one. This is because Stephen's epiphany, we invite our readers to consider, may not be understood as divine inspiration or a bolt from the blue, but rather as an artistic composition. From a ready collection of impressions, feelings, memories, sights, sounds and smells, Stephen, on some level of consciousness, selects, molds and composes elements of experience so as to produce a newly redesigned understanding of who Stephen Dedalus is and should be. And, just as a musical concerto is textual evidence of the composer's creative process, the phrase that Steven utters – *a day of dappled seaborne clouds* – is durable proof of his epiphany, reminding the 'artist' of his creative act and, if shared, perhaps precipitating further moments of inspiration in others, as Joyce's text has in fact done for so many.

Stephen Dedalus' 'experience' is fictional, of course. It is a creative act at least once-removed – a product of Joyce's capacity to imagine inspiration in the mind and words of an also imagined Stephen. However, Stephen's

---

[1]   To avoid confusion, we would point out that the artist whose work is examined here is also included among the authors of this chapter. In his artistic life, Randy Young prefers to use RelixStylz as his nom de plume and stage name.

example, we suggest, helpfully demonstrates how 'learning lives' may be creatively composed and revised one epiphany, one surprise, at a time. In this chapter, we explore the possibility that the learning that we do through and about our lives may happen not only as a function of accruing experience, knowledge and the like, but also of the creative, integrative, even disruptive 'a-ha moments' that punctuate this accrual. Furthermore, we suggest that artistic practice can be especially productive of these critical moments of emergent understanding and, as such, that creative expression might be seen as a central component of education and literacies for the twenty-first century. As a core theoretical lens through which to examine and conceptualise the creative, synthetic moment, we adopt Jerome S. Bruner's (1973) notion of 'effective surprise'. We draw, too, upon frameworks and concepts from the New Literacy Studies (Street, 1995; Gee, 1996, 1999; Lankshear & Knobel, 2003) and social semiotics (see e.g. Halliday, 1978; Hodge & Kress, 1988; Kress, 2003, 2010; van Leeuwen, 2005), which support a broadly meaning-focused (as opposed to principally language-focused) and multimodal view of literacy and learning. Empirically, this investigation is grounded in the work and inspiration of our long-time collaborator, a San Francisco Bay Area poet, musician and multimedia artist whose stage name is RelixStylz, and whose experiences we believe, may also shed a positive new light on the learning lives of adults.

THE NEW-LITERATE LIVES OF ADULTS: RELIXSTYLZ AS A PARADIGM CASE

It has become a commonplace now within socio-cultural perspectives on literacy to favor the plural of litera*cies*, which are understood to be fundamentally multisemiotic, multimodal and multimedial. What is not so common in accounts of new literacies (cf. Gee, 1996, 1999; Lankshear & Knobel, 2003; Street, 1995) or so-called twenty-first-century skills (cf. Lemke et al., 2003; Partnership for 21st Century Skills[2]) are theorisations and empirical examples that specifically characterise and illustrate the design and interpretation of meanings in our highly multimodal, digital age. Important questions that beg answers include: What are the habits of mind and the semiotic strategies that constitute such literacies? And, how might we go beyond lists of competencies, such as those provided by the Partnership for 21st Century Skills (as necessary a start as they have been) to capture or even to investigate the nature of what is new?

---

[2]   http://www.p21.org

We would like to draw special attention with our analysis to adults and to the learning lives of adults. In the United States, those who study learning largely ignore the 'learning lives' that occur after K–16 schooling (mostly after K–12 schooling). There are a few notable exceptions, to be sure, such as an interest in the changing literate demands of reconceptualised workplaces (see e.g. Gee, Hull & Lankshear, 1996) and research, carried out in the United Kingdom, that explores the 'abundance and diversity of possibilities for literacy' in further education contexts (Ivanic et al., 2007, p. 703). By and large, however, the question remains: How can we loosen the deficit-oriented straightjacket that adult learning often wears? How can we conceptualise learning lives in ways that acknowledge the human impulse and desire to make meanings that include, but also sometimes surpass, the purely instrumental? What might such a reconceptualisation look like in a digital, multimodal age?

An appropriate start, we believe, is to add the words 'creativity' and 'imagination' to our theoretical and practical vocabularies, both when thinking about new literacies and when thinking about adults. We are firmly fixed, in policy and practice around literacy, even as we attempt to celebrate things multi- and things digital, in the instrumental and the obviously utilitarian. We separate into different classes, or even into school and nonschool hours, literacy on the one hand and artistic endeavors on the other, if there is time made at all during the current historical moment, in school or nonschool realms, for the creative. This may be just another incarnation of a long tradition of separating the mind and the hand, cognition and feeling, and the disciplinary boundaries that have followed (cf. Rose, 2004). Yet, we are compelled now to ask how we might move past such deeply engrained dichotomies. In our conceptualisation, multimedia/multimodal literacies and artistic creativity are inextricable and result in texts and artefacts that appeal, communicate and help us to know in multiple ways (cf. Hull & Nelson, 2009). And, most significantly, it has been the work and words of RelixStylz that have led us to this line of thinking.

In 2001, RelixStylz attended a workshop on learning to create digital stories: brief movies that blend music, image and words, that tell a personal narrative recorded in the author's voice. Like many artists, he had a variety of day jobs (and sometimes no job) to support himself, but his true vocation was to make music, and rap music in particular. He was also a burgeoning photographer and videographer, and after he discovered multimedia composition, he started to create digital stories. He has created seven stories over the years, three of which we examine here. To begin with, he showed these stories only to friends or at community venues. Yet, over the past few years, he has made them available to the broader public on YouTube, and he has become aware that he has an audience for these works, as well as for his original music compositions, which are his primary artistic endeavor. Over the years, with the completion of each digital story, we have interviewed RelixStylz to capture his thoughts and impressions, and, in the summer of 2008, we recorded a semi-structured conversation with him as we viewed his body of work to date.

Without exception, his digital stories are his critical commentaries on his world. As an African American, a 'young black man' as he called himself, he was clearly aware of the stereotypes that people brought to their encounters with him, and he has aimed to challenge and defeat them in his creative work. He is a young man with a variety of critical and caring messages that he wants to have heard – about his community, the nation and the world. As he once commented, 'I'm not a preacher, I'm just trying to kick it from the heart'. And art provides his agency in the world. As he said on another occasion, 'art is my power against what I can't control'.

We analysed one of RelixStylz's stories in detail before – his first, called *Lyfe-N-Rhyme* – in order to try to 'locate' or characterise the aesthetic power that it seemed to hold for so many who had viewed it (Hull & Nelson, 2005). This chapter reports our initial attempt at looking analytically across RelixStylz's oeuvre, and at three stories in particular, entitled *Love Is in the Air, Blood Sweat and Tears* and *Lyfe-N-Rhyme* once again, which are briefly described in Table 13.1 below. (We also recommend viewing these pieces before reading the analysis that follows. They can be accessed at http://www.youtube.com/user/Relixstylz.) In so doing, again, our hope is to stimulate discussion of the nature, roles and development of multimodal literacies and artistic creativity in the lives of adults.[3]

MULTIMODALITY, 'EFFECTIVE SURPRISE' AND THE CREATIVE ENTERPRISE

As mentioned above, we locate our work broadly within what has come to be called the 'New Literacy Studies', which came about, as Gee (1999) describes, as a part of 'a larger "social turn" away from a focus on individuals and their "private" minds and towards interaction and social practice' (para. 1). In brief, the New Literacy Studies regard literacy as 'literacies', ideology-laden,

---

[3]   We recognize the raft of important scholarship around issues of narrative and identity (e.g., see Labov 1966, Linde 1993, Ochs & Capps 2001), including pivotal work by Bruner himself (1986, 2001). However, in this particular chapter, though we examine a related group of digital stories, we are not interested in narrative analysis or identity construction per se. Rather we confine our investigation to the multimodal composing process and attempt to describe what we see as a productive relationship between artistic practice and new literacies learning.

TABLE 13.1 *Descriptive summaries of RelixStylz's digital stories*

Title	Running Time m:s	Brief Description
Lyfe-N-Rhyme (2002)	2:12	*L-N-R* is a rap-style spoken-word poem, set against the jazz of Miles Davis and a driving drumbeat. Co-deployed are RelixStylz's own photos; title-like, print-only images; and graphics and photos appropriated from online sources. These resources are designed to speak to the struggles of urban life and personal and global interpretations of the African American male experience: themes include poverty, drugs, incarceration, family and love. http://www.youtube.com/watch?v=yfFg8zNkXZM
Love Is in the Air (2005)	3:41	*LIITA* features another original spoken-word piece, accompanied by an also original Reggae-inspired score. The imagery is comprised only of photos taken by RelixStylz himself, of his neighbourhood environment, family and community members. In each represented mode, the intended effect is very personal and autobiographical, explicitly detailing RelixStylz's own life and creative work, but, again, with an eye to the more global concerns of African American people. The mood of the piece, as the titles suggests, is optimistic. http://www.youtube.com/watch?v=iI4SkzBLgwE
Blood, Sweat and Tears (2008)	3:22	As with RelixStylz's other pieces, *BS&T* toggles between RelixStylz's own life experiences and those of his wider community, showing how each is reflective of the other. This piece features fast-paced original hip-hop music, a combination of appropriated and personal photographic images, and a spoken-word component that combine to a confident, pointed effect. This is the most directly politically engaged of RelixStylz's always political works, leveling criticism at the powers that be for their policies of neglect and destruction. http://www.youtube.com/watch?v=ABIX8sOeGZY

inherently social meaning-making practices, rather than a unitary set of 'autonomous' (viz. context- and purpose-independent) knowledge and skills (Street, 1995). A core concept within the New Literacy Studies is multimo-dality, referring to the diversity of modes (e.g. written language, visual imagery, music) that increasingly characterise contemporary texts and communication and the ways in which meanings are constructed in and in between these modes. Following on foundational work in this area by linguists and semioticians M. A. K. Halliday (1973, 1978), Gunther Kress (2000, 2003, 2010) and Theo van Leeuwen (1999, 2005), we understand meaning in multimodal representations to always be designed or constructed (rather than simply encoded and decoded) by composer-writers and viewer-readers alike, on the basis of 'semiotic resources' or 'available designs' (New London Group, 1996), which are the physical and conceptual stuff of representation and communication (e.g. paper, language, genres, memories, to name a very few). More, from a social semiotic viewpoint, it is the inventive combination and recombination of resources, the shifting of meaning across boundaries of mode, which drives the construction of new meanings, setting the stage for learning and literacy (in the 'new' sense, defined above). In a rather Vygotskian turn of phrase, Kress (2010) describes this 'synaesthetic' process of creative multimodal knowledge work in terms of '"inner" representation and the "inner" trade between different forms of representation' (p. 17; cf. Vygotsky, 1986). In this chapter, we attempt to shed a new light on the 'hugely neglected process of synaesthesia' (Kress, 2010, p. 17) by examining the utility of Jerome Bruner's (1973) notion of 'effective surprise' in conceptualising how new meanings and learning arise out of sustained multimodal artistic practice.

Lesser known among Bruner's highly influential writings is a brief essay entitled 'The Conditions of Creativity', in which he explores the nature and purposes of creativity as broadly construed across several disciplines – mathematics, science, literature, art. Bruner sees creativity as central to 'the ancient search of the humanist for the excellence of man' and 'the next creative act' as possessing the potential to 'bring man to a new dignity' (p. 208). This piece was originally published in the early sixties, but, just as the search for human excellence and dignity is as relevant and necessary as ever, so too are Bruner's theoretical recommendations for understanding and conducting this search. Actually, when we encountered this formulation for unpacking creativity, we were struck by its potential explanatory value in relation to the kinds of multimedial, multimodal texts and practices we had been thinking about for some time, especially the artistic work and life of RelixStylz.

As a working definition for creativity, Bruner proposes, 'an act that produces *effective surprise*'; and surprise he defines as 'the unexpected that strikes one with wonder and astonishment'. Bruner clarifies this broad definition of effective surprise in terms of two related conditions. First, effective surprise is not dependent on or necessarily a function of the intention to create. As Bruner writes, 'the road to banality is paved with creative intentions'. Second,

effective surprises are not special or rarified, but everyday kinds of occur-
rences. According to Bruner, 'they have the quality of *obviousness* about them
when they occur, producing a *shock of recognition*, following which there is no
longer astonishment' (p. 209, emphasis added). Harder to discern from
Bruner's writing is where and with whom he locates the surprise, with the
creator or with the receiver or consumer or audience – but in view of our
present project, this is not problematic. Again, aligning ourselves with current
ways of thinking about all meaning making as a process and product of
design, we assume it to potentially be either or both.

Bruner identifies three kinds of effectiveness or, in his terms, three forms of
'implicit self-evidence' for effective surprise. The first is 'predictive effectiveness' or the 'kind of surprise that yields high predictive value in its wake' (p.
210). Bruner concedes that 'predictive effectiveness does not always come
through surprise, but through the slow accretion of knowledge and urge' and
that 'the surprise may only come when we look back and see whence we have
come'. It may be, then, that the kind of creative surprise experienced by
Stephen Dedalus, to recall our earlier example from Joyce, could fairly be
characterised as predictive in that all of the uneasiness, aesthetic sensitivity,
longing and emotions that Stephen felt in his earlier life seem to coalesce in a
single decisive moment.

The second form of effectiveness Bruner calls 'formal', and this consists of
an 'ordering of elements in such a way that one sees relationships that were
not evident before, groupings that were not before present, ways of putting
things together not before within reach', the result of which is 'consistency or
harmony or depth of relationship'. Similarly, there is 'metaphoric effectiveness'. Bruner likens this to formal effectiveness, but associates formal effectiveness with mathematics, logic and science and locates metaphoric
effectiveness within the domain of art. For purposes of our analysis and
discussion, we deal with formal and metaphoric effectiveness together, as
related phenomena. This is appropriate given our interest in creativity that is
expressed in multimodal textual forms, which may integrate the semiotic
affordances, constraints and organising logics of music, visual imagery and
poetry, among other symbolic systems. And, it is most important to note that
the source of all of these forms of effective surprise, according to Bruner, is
'combinatorial activity', of a kind that 'takes one beyond common ways of
experiencing the world' (p. 212).

Coupled with a New Literacies perspective, this framework for understanding and articulating the nature and effects of creativity may go some
way towards illuminating what it means to be and become powerfully literate
in the multiple sense, apropos of the socially, culturally and textually diverse

literacy landscape in which we all live and interact. Further, we suggest that RelixStylz's creative practice, choices and works may be understood as a kind of bellwether, an exemplar of the sort of multisemiotic creative capacity that present and future literacies require and to which adults may be specially well disposed. In order to explain and concretise the brief theoretical outline just given and demonstrate its potential value, we next turn to an interpretation and application of these ideas within and across a grouping of RelixStylz's multimedia compositions. The structure of our analysis treats each of Bruner's three forms of effective surprise in turn, and, again, due to conceptual commonalities, considers formal and metaphorical effectiveness to be related. We highlight instances in which RelixStylz reports having himself experienced a creative epiphany of sorts along with cases of his attempts to engineer surprises on the parts of others; that is, to intentionally, prospectively create and configure the resources in his pieces so as to evoke very particular *shocks of recognition*, to adapt Bruner's phrase, in the minds of his audience.

IDENTIFYING EFFECTIVE SURPRISE IN MULTIMEDIA COMPOSING

Predictive Effectiveness

Once again, predictive effectiveness may be understood as a kind of creative newness or surprise that emerges in the 'review mirror', so to speak. Adapted to our particular interests and project, it characterises a new design for meaning formed of an accrued collection of diverse semiotic resources – memories, intentions, artefacts and the like – finally reconciled. In our analysis of RelixStylz's multimedia work and his commentary on that work, we found particular evidence of a sophisticated predictive meaning design capacity, in both expressive or productive and receptive senses.

By expressive or productive, we mean designs for meaning that invite the viewer, the audience, to reflect on resources provided as the digital story unfolds, as an assemblage of clues to suggest, in hindsight, a new and combinative quality of meaning. In his first piece, *Lyfe-N-Rhyme*, RelixStylz orchestrates several designs for meaning in order to predispose and equip each member of his audience to have a semiotic epiphany in the final seconds of the piece. As we discussed in a prior investigation of this work (Hull & Nelson, 2005), in *Lyfe-N-Rhyme*, through the repetition and reinforcement of a particular thematic pattern in the spoken language of the piece, along with the deployment and redeployment of photographs depicting life in his Oakland, California neighbourhood, RelixStylz progressively prepares his audience to make a creative leap, to experience a retrospective surprise. More specifically, his aim is to implicitly connect his own experiences of struggle, fear, frustration and love with the broader experience of African American people and humanity at large. He accomplishes this semiotically in part through engineering a recursive thematic movement in his spoken-word poem – or 'essay', as he described it in a more recent interview – from a more global, universal quality of meaning to a more personal one, most often signaled by first-person pronominal reference. For instance, consider the semantic movements from global to personal meanings in the following excerpts:

Life, love, truth, trust. Tribulation, that's what's up. The older *we* get, the harder a habit is to kick.

Section-Eight[4] living. Societies rivals. Freedom of speech. Who are *we* to teach? Friction. Failure. Function. Worth. *Me* and Mom Dukes, family first.

At the close of *Lyfe-N-Rhyme*, RelixStylz repeats several of the photographs he deploys earlier in the narrative; these are the only repeated images, and all are neighbourhood photos that RelixStylz himself took (see Figure 13.1.) The effect, the *surprise*, is meant to come when the audience sees these photos again, literally and metaphorically, in the absence of language (i.e. no words are spoken) and discovers a more global significance, a symbolic condensation of RelixStylz's big themes – poverty,

FIGURE 13.1 Final sequence from *Lyfe-N-Rhyme* (all photos by RelixStylz)

---

4   'Section Eight' refers to a public housing assistance program aimed at economically disadvantaged residents of California.

crime, social and institutional abuse, hope, love – in the highly particular images depicting his own life-world. This choice evidences an implicit understanding on RelixStylz's part of the generic characteristic of the photographic image, identified by Barthes (1977), to 'mask the constructed meaning under the appearance of the given meaning' (p. 46) – that is, until these photos are re-presented, resonating with RelixStylz's words, at which point the everyday scenes are surprisingly transformed into symbolic emblems.

An example of RelixStylz's own receptivity to predictive semiotic effect arose during an interview in which we asked him to discuss some of the choices he made in composing his second digital story, entitled *Love Is in the Air*:

GLYNDA: There were so many striking images. What was the meaning of, that you were getting at with the shoes hanging from the wire? Was that anything special or was it just a striking image? [See Figure 13.2.]

RELIXSTYLZ: I wouldn't say it was anything kind of, too complex method. Basically it's just that's what you kind of see there in the neighbourhood.

GLYNDA: And there was that moment when you have the earphones on the sidewalk with the crack. What was going on with that? [See Figure 13.3.]

RELIXSTYLZ: Right. Now that represents me as an underground artist, underground hip-hop. Another thing with the shoes, though,

FIGURE 13.2 Sneakers hanging from a power line (photo by RelixStylz)

FIGURE 13.3 Headphones on a cracked sidewalk (photo by RelixStylz)

> like, kind of like how a jersey hangs in the rafters, retired you
> know. Same kind of instance. My sound is good. In that case, it's
> pretty good. That's what underground hip-hop is.

Here, we notice an effective surprise on RelixStylz's own part. He admits not
having been cognizant of any special, intended significance within the
composition of the sneakers hanging from power lines, other than as a
common, enduring sight in his local landscape. However, in the process of
discussing the image of headphones on the sidewalk and underground
hip-hop, a surprising innovation occurs. RelixStylz apprehends and actual-
ises the meaning potential in the connection of the image of 'sneakers
hanging on a power line' to the discourse and practices – or 'semiotic
domain', to borrow Gee's (2003) term – of professional basketball and the
associated custom of 'retiring' the jerseys of all-star players by framing them
and hanging them in the rafters of the team's home court. In this highly
syncretic way, the image of the shoes comes to symbolise RelixStylz's
identity as an aspiring underground hip-hop all-star. This we might recognise as an example of 'predictability' afforded by earlier creative acts that
facilitates a retrospective moment of surprise. And language, in this case,
was the vehicle for consciously mapping connections between the images
and his own experience: the retrospective 'languaging' (qua discussion) of
these visual resources prompted RelixStylz to construct a new clarity,
coherence and relevance in his multimodal narrative.

Formal-Metaphorical Effectiveness

The essence of formal effectiveness is in revealing 'unsuspected kinship between   facts long known, but wrongly believed to be strangers to one another', writes Bruner (1973, p. 210), himself quoting from the mathematician Poincaré. Again, metaphorical effectiveness is similar to formal effectiveness, but also distinct in that it evokes a holistic kind of aesthetic or poetic kinship, which may not be explained by or reducible to formal arrangements or juxtapositions. In RelixStylz's case, of course, we are concerned not with facts as such, but with semiotic resources and meaning potential; still, the principle holds.

RelixStylz's approach to designing the formal aspects of his stories might be described as quite deliberate and even economical. He is keenly aware of the complexities of orchestrating multimodal meaning and strictly avoids the inclusion in his compositions of anything extraneous, any feature that doesn't seem to specifically contribute to the realisation in the minds of his audience of his meaning design. One salient example of this design economy is RelixStylz's disposition toward omitting altogether the kind of visual transition effects commonly used to segue between the sequenced images or video clips in a digital story or filmic text (e.g. fade, wipe and iris effects). When asked why he eschews all such transitions, RelixStylz explained:

See, that's the crossroads you come to. So when I'm finished, with these images, with the beat, and I got the rhyme, and I could go throw in some effects. But I don't need to. I don't want to over-complex it anyway. Because it's enough, it's three different entities that have to work together. That's complex enough!

And this artist is equally concerned with economy and specificity within particular modes. In one of our conversations with him, RelixStylz recounted a design decision he made in regard to another of the images that appears in *Love Is in the Air*, a photograph of a diamond advertisement on a billboard (see Figure 13.4):

These photos were photos that were just taken. This is making your image, almost creating photography art with just life as it happens. When I really think about it, that's kind of what it is. I'm walking down the street. I see that sign. It's an artistic sign, and I can get something from it. But I don't want everything that's in it, so yeah I just cut the diamond out, keep the other part, and it totally supports the art of what I'm saying. And I didn't even tell them to put the sign up!

FIGURE 13.4 Billboard, "Love Is Outperforming Everything This Year" (photo by RelixStylz)

In the interview extract above, RelixStylz alludes to visually cropping the billboard in Figure 13.4 to exclude the image of a diamond ring, which the sign was intended to advertise. Revisiting the expression-reception distinction introduced earlier, we regard RelixStylz's experience of conceptually, visually and photographically 'cropping life into art' as a formal effective surprise of the receptive type. And in reshaping and repurposing this resource, he also shapes its potential to elicit an ensuing act of creativity on the part of his audience (cf. Bauman & Briggs's [1990] notion of 'reappropriation'). Through changing the formal aspects of the sign in the way that he does, he expects that his viewer will be more inclined to see what he sees, and to motivate the subtle connections – reveal for themselves the 'unsuspected kinships' that Bruner discusses – that designfully convey his message.

Still, for RelixStylz, the art is in conveying his message indirectly, symbolically, metaphorically, such that his audience is impressed both with the seeming naturalness and self-evidentiary nature of the relationships of meaning he designs as with the novelty and freshness of the combination. On this point he says,

Making it work is the fun part of it. That's the challenge. That's the work to be done. So it's a welcome challenge. Now can I make this work to someone else? Not just me, because I'm gonna get it. But someone else has to get it. That's the challenge right there.

Discussing a third pivotal multimedia piece among his compositions, *Blood,
Sweat and Tears*, RelixStylz describes his strategy for assembling the corpus of
images that are deployed in the story and designing the relationships that tie
these to other elements of the work. He explains,

I knew what it was going to be about. I knew *Blood, Sweat and Tears* was gonna be
about things like oppression, genocide, also peace   when a person is creating
something like this, not just me but when a person is doing it, they want to be
mindful of the words that also support the title.

In this case, RelixStylz's strategy for approaching his 'welcome challenge' is a
simple but cleverly effective one. Nearly all of the images that appear in this
piece were obtained via Google image searches. And the linguistic terms that
he chose to mediate these searches relate mainly to the big, broad, abstractly
stated themes of the story – 'oppression', 'genocide', 'peace', as he mentions –
and much less to the particular words or phrases that he speaks. Although
there are a number of evidently direct, iconic language-image relationships in
the piece, as an artefact of this image collection method, the story is mainly
characterised, almost by default, by more abstract, symbolic and metaphorical
relationships between what is 'narrated' (or spoken, in language) and what is
'displayed' (or depicted visually), to apply Kress's (2003) terminology. In this
way, RelixStylz's design leaves open opportunities for his audience to unpack
the ambiguities of the intersemiotic relationships, to experience effective
surprises of their own, but according to the constraints of the meaning-
making potentials and parameters that his choices make available.

By way of example, consider four images that appear in a three-second
sequence (1:19–1:21) in *Blood, Sweat and Tears* along with the spoken text
'Just trying to live and make it through these years'. The first two images are
a sub-sequence of photographic depictions of the events of September 11, 2001,
at the World Trade Center, in New York City. The first image is a mid-range,
centred perspective onto the scene of an airplane about to strike the second
Tower, with the view of first Tower partly obscured by billowing black smoke.
The second image is of the aftermath: smoke and dust spewing upward and
outward as one Tower collapses. The third image is of a framed painting of a
bleak, surrealistic, seemingly allegorical landscape inhabited by caricatures of
Saddam Hussein, in a torn military uniform, and Bill Clinton, roughly grasping
Saddam's shirt and pointing a finger cryptically toward the right of picture
plane. Perhaps evoking the style of Orozco and Mexican Muralism, the painting also depicts human and animal skulls, a nuclear missile, a drab-green
military vehicle, a nuclear reactor apparently melting down and other

conventional symbols of death and destruction. The fourth image in the sequence shows a crowded city street in one-point perspective. The low-chroma, low-definition figures, signs and buildings blend together to suggest an uneasy hybrid of photography and illustration. These images stand in rather ambiguous relation to what is simultaneously being said: again, 'just trying to live and make it through these years'. Obliquely, however, these images are interpreted to express the above-mentioned global themes in the piece.

SUMMARY

These are but a few examples of the effective surprises that RelixStylz in his digital storytelling work has experienced for himself and designed, in the form of meaning potential, for his audience. Our analysis of his body of work is still quite preliminary. Here, we haven't described any developmental trajectory that RelixStylz's work could evince, nor was that our intention. In point of fact, an epiphany that we ourselves have come to in doing this work, in collaborating with and learning from RelixStylz, is that influences on and development in new literacy capacities may be best understood by taking notice of the bumps, potholes, passersby and impressive vistas one encounters along the path, rather than attending mainly to the developmental pathway itself. RelixStylz's artistic engagements with digital media have been about repeatedly grappling with, assembling, synthesising and then re-presenting his experience, in a variety of integrated forms, to others and to himself; and this kind of reflexive, surprise-studded learning journey, we think, may point the way towards useful, tangible understandings of how lived experience, social and semiotic awareness and the application of symbolic creativity (Willis, 1990) over time are imbricated in meaning-making dispositions and literacy practices vital to learning in the twenty-first century.

We want to suggest, too, that the notion of effective surprise, in conversation with a social semiotic approach to research on multimodality (cf. Jewitt, 2009, pp. 37–8), might well serve not only as a helpful unit of analysis, but also as a touchstone for understanding and evaluating creativity, imagination and learning in new media literacy practices and events. If there is something special about new media composers like RelixStylz – who possess a particular sensitivity towards how meanings are actualised in receptive and productive ways and across different modes, audiences and contexts – Bruner's concept of effective surprise may afford a firmer kind of purchase on the mechanisms and implications of such sensitivity.

Finally, RelixStylz's example has led us to believe that adults may enjoy a significant advantage in the development and practice of new media literacies defined in terms of effective surprise. As Bruner explains and RelixStylz's life and work exemplify, creativity fundamentally involves combination, recombination and reconfiguration of available resources for making meaning. And combination, in a sense that is nontrivial or not merely additive, necessarily involves the ability to notice, create and motivate potential connections and relationships of meaning in, between and among resources. (It could well be that the image-text of the billboard – 'Love is outperforming everything this year' – held for RelixStylz the same kind of life-enhancing potency that 'a day of dappled seaborne clouds' held for Stephen Dedalus!) In addition to talent and passion, RelixStylz has a very rich store of memories and experiences, and what might be called 'accrued connections' among these, to draw upon in actualising meaning potential, as do practically all adults. This recognition should help us to rethink adult literacy and education as we rethink literacy and education more broadly. In this and other research, we have witnessed how adult learners – whose literacy needs are presumed to be purely functional and often remedial – can, given the opportunity and encouragement, leverage new media composing to 'radically self-altering' effects (Hull, Jury & Zacher, 2007, p. 314). This has been so, we now propose, because digital storytelling and other multimedia meaning-making work fundamentally involve designing new meanings from the entire collection of life's resources, integrating photos, feelings, words and memories in new ways, perhaps with previously unconsidered images and possibilities, and often with unexpected, *surprising* outcomes. According to the New London Group (1996), education and literacy should now have one overarching aim: preparing individuals to design for themselves their 'social futures', by which the authors essentially mean fulfilling, enriching, positive lives. Redesigning and re-presenting the elements of one's life-world at present, as RelixStylz has done and continues to do, may importantly, even suddenly, prompt a creative reimagining of what also could be.

REFERENCES

Barthes, R. (1977). *Image-music-text*. New York: Hill & Wang.

Bauman, R., & Briggs, C. L. (1990). Poetics and performance as critical perspectives on language and social life. *Annual Review of Anthropology, 19,* 59–88.

Bruner, J. S. (1973). *Beyond the information given: Studies in the psychology of knowing.* New York: W.W. Norton & Co.

Bruner, J. S. (1986). *Actual minds, possible worlds.* Cambridge, MA: Harvard University Press.

Bruner, J. S. (2001). Self-making and world-making. In J. Brockmeier & D. Carbaugh (Eds.), *Narrative and identity: Studies in autobiography, self and culture* (pp. 25–37). Amsterdam: John Benjamins.

Gee, J. P. (1996). *Social linguistics and literacies: Ideology in discourse.* London: Taylor and Francis.

Gee, J. P. (1999). *The new literacy studies and the 'social turn'.* ERIC Opinion Paper (ED442118). Retrieved October 20, 2010, from http://www.schools.ash.org.au/lit-web/page300.html

Gee, J. P. (2003). *What video games have to teach us about learning and literacy.* New York: Palgrave Macmillan.

Gee, J. P., Hull, G. A., & Lankshear, C. (1996). *The new work order: Behind the language of the new capitalism.* Boulder, CO: Westview Press.

Halliday, M. A. K. (1973). *Explorations in the functions of language.* London: Edward Arnold.

Halliday, M. A. K. (1978). *Language as social semiotic: The social interpretation of language and meaning.* London: Edward Arnold.

Hodge, R., & Kress, G. (1988). *Social semiotics.* Ithaca, NY: Cornell University Press.

Hull, G. A., & Nelson, M. E. (2005). Locating the semiotic power of multimodality. *Written Communication, 22*(2), 224–61.

Hull, G. A., & Nelson, M. E. (2009). Literacy, media, and morality: Making the case for an aesthetic turn. In M. Baynham & M. Prinsloo (Eds.), *The future of literacy studies* (pp. 199–227). London: Palgrave Macmillan.

Hull, G. A., Jury, M., & Zacher, J. (2007). Possible selves: Literacy, identity, and development in work, school, and community. In A. Belzer (Ed.), *Improving and defining quality in adult basic education: Issues and challenges* (pp. 299–317). Mahwah, NJ: Lawrence Erlbaum.

Jewitt, C. (2009). Different approaches to multimodality. In C. Jewitt (Ed.), *The Routledge handbook of multimodal analysis* (pp. 28–39). London: Routledge.

Ivanic, R., Edwards, R., Satchwell, C. & Smith, J. (2007). Possibilities for pedagogy in further education: Harnessing the abundance of literacy. *British Educational Research Journal, 33*(5), 703–21.

Joyce, J. (1916/1988). *Portrait of the artist as a young man.* New York: Penguin. (Original work published in 1916.)

Kress, G. (2000). Multimodality. In B. Cope & M. Kalantzis (Eds.), *Multiliteracies: Literacy learning and the design of social futures* (pp. 182–202). London: Routledge.

Kress, G. (2003). *Literacy in the new media age.* London: Routledge.

Kress, G. (2010). *Multimodality: A social semiotic approach to contemporary communication.* London: Routledge.

Labov, W. (1966). *The social stratification of English in New York City.* Washington DC: The Center for Applied Linguistics.

Lankshear, C., & Knobel, M. (2003). *New literacies: Changing knowledge and classroom Learning.* Berkshire: Open University Press.

Lemke, C., Coughlin, E., Thadani, V. & Martin, C. (2003). *enGauge 21st century skills: Literacy in the digital age.* Naperville, IL: NCREL. Retrieved June 5, 2010, from http://www.metiri.com/features.html

Linde, C. (1993). *Life stories: The creation of coherence.* Oxford: Oxford University Press.

New London Group. (1996). A pedagogy of multiliteracies: Designing social futures. *Harvard Educational Review, 66,* 60–92.

Ochs, E., & Capps, L. (2001). *Living narrative: Creating lives in everyday storytelling.* Cambridge, MA: Harvard University Press.

Rose, M. (2004). *The mind at work: Valuing the intelligence of the American worker*. New York: Viking.

Street, B. (1995). *Social literacies: Critical approaches to literacy in development, ethnography, and education*. London: Longman.

Van Leeuwen, T. (1999). *Speech, music, sound*. London: Palgrave Macmillan.

Van Leeuwen, T. (2005). *Introducing social semiotics*. London: Routledge.

Vygotsky, L. (1986). *Thought and language*. Cambridge, MA: MIT Press.

Willis, P. (1990). *Common culture: Symbolic work at play in the everyday cultures of the young*. Milton Keynes, UK: Open University Press.

Index